MULTI-LEVEL HOMES
Split-Level • Bi-Level • Hillside Designs

HOME PLANNERS, INC.

Contents

	Page
Index to Designs	3
How to Read Floor Plans and Blueprints	4
How to Choose a Contractor	5
How to Shop for Mortgage Money	6
Traditional Split-Levels	7
Contemporary Split-Levels	45
Bi-Level Designs	73
Leisure Living Multi-Levels	103
Lower Level Utility	115
Sunken Living Areas	127
Third-Story Livability	143
Home Planners' Services	151
The Plan Books	152
The Complete Blueprint Package	154
Before You Order	156
Hillside Homes	157

Edited by: Net Gingras

Published by Home Planners, Inc., 23761 Research Drive, Farmington Hills, Michigan 48024.
All designs and illustrative material Copyright © MCMLXXXVI by Home Planners, Inc. All
rights reserved. Reproduction in any manner or form not permitted. Printed in the United
States of America. International Standard Book Number (ISBN): 0-918894-53-0.

Index to Designs

DESIGN NO.	PAGE NO.	DESIGN NO.	PAGE NO.	DESIGN NO.	PAGE NO.	DESIGN NO.	PAGE NO.	DESIGN NO.	PAGE NO.
41093	66	41783	131	42296	65	42560	170	42763	68
41210	90	41789	70	42300	63	42562	118	42769	187
41220	98	41822	94	42319	98	42566	53	42770	176
41223	136	41842	100	42324	128	42567	98	42773	13
41230	33	41850	90	42331	26	42574	62	42774	150
41265	41	41882	22	42334	92	42576	171	42786	8
41267	86	41927	14	42354	18	42578	161	42787	9
41270	15	41930	36	42361	34	42579	81	42788	86
41292	35	41935	40	42366	32	42580	73	42789	127
41298	185	41961	28	42372	130	42583	186	42794	132
41308	24	41963	182	42373	33	42584	48	42823	140
41310	100	41974	184	42375	66	42588	49	42827	79
41324	34	41976	188	42377	47	42589	86	42830	123
41341	92	41977	30	42379	142	42608	20	42832	139
41347	38	41978	72	42392	190	42624	19	42834	122
41348	37	41981	24	42393	46	42625	133	42835	192
41353	72	41985	30	42394	96	42628	20	42836	50
41358	22	42100	150	42429	112	42633	148	42837	50
41375	88	42111	60	42433	114	42645	143	42842	74
43176	89	42125	31	42435	107	42659	149	42843	75
41377	88	42137	27	42438	109	42660	146	42844	77
41378	89	42143	10	42455	104	42662	145	42845	66
41386	90	42169	174	42463	103	42709	119	42846	181
41391	35	42171	26	42465	108	42710	115	42847	180
41445	106	42173	54	42470	114	42712	70	42848	164
41457	104	42192	144	42482	106	42715	80	42849	36
41460	110	42205	167	42485	104	42716	162	42850	11
41474	113	42212	137	42502	168	42717	134	42856	76
41475	111	42213	179	42504	169	42719	160	42858	141
41498	108	42216	28	42511	157	42721	116	42858	141
41704	102	42218	7	42512	21	42723	84	42868	78
41705	28	42219	97	42514	94	42725	173	42885	100
41712	129	42243	16	42516	71	42726	42	42887	126
41713	134	42247	61	42526	59	42727	42	42893	45
41717	38	42248	55	42536	58	42730	117	42894	82
41721	43	42251	138	42546	176	42734	64	42895	158
41737	69	42254	16	42547	94	42735	85	42896	159
41739	189	42272	120	42548	177	42756	134	42901	44
41743	96	42273	124	42549	178	42758	12	43148	38
41768	24	42279	125	42551	52	42759	83	43151	56
41770	22	42282	121	42552	163	42760	172	43179	57
41778	102	42291	40	42556	147	42761	166	43198	92

On the Cover: Cover design can be found on page 76.

How To Read Floor Plans and Blueprints

Selecting the most suitable house plan for your family is a matter of matching your needs, tastes, and life-style against the many designs we offer. When you study the floor plans in this issue, and the blueprints that you may subsequently order, remember that they are simply a two-dimensional representation of what will eventually be a three-dimensional reality.

Floor plans are easy to read. Rooms are clearly labeled, with dimensions given in feet and inches. Most symbols are logical and self-explanatory: The location of bathroom fixtures, planters, fireplaces, tile floors, cabinets and counters, sinks, appliances, closets, sloped or beamed ceilings will be obvious.

A blueprint, although much more detailed, is also easy to read; all it demands is concentration. The blueprints that we offer come in many large sheets, each one of which contains a different kind of information. One sheet contains foundation and excavation drawings, another has a precise plot plan. An elevations sheet deals with the exterior walls of the house; section drawings show precise dimensions, fittings, doors, windows, and roof structures. Our detailed floor plans give the construction information needed by your contractor. And each set of blueprints contains a lengthy materials list with size and quantities of all necessary components. Using this list, a contractor and suppliers can make a start at calculating costs for you.

When you first study a floor plan or blueprint, imagine that you are walking through the house. By mentally visualizing each room in three dimensions, you can transform the technical data and symbols into something more real.

Start at the front door. It's preferable to have a foyer or entrance hall in which to receive guests. A closet here is desirable; a powder room is a plus.

Look for good traffic circulation as you study the floor plan. You should not have to pass all the way through one main room to reach another. From the entrance area you should have direct access to the three principal areas of a house—the living, work, and sleeping zones. For example, a foyer might provide separate entrances to the living room, kitchen, patio, and a hallway or staircase leading to the bedrooms.

Study the layout of each zone. Most people expect the living room to be protected from cross traffic. The kitchen, on the other hand, should connect with the dining room—and perhaps also the utility room, basement, garage, patio or deck, or a secondary entrance. A homemaker whose workday centers in the kitchen may have special requirements: a window that faces the backyard; a clear view of the family room where children play; a garage or driveway entrance that allows for a short trip with groceries; laundry facilities close at hand. Check for efficient placement of kitchen cabinets, counters, and appliances. Is there enough room in the kitchen for additional appliances, for eating in? Is there a dining nook?

Perhaps this part of the house contains a family room or a den/bedroom/office. It's advantageous to have a bathroom or powder room in this section.

As you study the plan, you may encounter a staircase, indicated by a group of parallel lines, the number of lines equaling the number of steps. Arrows labeled "up" mean that the staircase leads to a higher level, and those pointing down mean it leads to a lower one. Staircases in a split-level will have both up and down arrows on one staircase because two levels are depicted in one drawing and an extra level in another.

Notice the location of the stairways. Is too much floor space lost to them? Will you find yourself making too many trips?

Study the sleeping quarters. Are the bedrooms situated as you like? You may want the master bedroom near the kids, or you may want it as far away as possible. Is there at least one closet per person in each bedroom or a double one for a couple? Bathrooms should be convenient to each bedroom—if not adjoining, then with hallway access and on the same floor.

Once you are familiar with the relative positions of the rooms, look for such structural details as:

• Sufficient uninterrupted wall space for furniture arrangement.

• Adequate room dimensions.

• Potential heating or cooling problems—i.e., a room over a garage or next to the laundry.

• Window and door placement for good ventilation and natural light.

• Location of doorways—avoid having a basement staircase or a bathroom in view of the dining room.

• Adequate auxiliary space—closets, storage, bathrooms, countertops.

• Separation of activity areas. (Will noise from the recreation room disturb sleeping children or a parent at work?)

As you complete your mental walk through the house, bear in mind your family's long-range needs. A good house plan will allow for some adjustments now and additions in the future.

Each member of your family may find the listing of his, or her, favorite features a most helpful exercise. Why not try it?

How To Choose a Contractor

A contractor is part craftsman, part businessman, and part magician. As the person who will transform your dreams and drawings into a finished house, he will be responsible for the final cost of the structure, for the quality of the workmanship, and for the solving of all problems that occur quite naturally in the course of construction. Choose him as carefully as you would a business partner, because for the next several months that will be his role in your life.

As soon as you have a building site and house plans, start looking for a contractor, even if you do not plan to break ground for several months. Finding one suitable to build your house can take time, and once you have found him, you will have to be worked into his schedule. Those who are good are in demand and, where the season is short, they are often scheduling work up to a year in advance.

There are two types of residential contractors: the construction company and the carpenter-builder, often called a general contractor. Each of these has its advantages and disadvantages.

The carpenter-builder works directly on the job as the field foreman. Because his background is that of a craftsman, his workmanship is probably good—but his paperwork may be slow or sloppy. His overhead—which you pay for—is less than that of a large construction company. However, if the job drags on for any reason, his interest may flag because your project is overlapping his next job and eroding his profits.

Construction companies handle several projects concurrently. They have an office staff to keep the paperwork moving and an army of subcontractors they know they can count on. Though you can be confident that they will meet deadlines, they may sacrifice workmanship in order to do so. Because they emphasize efficiency, they are less personal to work with than a general contractor. Many will not work with an individual unless he is represented by an architect. The company and the architect speak the same language; it requires far more time to deal directly with a homeowner.

To find a reliable contractor, start by asking friends who have built homes for recommendations. Check with local lumber yards and building supply outlets for names of possible candidates.

Once you have several names in hand, ask the Chamber of Commerce, Better Business Bureau, or local department of consumer affairs for any information they might have on each of them. Keep in mind that these watchdog organizations can give only the number of complaints filed; they cannot tell you what percent of those claims were valid. Remember, too, that a large-volume operation is logically going to have more complaints against it than will an independent contractor.

Set up an interview with each of the potential candidates. Find out what his specialty is—custom houses, development houses, remodeling, or office buildings. Ask each to take you into—not just to the site of—houses he has built. Ask to see projects that are complete as well as work in progress, emphasizing that you are interested in projects comparable to yours. A $300,000 dentist's office will give you little insight into a contractor's craftsmanship.

Ask each contractor for bank references from both his commercial bank and any other lender he has worked with. If he is in good financial standing, he should have no qualms about giving you this information. Also ask if he offers a warranty on his work. Most will give you a one-year warranty on the structure; some offer as much as a ten-year warranty.

Ask for references, even though no contractor will give you the name of a dissatisfied customer. While previous clients may be pleased with a contractor's work overall, they may, for example, have had to wait three months after they moved in before they had any closet doors. Ask about his follow-through. Did he clean up the building site, or did the owner have to dispose of the refuse? Ask about his business organization. Did the paperwork go smoothly, or was there a delay in hooking up the sewer because he forgot to apply for a permit?

Talk to each of the candidates about fees. Most work on a "cost plus" basis; that is, the basic cost of the project—materials, subcontractors' services, wages of those working directly on the project, but not office help—plus his fee. Some have a fixed fee; others work on a percentage of the basic cost. A fixed fee is usually better for you if you can get one. If a contractor works on a percentage, ask for a cost breakdown of his best estimate and keep very careful track as the work progresses. A crafty contractor can always use a cost overrun to his advantage when working on a percentage.

Do not be overly suspicious of a contractor who won't work on a fixed fee. One who is very good and in great demand may not be willing to do so. He may also refuse to submit a competitive bid.

If the top two or three candidates are willing to submit competitive bids, give each a copy of the plans and your specifications for materials. If they are not each working from the same guidelines, the competitive bids will be of little value. Give each the same deadline for turning in a bid; two or three weeks is a reasonable period of time. If you are willing to go with the lowest bid, make an appointment with all of them and open the envelopes in front of them.

If one bid is remarkably low, the contractor may have made an honest error in his estimate. Do not try to hold him to it if he wants to withdraw his bid. Forcing him to build at too low a price could be disastrous for both you and him.

Though the above method sounds very fair and orderly, it is not always the best approach, especially if you are inexperienced. You may want to review the bids with your architect, if you have one, or with your lender to discuss which to accept. They may not recommend the lowest. A low bid does not necessarily mean that you will get quality with economy.

If the bids are relatively close, the most important consideration may not be money at all. How easily you can talk with a contractor and whether or not he inspires confidence are very important considerations. Any sign of a personality conflict between you and a contractor should be weighed when making a decision.

Once you have financing, you can sign a contract with the builder. Most have their own contract forms, but it is advisable to have a lawyer draw one up or, at the very least, review the standard contract. This usually costs a small flat fee.

A good contract should include the following:

• Plans and sketches of the work to be done, subject to your approval.

• A list of materials, including quantity, brand names, style or serial numbers. (Do not permit any "or equal" clause that will allow the contractor to make substitutions.)

• The terms—who (you or the lender) pays whom and when.

• A production schedule.

• The contractor's certification of insurance for workmen's compensation, damage, and liability.

• A rider stating that all changes, whether or not they increase the cost, must be submitted and approved in writing.

Of course, this list represents the least a contract should include. Once you have signed it, your plans are on the way to becoming a home.

A frequently asked question is: "Should I become my own general contractor?" Unless you have knowledge of construction, material purchasing, and experience supervising subcontractors, we do not recommend this route.

How To Shop For Mortgage Money

Most people who are in the market for a new home spend months searching for the right house plan and building site. Ironically, these same people often invest very little time shopping for the money to finance their new home, though the majority will have to live with the terms of their mortgage for as long as they live in the house.

The fact is that all banks are not alike, nor are the loans that they offer—and banks are not the only financial institutions that lend money for housing. The amount of down payment, interest rate, and period of the mortgage are all, to some extent, negotiable.

• Lending practices vary from one city and state to another. If you are a first-time builder or are new to an area, it is wise to hire a real estate (not divorce or general practice) attorney to help you unravel the maze of your specific area's laws, ordinances, and customs.

• Before talking with lenders, write down all your questions. Take notes during the conversation so you can make accurate comparisons.

• Do not be intimidated by financial officers. Keep in mind that *you are not begging for money*, you are buying it. Do not hesitate to reveal what other institutions are offering; they may be challenged to meet or better the terms.

• Use whatever clout you have. If you or your family have been banking with the same firm for years, let them know that they could lose your business if you can get a better deal elsewhere.

• Know your credit rights. The law prohibits lenders from considering only the husband's income when determining eligibility, a practice that previously kept many people out of the housing market. If you are turned down for a loan, you have a right to see a summary of the credit report and change any errors in it.

A GUIDE TO LENDERS

Where can you turn for home financing? Here is a list of sources for you to approach:

Savings and loan associations are the best place to start because they write well over half the mortgages in the United States on dwellings that house from one to four families. They generally offer favorable interest rates, require lower down payments, and allow more time to pay off loans than do other banks.

Savings banks, sometimes called mutual savings banks, are your next best bet. Like savings and loan associations, much of their business is concentrated in home mortgages.

Commercial banks write mortgages as a sideline, and when money is tight many will not write mortgages at all. They do hold about 15 percent of the mortgages in the country, however, and when the market is right, they can be very competitive.

Mortgage banking companies use the money of private investors to write home loans. They do a brisk business in government-backed loans, which other banks are reluctant to handle because of the time and paperwork required.

Some credit unions are now allowed to grant mortgages. A few insurance companies, pension funds, unions, and fraternal organizations also offer mortgage money to their membership, often at terms more favorable than those available in the commercial marketplace.

A GUIDE TO MORTGAGES

The types of mortgages available are far more various than most potential home buyers realize.

Traditional Loans

Conventional home loans have a fixed interest rate and fixed monthly payments. About 80 percent of the mortgage money in the United States is lent in this manner. Made by private lending institutions, these fixed rate loans are available to anyone whom the bank officials consider a good credit risk. The interest rate depends on the prevailing market for money and is slightly negotiable if you are willing to put down a large down payment. Most down payments range from 15 to 33 percent.

You can borrow as much money as the lender believes you can afford to pay off over the negotiated period of time—usually 20 to 30 years. However, a 15 year mortgage can save you considerably and enable you to own your home in half the time. For example, a 30 year, $60,800 mortgage at 12% interest will have a monthly payment of $625.40 per month vs $729.72 per month for a 15 year loan at the same interest rate. At the end of 30 years you have paid $164,344 in interest vs $70,550 for the 15 year. Remember - this is only $104.32 more per month. Along with saving with a 15 year mortgage, additional savings

can be realized with a biweekly payment plan. So be sure to consult your borrowing institution for all of your options.

The FHA does not write loans; it insures them against default in order to encourage lenders to write loans for first-time buyers and people with limited incomes. The terms of these loans make them very attractive, and you may be allowed to take as long as 25 to 30 years to pay it off.

The down payment also is substantially lower with an FHA-backed loan. At present it is set at 3 percent of the first $25,000 and 5 percent of the remainder, up to the $75,300 limit. This means that a loan on a $75,300 house would require a $750 down payment on the first $25,000 plus $2,515 on the remainder, for a total down payment of $3,265. In contrast, the down payment for the same house financed with a conventional loan could run as high as $20,000.

Anyone may apply for an FHA-insured loan, but both the borrower and the house must qualify.

The VA guarantees loans for eligible veterans, and the husbands and wives of those who died while in the service or from a service-related disability. The VA guarantees up to 60 percent of the loan or $27,500, whichever is less. Like the FHA, the VA determines the appraised value of the house, though with a VA loan, you can borrow any amount up to the appraised value.

The Farmers Home Administration offers the only loans made directly by the government. Families with limited incomes in rural areas can qualify if the house is in a community of less than 10,000 people and is outside of a large metropolitan area; if their income is less than $18,000; and if they can prove that they do not qualify for a conventional loan.

For more information, write Farmers Home Administration, Department of Agriculture, Washington, D.C. 20250, or your local office.

New loan instruments

If you think that the escalating cost of housing has squeezed you out of the market, take a look at the following new types of mortgages.

The graduated payment mortgage features a monthly obligation that gradually increases over a negotiated period of time—usually five to ten years. Though the payments begin lower, they stabilize at a higher monthly rate than a standard fixed rate mortgage. Little or no equity is built in the first years, a disadvantage if you decide to sell early in the mortgage period.

These loans are aimed at young people who can anticipate income increases that will enable them to meet the escalating payments. The size of the down payment is about the same or slightly higher than for a conventional loan, but you can qualify with a lower income. As of last year, savings and loan associations can write these loans, and the FHA now insures five different types.

The flexible loan insurance program (FLIP) requires that part of the down payment, which is about the same as a conventional loan, be placed in a pledged savings account. During the first five years of the mortgage, funds are drawn from this account to supplement the lower monthly payments.

The deferred interest mortgage, another graduated program, allows you to pay a lower rate of interest during the first few years and a higher rate in the later years of the mortgage. If the house is sold, the borrower must pay back all the interest, often with a prepayment penalty. Both the FLIP and deferred interest loans are very new and not yet widely available.

The variable rate mortgage is most widely available in California, but its popularity is growing. This instrument features a fluctuating interest rate that is linked to an economic indicator—usually the lender's cost of obtaining funds for lending. To protect the consumer against a sudden and disastrous increase, regulations limit the amount that the interest rate can increase over a given period of time.

To make these loans attractive, lenders offer them without prepayment penalties and with "assumption" clauses that allow another buyer to assume your mortgage should you sell.

Flexible payment mortgages allow young people who can anticipate rising incomes to enter the housing market sooner. They pay only the interest during the first few years; then the mortgage is amortized and the payments go up. This is a valuable option only for those people who intend to keep their home for several years because no equity is built in the lower payment period.

The reverse annuity mortgage is targeted for older people who have fixed incomes. This new loan allows those who qualify to tap into the equity on their houses. The lender pays them each month and collects the loan when the house is sold or the owner dies.

TRADITIONAL SPLIT-LEVELS . . . *have*

been included in this section that reflect exteriors of a variety of classic styles. Tudor, Spanish, Western, French and Early American versions have been adapted to the split-level type of floor plan. The split-level house may be built on a flat or sloping site. It is a favorite of many because it features a desirable separation of functions. The main level is generally the living level and contains the living, dining and breakfast rooms, plus kitchen. The upper level is exclusively the sleeping level with its baths. The lower level is devoted to laundry and family room. Some split-levels feature a fourth basement level.

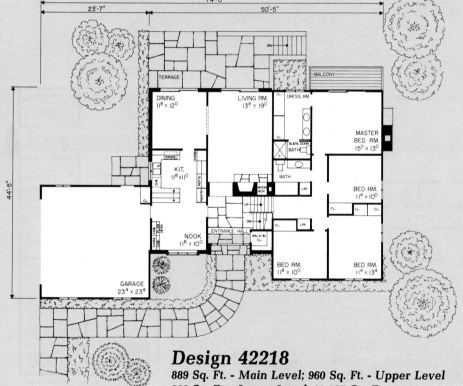

Design 42218
889 Sq. Ft. - Main Level; 960 Sq. Ft. - Upper Level
936 Sq. Ft. - Lower Level; 33,865 Cu. Ft.

● Styled in the Tudor tradition, the warmth and charm of the exterior sets the tone for an exceptionally livable interior. Were you to ask each member of your family to choose his/her favorite feature there would be many outstanding highlights to consider.

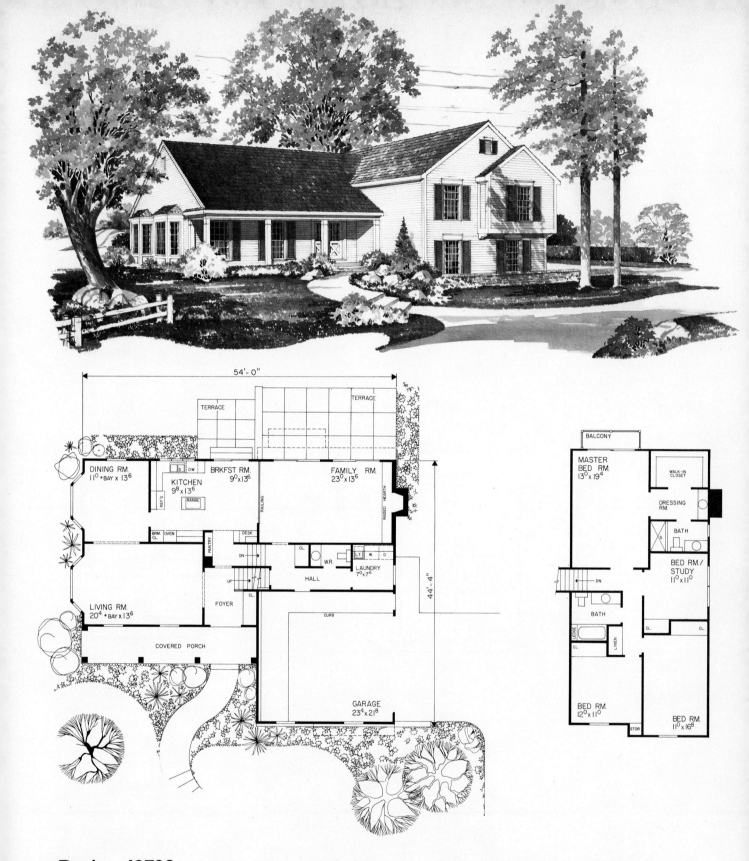

Design 42786 871 Sq. Ft. - Main Level; 1,132 Sq. Ft. - Upper Level; 528 Sq. Ft. - Lower Level; 44,000 Cu. Ft.

● A bay window in each the formal living room and dining room. A great interior and exterior design feature to attract attention to this tri-level home. The exterior also is enhanced by a covered front porch to further the Colonial charm. The interior livability is outstanding, too. An abundance of built-ins in the kitchen create an efficient work center. Features include an island range, pantry, broom closet, desk and breakfast room with sliding glass doors to the rear terrace. The lower level houses the informal family room, wash room and laundry. Further access is available to the outdoors by the family room to the terrace and laundry room to the side yard.

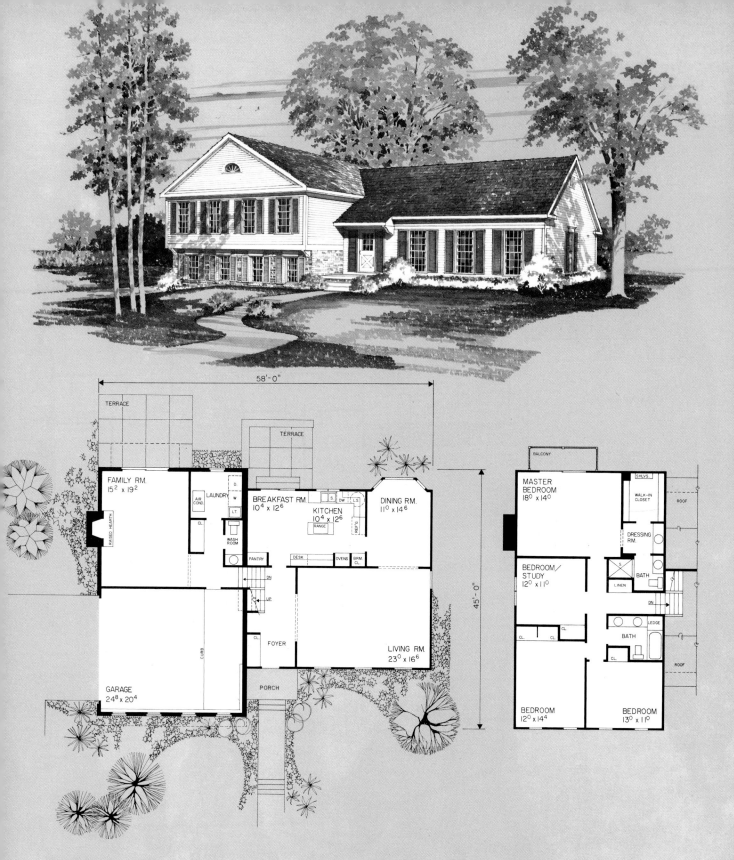

Design 42787 976 Sq. Ft. - Main Level; 1,118 Sq. Ft. - Upper Level; 524 Sq. Ft. - Lower Level; 36,110 Cu. Ft.

● Three level living! Main, upper and lower levels to serve you and your family with great ease. Start from the bottom and work your way up. Family room with raised hearth fireplace, laundry and wash room on the lower level. Formal living and dining rooms, kitchen and breakfast room on the main level. Stop and take note at the efficiency of the kitchen with its many outstanding extras. The upper level houses the three bedrooms, study (or fourth bedroom if you prefer) and two baths. This design has really stacked up its livability to serve its occupants to their best advantage. This design has great interior livability and exterior charm.

Design 42143 832 Sq. Ft. - Main Level; 864 Sq. Ft. - Upper Level; 864 Sq. Ft. - Lower Level; 27,473 Cu. Ft.

● Here the Spanish Southwest comes to life in the form of an enchanting multi-level home. There is much to rave about. The architectural detailing is delightful, indeed. The entrance courtyard, the twin balconies and the roof treatment are particular-ly noteworthy. Functioning at the rear of the house are the covered patio and the balcony with its lower patio. Well zoned, the upper level has three bedrooms and two baths; the main level has its formal living and dining rooms to the rear and kitchen area looking onto the courtyard; the lower level features the family room, study and laundry. Be sure to notice the extra wash room and the third full bath. There are two fireplaces each with a raised hearth. A dramatic house wherever built!

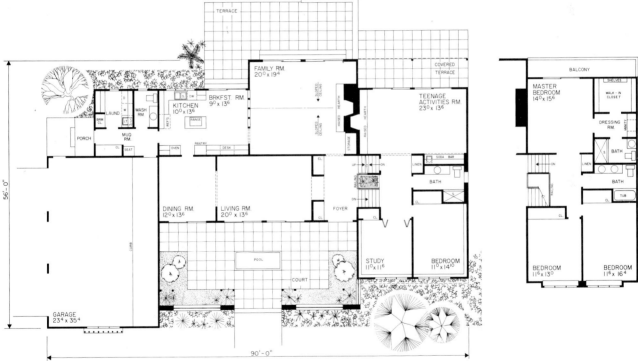

Design 42850

1,530 Sq. Ft. - Main Level; 984 Sq. Ft. - Upper Level; 951 Sq. Ft. - Lower Level; 53,780 Cu. Ft.

● Entering through the entry court of this Spanish design is very impressive. Partially shielded from the street, this court features planting areas and a small pool. Enter into the foyer and this split-level interior will begin to unfold. Down six steps from the foyer is the lower level housing a bedroom and full bath, study and teenage activities room. Adults, along with teenagers, will enjoy the activities room which has a raised hearth fireplace, soda bar and sliding glass doors leading to a covered terrace. Six steps up from the foyer is the upper level bedroom area. The main level has the majority of the living areas. Formal living and dining rooms, informal family room, kitchen with accompanying breakfast room and mud room consisting of laundry and wash room. This home even has a three-car garage. Livability will be achieved with the greatest amount of comfort in this home.

Design 42758

1,143 Sq. Ft. - Main Level
792 Sq. Ft. - Upper Level
770 Sq. Ft. - Lower Level
43,085 Cu. Ft.

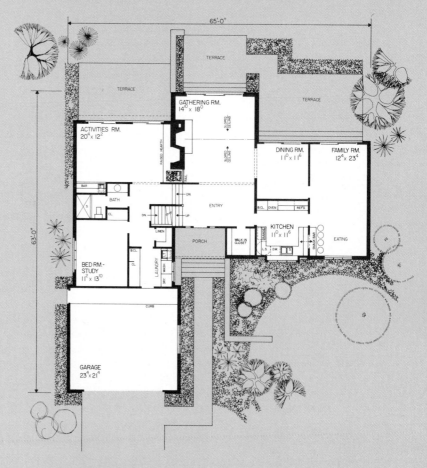

● An outstanding Tudor with three levels of exceptional livability, plus a basement. A careful study of the exterior reveals many delightful architectural details which give this home a character of its own. Notice the appealing recessed front entrance. Observe the overhanging roof with the exposed rafters. Don't miss the window treatment, the use of stucco and simulated beams, the masses of brick and the stylish chimney. Inside, the living potential is unsurpassed. Imagine, there are three living areas - the gathering, family and activities rooms. Having a snack bar, informal eating area and dining room, eating patterns can be flexible. In addition to the three bedrooms, two-bath upper level, there is a fourth bedroom with adjacent bath on the lower level.

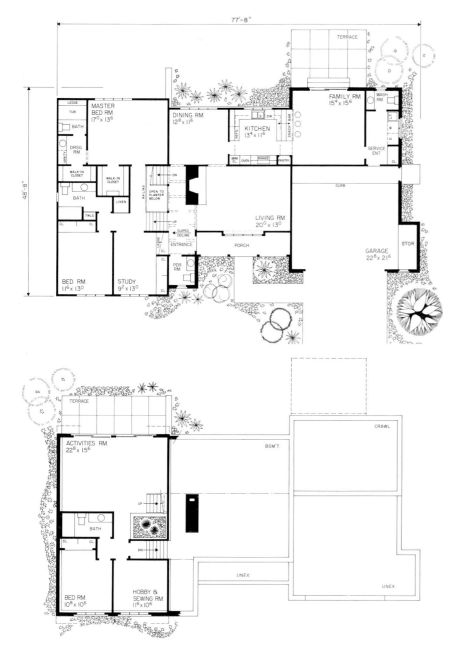

Design 42773

1,157 Sq. Ft. - Main Level
950 Sq. Ft. - Upper Level
912 Sq. Ft. - Lower Level
44,354 Cu. Ft.

● Here is another exquisitely styled Tudor tri-level designed to serve its happy occupants for many years. The contrasting use of material surely makes the exterior eye-catching. Another outstanding feature will be the covered front porch. A delightful way to enter this home. Many fine features also will be found inside this design. Formal living and dining room, U-shaped kitchen with snack bar and family room find themselves located on the main level. Two of the three bedrooms are on the upper level with two baths. Activities room, third bedroom and hobby/sewing room are on the lower level. Notice the built-in planter on the lower level which is visible from the other two levels. A powder room and a wash room both are on the main level. A study is on the upper level which is a great place for a quiet retreat. The basement will be convenient for the storage of any bulk items.

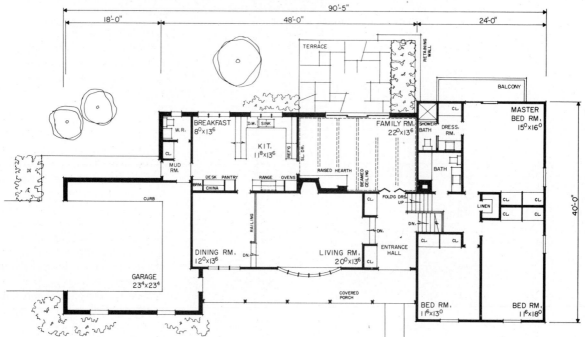

Design 41927

1,272 Sq. Ft. - Main Level; 960 Sq. Ft. - Upper Level
936 Sq. Ft. - Lower Level; 36,815 Cu. Ft.

● Living in this traditional split level home will be a great experience. For here is a design that has everything. It has good looks and an abundance of livability features. The long, low appearance is accentuated by the large covered porch which shelters the bowed window and the inviting double front doors. Whatever your preference for exterior materials they will show well on this finely proportioned home. They start with four bedrooms and three full baths and continue with: beamed ceiling family room, sunken living room, formal dining room, informal breakfast room, extra wash room, outstanding kitchen and two attractive fireplaces.

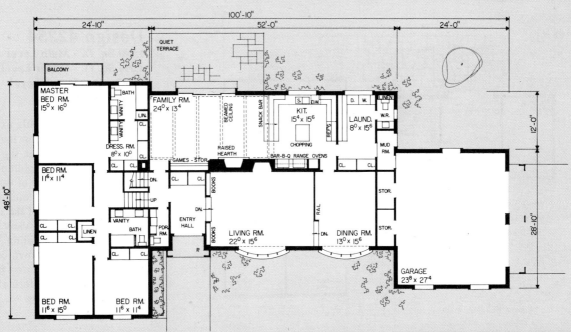

Design 41270
**1,648 Sq. Ft. - Main Level; 1,200 Sq. Ft. - Upper Level
1,200 Sq. Ft. - Lower Level; 48,856 Cu. Ft.**

● A French Provincial adaptation with an enormous amount of livability on three levels. Whether called upon to function as a four or six bedroom home, there will be plenty of space in which to move around. Whatever the activities of the family–formal or informal–this floor plan contains the facilities to cater to them. For instance, there is the family room of the main level and the recreation room of the lower level to more than adequately serve informal persuits. Then there is the sunken living room. The main level laundry will save many steps. There are two fireplaces and exceptional storage facilities. Four bedrooms highlights upper level.

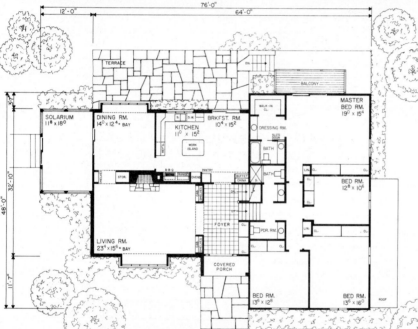

Design 42254

1,220 Sq. Ft. - Main Level
1,344 Sq. Ft. - Upper Level
659 Sq. Ft. - Lower Level
56,706 Cu. Ft.

● Tudor charm is deftly exemplified by this outstanding four level design. The window treatment, the heavy timber work and the chimney pots help set the character of this home. Contributing an extra measure of appeal is the detailing of the delightful solarium. The garden view of this home is equally appealing. The upper level balcony looks down onto the two terraces. The covered front entry leads to the spacious formal entrance hall with its slate floor. . .

Design 42243

1,274 Sq. Ft. - Main Level; 960 Sq. Ft. - Upper Level
936 Sq. Ft. - Lower Level; 42,478 Cu. Ft.

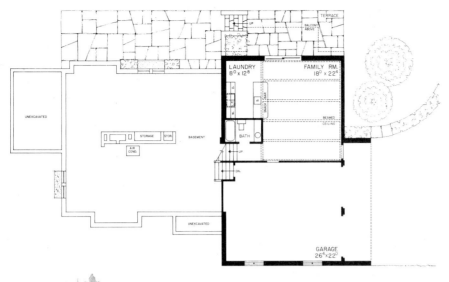

. . . Straight ahead is the kitchen and nook. The open planning of this area results in a fine feeling of spaciousness. Both living and dining rooms are wonderfully large. Each room highlights a big bay window. Notice the built-in units. Upstairs there are four bedrooms, two full baths and a powder room. Count the closets. The lower level is reserved for the all-purpose room, the separate laundry and a third full bath. The garage is adjacent. A fourth level is a basement with an abundance of space for storage and hobbies.

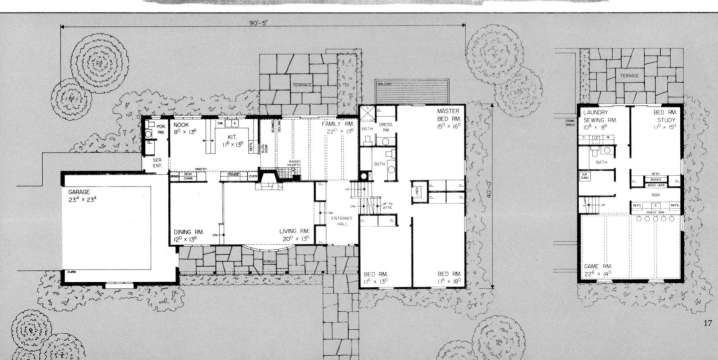

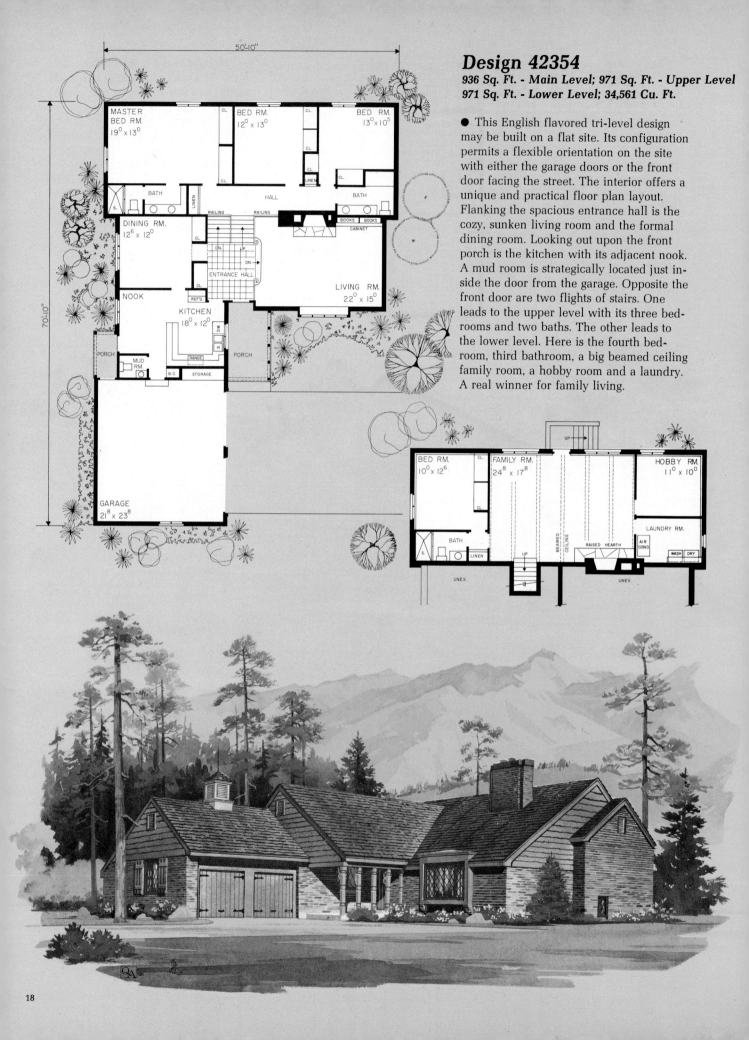

Design 42354

936 Sq. Ft. - Main Level; 971 Sq. Ft. - Upper Level
971 Sq. Ft. - Lower Level; 34,561 Cu. Ft.

● This English flavored tri-level design may be built on a flat site. Its configuration permits a flexible orientation on the site with either the garage doors or the front door facing the street. The interior offers a unique and practical floor plan layout. Flanking the spacious entrance hall is the cozy, sunken living room and the formal dining room. Looking out upon the front porch is the kitchen with its adjacent nook. A mud room is strategically located just inside the door from the garage. Opposite the front door are two flights of stairs. One leads to the upper level with its three bedrooms and two baths. The other leads to the lower level. Here is the fourth bedroom, third bathroom, a big beamed ceiling family room, a hobby room and a laundry. A real winner for family living.

Floor plan labels

Upper level
- MASTER BED RM. $19^0 \times 13^0$
- BED RM. $12^0 \times 13^0$
- BED RM. $13^0 \times 10^5$
- BATH
- HALL
- LINEN
- CL.
- BOOKS
- CABINET
- RAILING

Main level
- DINING RM. $12^6 \times 12^0$
- NOOK
- KITCHEN $18^0 \times 12^0$
- ENTRANCE HALL
- LIVING RM. $22^0 \times 15^0$
- DN. UP
- DN.
- REF'G.
- D.W.
- RANGE
- S.
- B.C. STORAGE
- MUD RM.
- PORCH
- GARAGE $21^8 \times 23^8$

Dimensions: 50'-10", 70'-10"

Lower level
- BED RM. $10^0 \times 12^6$
- FAMILY RM. $24^8 \times 17^8$
- HOBBY RM. $11^0 \times 10^0$
- BATH
- LINEN
- LAUNDRY RM.
- BEAMED CEILING
- RAISED HEARTH
- AIR COND.
- WASH DRY
- UP
- UNEX.

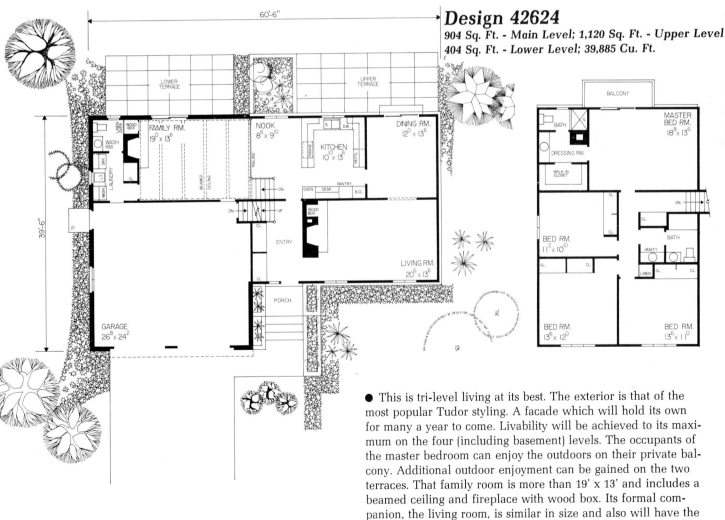

60'-6"

39'-6"

LOWER TERRACE

UPPER TERRACE

LINEN / OVEN

WOOD BOX

FAMILY RM.
19'⁰ x 13'⁶

NOOK
8'⁶ x 9'¹⁰

DINING RM.
12'⁰ x 13'⁶

KITCHEN
10' x 13'

WASH RM.

LAUNDRY

CL.

BEAMED CEILING

RAILING

RANGE

REFG.

S.

D.W.

OVEN

DESK

PANTRY

B.CL.

WOOD BOX

DN.

UP

DN.

CL.

ENTRY

LIVING RM.
20'⁶ x 13'⁶

CL.

P

PORCH

GARAGE
26'⁸ x 24'²

BALCONY

BATH

S.

MASTER BED RM.
18'⁸ x 13'⁶

DRESSING RM.

WALK-IN CLOSET

CL.

CL.

DN.

CL.

BED RM.
11'² x 10'¹⁰

BATH

VANITY

CL.

CL.

LINEN

CL.

BED RM.
13'⁶ x 12'⁰

BED RM.
13'⁶ x 11'⁰

Design 42624
904 Sq. Ft. - Main Level; 1,120 Sq. Ft. - Upper Level
404 Sq. Ft. - Lower Level; 39,885 Cu. Ft.

● This is tri-level living at its best. The exterior is that of the most popular Tudor styling. A facade which will hold its own for many a year to come. Livability will be achieved to its maximum on the four (including basement) levels. The occupants of the master bedroom can enjoy the outdoors on their private balcony. Additional outdoor enjoyment can be gained on the two terraces. That family room is more than 19' x 13' and includes a beamed ceiling and fireplace with wood box. Its formal companion, the living room, is similar in size and also will have the added warmth of a fireplace.

Design 42608

728 Sq. Ft. - Main Level; 874 Sq. Ft. - Upper Level
310 Sq. Ft. - Lower Level; 27,705 Cu. Ft.

● Here is tri-level livability with a fourth basement level for bulk storage and, perhaps, a shop area. There are four bedrooms, a handy laundry, two eating areas, formal and informal living areas and two fireplaces. Sliding glass doors in the formal dining room and the family room open to a terrace. The U-shaped kitchen has a built-in range/oven and storage pantry. The breakfast nook overlooks the family room.

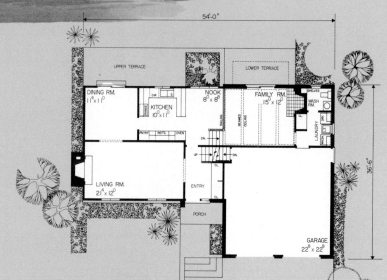

Design 42628

649 Sq. Ft. - Main Level; 672 Sq. Ft. - Upper Level
624 Sq. Ft. - Lower Level; 25,650 Cu. Ft.

● Traditional, yet contemporary! With lots of extras, too. Like a wet bar and game storage in the family room. A beamed ceiling, too, and a sliding glass door onto the terrace. In short, a family room designed to make your life easy and enjoyable. There's more. A living room with a traditionally styled fireplace and built-in bookshelves. And a dining room with a sliding glass door that opens to a second terrace. Here's the appropriate setting for those times when you want a touch of elegance.

Design 42512 2,074 Sq. Ft. - First Floor
1,116 Sq. Ft. - Second Floor; 41,500 Cu. Ft.

Second Floor Plan:

- BED RM. 22⁰ x 13⁰
- BALCONY
- CL
- CL
- CL
- BATH
- LINEN
- UPPER LIVING RM.
- SLOPED CEILING
- RAILING
- BALCONY
- DN
- OPEN TO FOYER
- RAILING
- SLOPED CEILING
- CL
- CL
- CL
- CL
- BALCONY
- BALCONY
- BED RM. 13⁸ x 15⁰
- BED RM. 10⁴ x 15⁰

First Floor Plan:

- 78'-8"
- 51'-0"
- TERRACE
- DINING RM. 15⁰ x 12⁰
- BRKFST RM. 9⁰ x 11⁶
- RAISED HEARTH
- RAISED HEARTH
- KITCHEN 12⁰ x 10⁰
- SHELVES CABINET
- REF'G
- PANTRY
- RANGE
- OVEN
- SNACK BAR
- FAMILY RM. 19⁸ x 13⁶
- WOOD BOX
- RAISED HEARTH
- WOOD BOX
- CURB
- LIVING RM. 20⁰ x 20⁰
- DN
- DN
- UP
- HALL
- DN
- TERRACE
- FOYER
- CL
- PDR. RM.
- LAUNDRY
- FLT. WASH. DRY.
- GARAGE 22⁸ x 23⁴
- BATH
- DRESSING
- VANITY
- MASTER BED RM. 15 x 15
- CL
- WALK-IN CLOSET
- PORCH
- ENTRANCE COURT
- DN

21

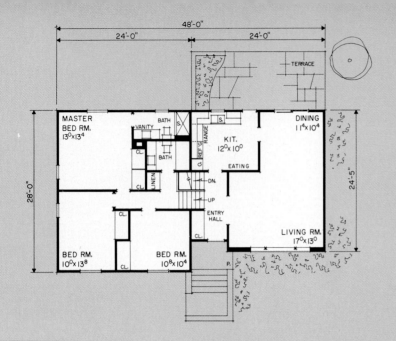

● Here are three charming split-levels designed for the modest budget. They will not require a large, expensive piece of property. Nevertheless, each is long on livability and offers all the features necessary to guarantee years of convenient living.

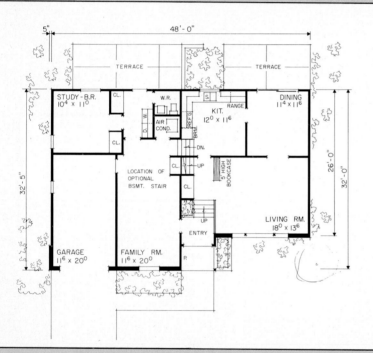

● Charming? It certainly is. And with good reason, too. This delightfully proportioned split level is highlighted by fine window treatment, interesting roof lines, an attractive use of materials and an inviting front entrance with double doors.

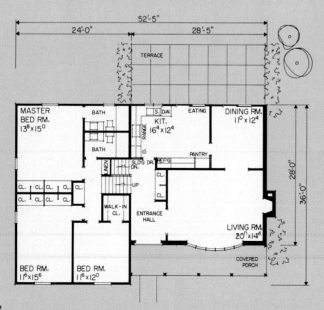

● Four level livability. And what livability it will be! This home will be most economical to build. As the house begins to take form you'll appreciate even more all the livable space you and your family will enjoy. List features that appeal to you.

Design 41358 576 Sq. Ft. - Main Level; 672 Sq. Ft. - Upper Level; 328 Sq. Ft. - Lower Level; 20,784 Cu. Ft.

Design 41770 636 Sq. Ft. - Main Level; 672 Sq. Ft. - Upper Level; 528 Sq. Ft. - Lower Level; 19,980 Cu. Ft.

Design 41882 800 Sq. Ft. - Main Level; 864 Sq. Ft. - Upper Level; 344 Sq. Ft. - Lower Level; 28,600 Cu. Ft.

● Projecting over the lower level in Garrison Colonial style is the upper level containing three bedrooms a compartmented bath with twin lavatories and two handy linen closets. The main level consists of an L-shaped kitchen with convenient eating space, a formal dining room with sliding glass doors to the terrace and a sizable living room. On the lower level there is access to the outdoors, a spacious family room and a laundry-washroom area.

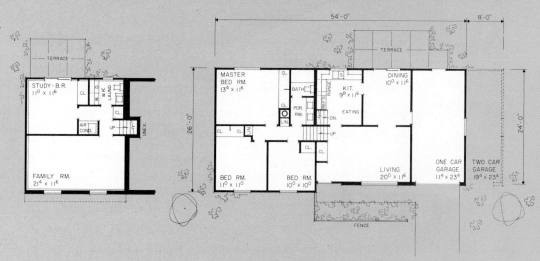

● Here are four levels just waiting for the opportunity to serve the living requirements of the active family. The traditional appeal of the exterior will be difficult to beat. Observe the window treatment, the double front doors, the covered front porch and the wrought iron work.

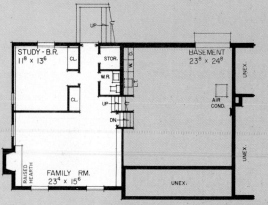

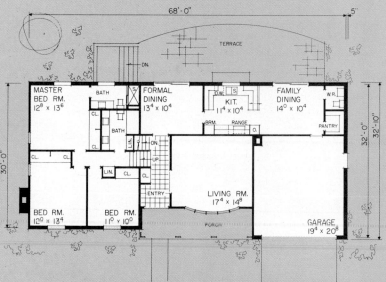

Design 41308 496 Sq. Ft. - Main Level; 572 Sq. Ft. - Upper Level; 537 Sq. Ft. - Lower Level; 16,024 Cu. Ft.

Design 41981
784 Sq. Ft. - Main Level; 912 Sq. Ft. - Upper Level
336 Sq. Ft. - Lower Level; 26,618 Cu. Ft.

● Here are three multi-level designs which are ideal for those who wish to build on a relatively narrow site. These split-levels have delightful exteriors and each offers exceptional family livability. Formal and informal areas are in each along with efficiently planned work centers. Outdoor areas are easily accessible from various rooms in these plans. Note that two of the upper level plans even have balconies.

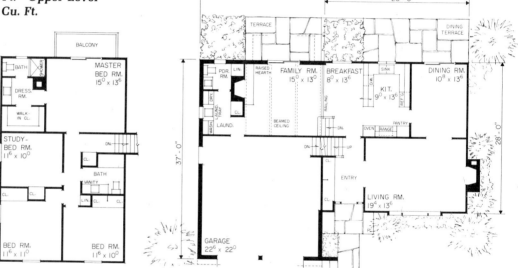

Design 41768 844 Sq. Ft. - Main Level; 740 Sq. Ft. - Upper Level; 740 Sq. Ft. - Lower Level; 29,455 Cu. Ft.

Design 42171

795 Sq. Ft. - Main Level
912 Sq. Ft. - Upper Level
335 Sq. Ft. - Lower Level; 33,243 Cu. Ft.

● This English Tudor, split-level adaptation has much to recommend it. Perhaps, its most significant feature is that it can be built economically on a relatively small site. The width of the house is just over 52 feet. But its size does not inhibit its livability. There are many fine qualities. Observe the living room fireplace in addition to the one in the family room with a wood box. The breakfast room overlooks the lower level family room. It also has a pass-thru to the kitchen. Don't miss the balcony off the master bedroom. Also worthy of note, a short flight of stairs leads to the huge attic storage area.

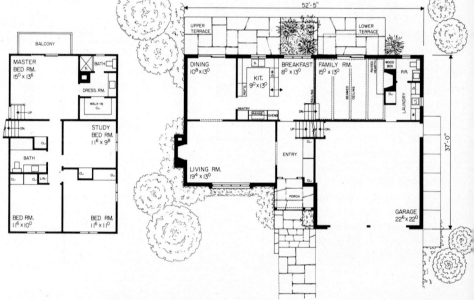

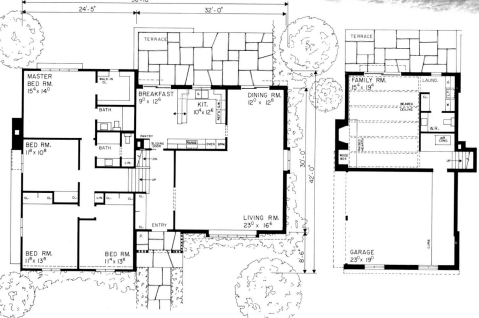

Design 42137
987 Sq. Ft. - Main Level
1,043 Sq. Ft. - Upper Level
463 Sq. Ft. - Lower Level; 29,382 Cu. Ft.

● Tudor design adapts to split-level living. The result is a unique charm for all to remember. As for the livability, the happy occupants of this tri-level home will experience wonderful living patterns. A covered porch protects the front entry. The center hall routes traffic coveniently to the spacious formal living and dining area; the informal breakfast room and kitchen zone; the upper level bedrooms and the lower level all-purpose family room. List the numerous features that contribute to fine living.

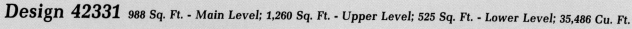

Design 42331 988 Sq. Ft. - Main Level; 1,260 Sq. Ft. - Upper Level; 525 Sq. Ft. - Lower Level; 35,486 Cu. Ft.

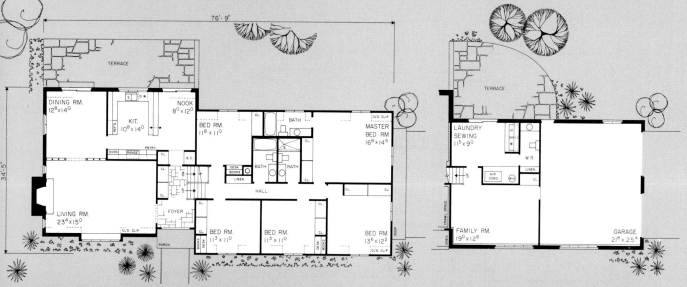

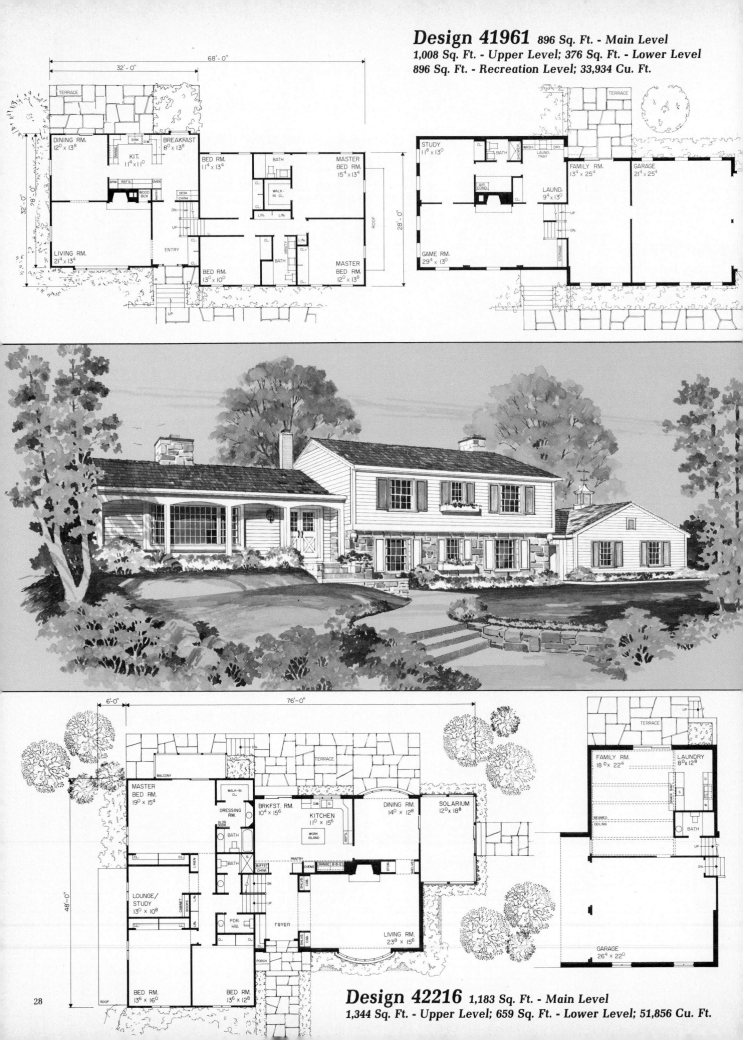

Design 41961
896 Sq. Ft. - Main Level
1,008 Sq. Ft. - Upper Level; 376 Sq. Ft. - Lower Level
896 Sq. Ft. - Recreation Level; 33,934 Cu. Ft.

Main Level (left plan):

68'-0"
32'-0"
32'-0"
28'-0"

TERRACE

DINING RM.
12⁰ x 13⁸

KIT.
11⁴ x 11⁰

SINK
D.W.
RANGE
BRM. REF'S. OVEN
WOOD BOX
PANTRY

BREAKFAST
8⁰ x 13⁸

BED RM.
11⁴ x 13⁴

BATH

MASTER BED RM.
15⁴ x 13⁴

WALK-IN CL.

DESK
CHINA
CL.
DN.
UP
LIN.
LIN.

LIVING RM.
21⁴ x 13⁴

ENTRY

CL.

BED RM.
13⁰ x 10⁰

VANITY
BATH
CL.
LIN.
CL.

MASTER BED RM.
12⁰ x 13⁸

ROOF

UP

Upper Level (right plan):

28'-0"

TERRACE

STUDY
11⁸ x 13⁰

CL.
BATH
SHOWER
WASH.
LAUND. TRAY
DRY.

FAMILY RM.
13⁴ x 25⁴

GARAGE
21⁴ x 25⁴

AIR COND.
CL.

LAUND.
9⁴ x 13⁰

GAME RM.
29⁴ x 13⁰

STORAGE
UP
DN.

Design 42216
1,183 Sq. Ft. - Main Level
1,344 Sq. Ft. - Upper Level; 659 Sq. Ft. - Lower Level; 51,856 Cu. Ft.

6'-0"
76'-0"
48'-0"

BALCONY

MASTER BED RM.
19⁰ x 15⁴

WALK-IN CL.

DRESSING RM.

SLDG. DOOR

BATH

BRKFST. RM.
10⁴ x 15⁶

TERRACE

KITCHEN
11⁰ x 15⁶

WORK ISLAND

DINING RM.
14⁰ x 12⁸

SOLARIUM
12⁰ x 18⁸

CL.
CL.
LINEN
BATH
S
BUFFET
CHINA
PANTRY
OVENS
RANGE B-B-Q
STOR.
SHELVES

LOUNGE/ STUDY
13⁰ x 10⁸

CABINET
BOOKS
DN.
UP
SHLVS.
CAB.

PDR.
HW.
FOYER
CAB.

LIVING RM.
23⁸ x 15⁶

PORCH
ROOF

BED RM.
13⁶ x 16⁰

BED RM.
13⁶ x 12⁸

Upper Level (right plan):

TERRACE
UP

FAMILY RM.
18⁰ x 22⁴

LAUNDRY
8⁰ x 12⁸

D.
SNACK BAR
BATH

BEAMED CEILING

UP
DN.

GARAGE
26⁴ x 22⁰

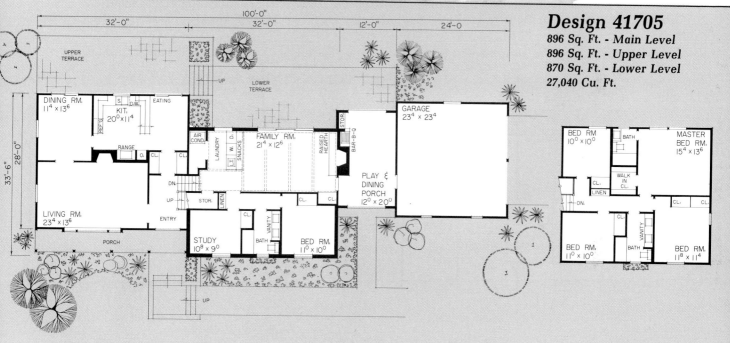

Design 41705

896 Sq. Ft. - Main Level
896 Sq. Ft. - Upper Level
870 Sq. Ft. - Lower Level
27,040 Cu. Ft.

Design 41977 *896 Sq. Ft. - Main Level; 884 Sq. Ft. - Upper Level; 896 Sq. Ft. - Lower Level; 36,718 Cu. Ft.*

● This split-level is impressive. It has a two-story center portion, flanked by a projecting living wing on one side and a garage on the other side, yet it still maintains that ground-hugging quality. There is an orderly flow of traffic. You will go up to the sleeping zone; down to the hobby/recreation level; straight ahead to the kitchen and breakfast room; left to the living room.

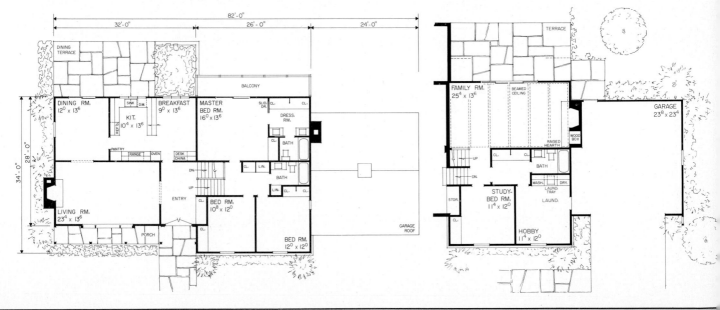

Design 42125
728 Sq. Ft. - Main Level; 672 Sq. Ft. - Upper Level; 656 Sq. Ft. - Lower Level; 28,315 Cu. Ft.

● A long list of features are available to recommend this four level, traditional home. First of all, it is a real beauty. The windows, shutters, doorway, horizontal siding and stone all go together with great proportion to project an image of design excellence. Inside, the livability is outstanding. There are three bedrooms, plus a study (make it the fourth bedroom if you wish); two full baths and a washroom; a fine kitchen with eating space; formal living and dining areas and an all-purpose family room.

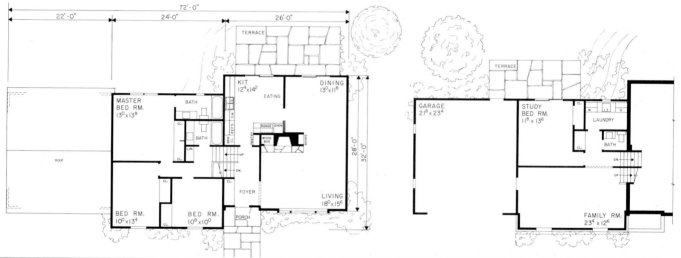

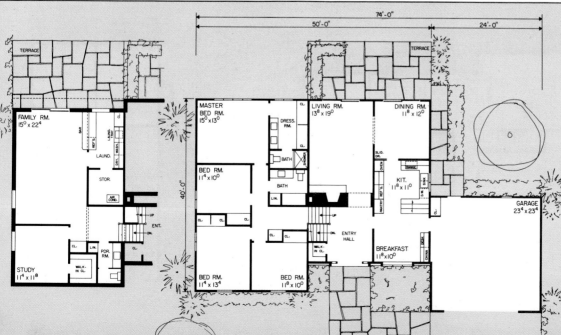

Design 41985
884 Sq. Ft. - Main Level
960 Sq. Ft. - Upper Level
888 Sq. Ft. - Lower Level
29,743 Cu. Ft.

● Here is a split-level that expresses all that is warm and inviting in the traditional vein. Delightfully proportioned, the projecting wings add that desired look of distinction. The double front doors open into a spacious entry hall. Straight ahead is the living room with the dining room but a step away. The kitchen is strategically located with a pass-thru to the breakfast room.

31

● Here are three optional elevations that function with the same basic floor plan. No need to decide now which is your favorite since the blueprints for this design include details for each optional exterior.

If yours is a restricted building budget, your construction dollar could hardly return greater dividends in the way of exterior appeal and interior livability. Also, you won't need a big, expensive site on which to build.

In addition to the four bedrooms and 2½ baths, there are two living areas, two places for dining, a fireplace and a basement. Notice the fine accessibility of the rear outdoor terrace.

Design 42366
1,078 Sq. Ft. - First Floor
880 Sq. Ft. - Second Floor
27,242 Cu. Ft.

Design 41230

728 Sq. Ft. - Main Level
728 Sq. Ft. - Recreation Level
792 Sq. Ft. - Upper Level
316 Sq. Ft. - Study Level
28,880 Cu. Ft.

● Here is a side-to-side split-level. It has a bow window that enlivens the front of the house. Note that the basement area has a workshop and recreation room. The bedroom area provides the master bedroom with its own private bath.

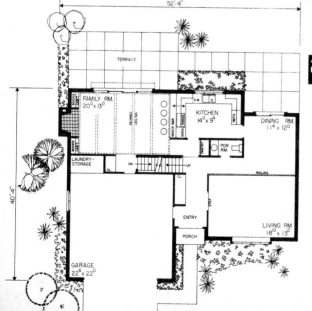

Design 42373

1,160 Sq. Ft. - First Floor
1,222 Sq. Ft. - Second Floor
33,775 Cu. Ft.

● It would be difficult to find more livability wrapped in such an attractive facade. This charming, Tudor adaptation will return big dividends per construction dollar. It is compact and efficient. And, of course, it will not require a big, expensive piece of property. The two-car garage is an integral part of the structure for convenience and economic advantages.

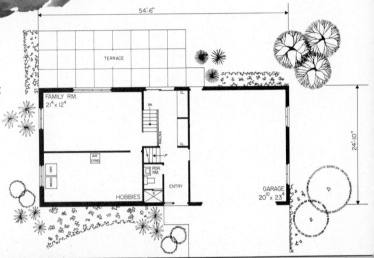

Design 42361 257 Sq. Ft. - Entry Level
575 Sq. Ft. - Main Level; 896 Sq. Ft. - Upper Level
304 Sq. Ft. - Lower Level; 23,500 Cu. Ft.

● Here is a great example of how much livability a modest sized, multi-level home really can deliver. Each of the four levels make a vital contribution to convenient living patterns. The entry level is on grade with the two-car garage. The family and hobby rooms are down on the lower level. Up from the entry level is the spacious living and dining area, plus the kitchen with its eating space. Stairs lead to the upper, sleeping level from this living level. Imagine, four bedrooms, two full baths and plenty of storage potential to serve the large and growing family. Don't miss the overall width of this house which can be built on a relatively narrow site.

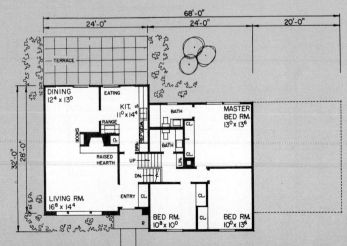

● Wonderfully proportioned, this tri-level has delightful symmetry. Designed to satisfy the requirements of the medium-sized building budget, the exterior houses an extremely practical floor plan. Although the upper level, sleeping area features three bedrooms and two full baths, this home could function admirably as a four bedroom. The fourth bedroom is acquired by utilizing the extra bedroom on the lower level. In addition to the study/bedroom of the lower level, there is the separate laundry, the extra washroom and the multi-purpose family room.

Design 41324 682 Sq. Ft. - Main Level
672 Sq. Ft. - Upper Level; 656 Sq. Ft. - Lower Level; 24,208 Cu. Ft.

● This compact tri-level will build economically. Its charming, traditional facade will never fail to elicit enthusiastic comment. Designed to assure the most economical use of lumber, this house is a perfect rectangle. When built on a site which slopes to the rear, the lower level can become exposed. This permits the family room to function with the outdoor terrace. The extra bedroom becomes completely livable. This house then features four bedrooms and two full baths.

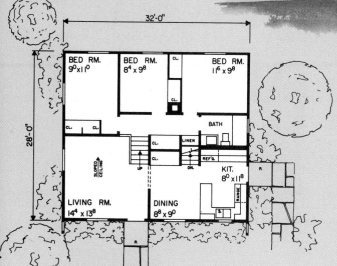

Design 41391 413 Sq. Ft. - Main Level
483 Sq. Ft. - Upper Level; 495 Sq. Ft. - Lower Level; 13,715 Cu. Ft.

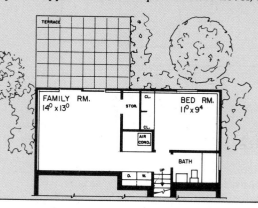

Design 41292 640 Sq. Ft. - Main Level
672 Sq. Ft. - Upper Level; 646 Sq. Ft. - Lower Level; 20,537 Cu. Ft.

● A traditionally styled tri-level design that is perfect for you and your family. Upon entering this home, you will find a raised living room. Just a few steps away, there is a nice-sized kitchen-eating area. It will make feeding the family a breeze. An adjacent dining room is for formal dining. To your left of the entryway, a conveniently situated office/study is available. It is ideal for a home business. Another convenience is the first floor laundry and washroom. Note the spacious family room with fireplace and sliding glass doors leading to the terrace. Two bedrooms, a full bath and a master bedroom will be found on the upper level.

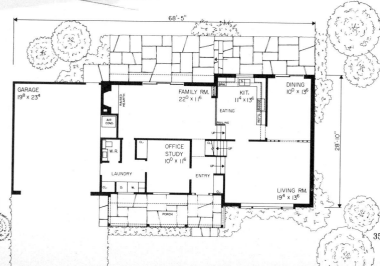

35

Design 42849 *1,003 Sq. Ft. - Main Level*
936 Sq. Ft. - Upper Level; 832 Sq. Ft. - Lower Level; 36,250 Cu. Ft.

● Enter into the front foyer of this traditional design and you will be impressed by the dramatic sloped ceiling. Sunken two steps, the formal living room is to the right. This room is highlighted by a fireplace with adjacent wood box, sloped ceiling and a multi-paned bay window. Formal and informal dining, kitchen, laundry and washroom also share the main level with the living room and foyer. The lower level houses the family room, bedroom/study, full bath and mechanical room; the upper level, three bedrooms and two more full baths. Notice the excellent indoor-outdoor living relationships. There is a side terrace accessible from each of the dining areas plus a rear terrace. The front projecting garage reduces the size of the lot required for this home.

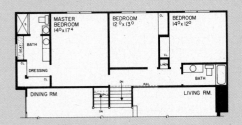

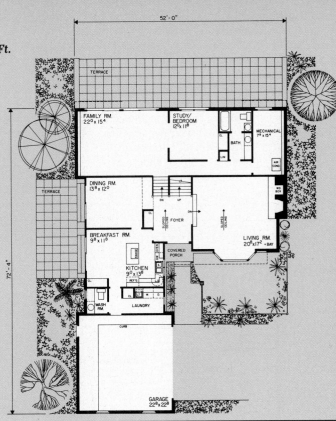

Design 41930 947 Sq. Ft. - Main Level; 768 Sq. Ft. - Upper Level; 740 Sq. Ft. - Lower Level; 25,906 Cu. Ft.

● The warmth of this inspiring Colonial adaptation is not restricted to the exterior. Its charm is readily apparent upon stepping through the double front doors. The sunken living room and family room will be in great demand.

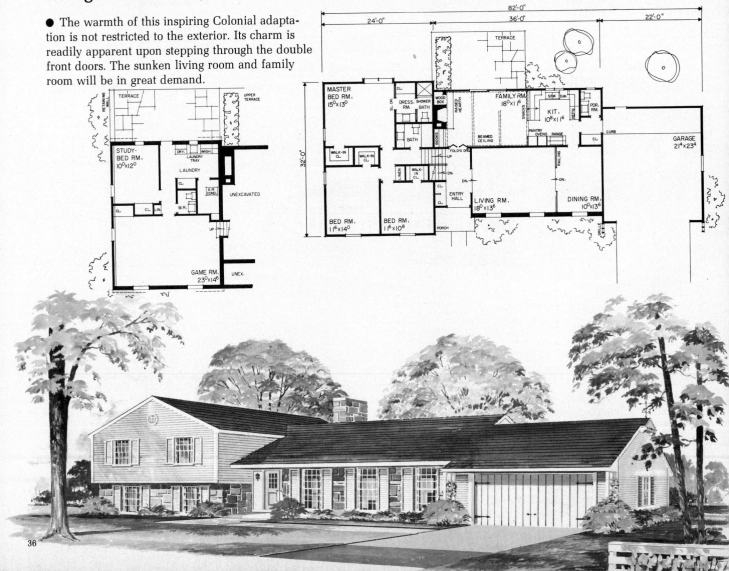

Design 41348 750 Sq. Ft. - Main Level; 672 Sq. Ft. - Upper Level; 664 Sq. Ft. - Lower Level; 22,143 Cu. Ft.

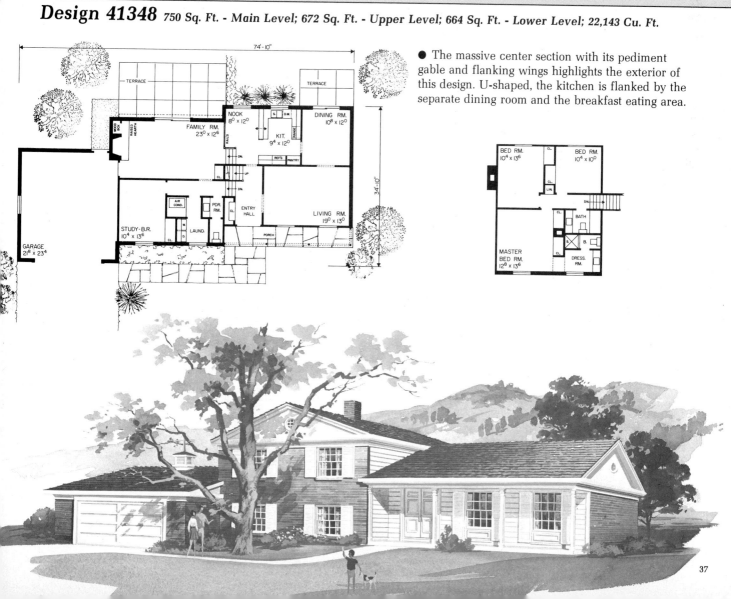

● The massive center section with its pediment gable and flanking wings highlights the exterior of this design. U-shaped, the kitchen is flanked by the separate dining room and the breakfast eating area.

74'-10"

TERRACE

TERRACE

NOOK
8⁰ x 12⁰

DINING RM.
10⁸ x 12⁰

FAMILY RM.
23⁰ x 12⁶

KIT.
9⁴ x 12⁰

WOOD BOX

RAISED HEARTH

DN.

REF'S

PANTRY

UP

DN.

CL.

AIR COND.

PDR. RM.

LAUND.

ENTRY HALL

LIVING RM.
19⁰ x 13⁰

STUDY-B.R.
10⁴ x 13⁶

CL.

PORCH

34'-10"

GARAGE
21⁸ x 23⁴

BED RM.
10⁴ x 13⁶

CL.

BED RM.
10⁴ x 10⁰

CL.

LIN.

DN.

CL.

BATH

B.

MASTER
BED RM.
12⁸ x 13⁶

CL.

DRESS. RM.

● A relatively small split-level that will surely return loads of livability for the building dollar. Certainly your building budget will purchase a well designed home. One that will be hard to beat for exterior appeal.

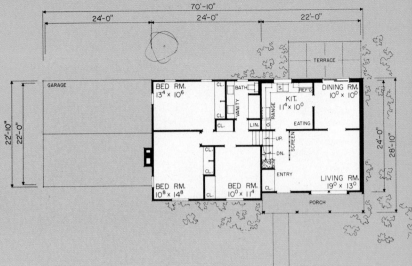

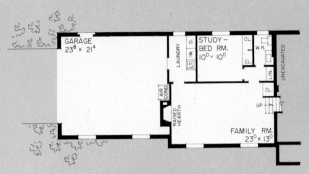

● Impressive, indeed, wherever located. Gabled roofs, muntined windows with shutters, a covered front porch, paneled double doors and a cupola over the garage give a Colonial touch to the exterior of this smartly, planned split-level.

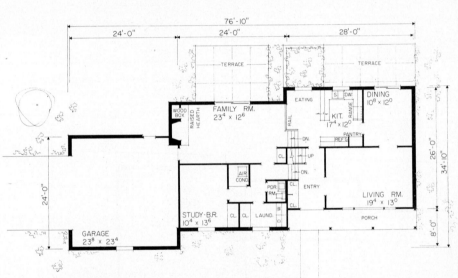

● You'll have fun living in this home. There will be four bedrooms, three baths, large formal living and dining rooms, an efficient kitchen with breakfast nook, a covered porch and much more to serve your family.

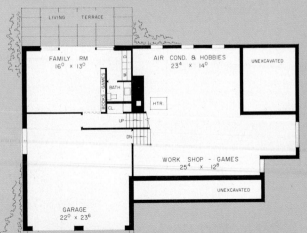

Design 41717 556 Sq. Ft. - Main Level; 624 Sq. Ft. - Upper Level; 596 Sq. Ft. - Lower Level; 17,975 Cu. Ft.

Design 41347 750 Sq. Ft. - Main Level; 672 Sq. Ft. - Upper Level; 664 Sq. Ft. - Lower Level; 21,646 Cu. Ft.

Design 43148 808 Sq. Ft. - Main Level; 960 Sq. Ft. - Upper Level; 374 Sq. Ft. - Lower Level; 33,931 Cu. Ft.

Design 41935 904 Sq. Ft. - Main Level; 864 Sq. Ft. - Upper Level; 840 Sq. Ft. - Lower Level; 26,745 Cu. Ft.

● This design will adapt equally well to a flat or sloping site. There would be no question about the family's ability to adapt to what the interior has to offer. Everything is present to satisfy the family's desire to "live a little". There are features such as the covered porch, balcony, two fireplaces, extra study, family room with beamed ceiling, complete laundry and a basement level for added recreational and storage space. Blueprints for this design include optional non-basement details.

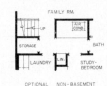

OPTIONAL NON-BASEMENT

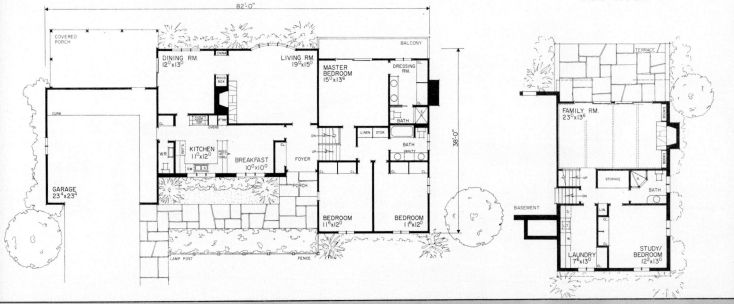

Design 42291 942 Sq. Ft. - Main Level
1,101 Sq. Ft. - Upper Level; 534 Sq. Ft. - Lower Level; 40,932 Cu. Ft

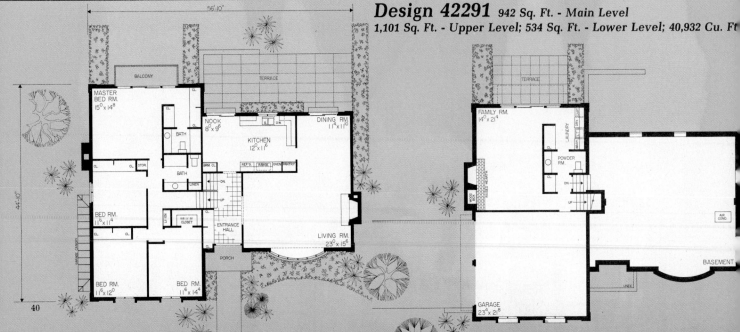

Design 41265 *1,298 Sq. Ft. - Main Level; 964 Sq. Ft. - Upper Level; 964 Sq. Ft. - Lower Level; 48,588 Cu. Ft.*

● Impressive, may be just the word to describe this appealingly formal, traditional tri-level. Changes in level add interest to its plan and make this already spacious house seem even larger. A glamorous living room, two steps below entry level, features a handsome fireplace and a broad, bay window. Raised two additional steps to emphasize the sunken area, the formal dining room is partitioned from the living room by a built-in planter. Up a few stairs from the entry hall, the sleeping level houses three bedrooms and two baths. The lower level has areas which will lend themselves to flexible living patterns.

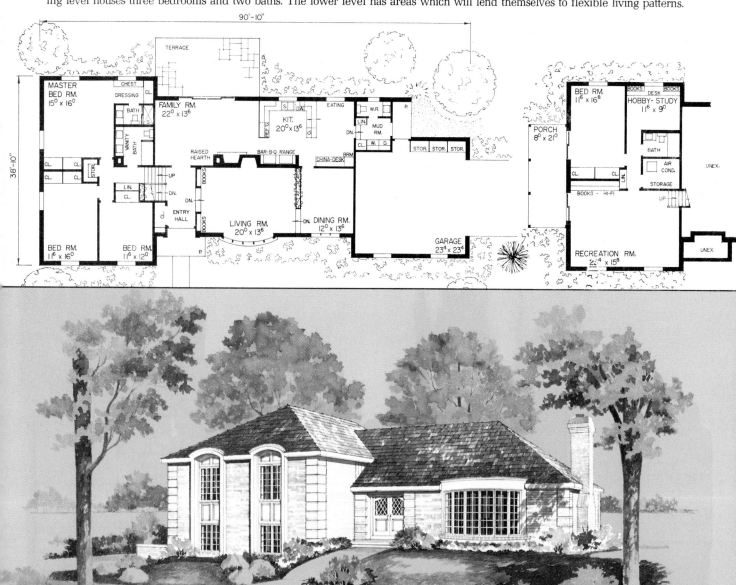

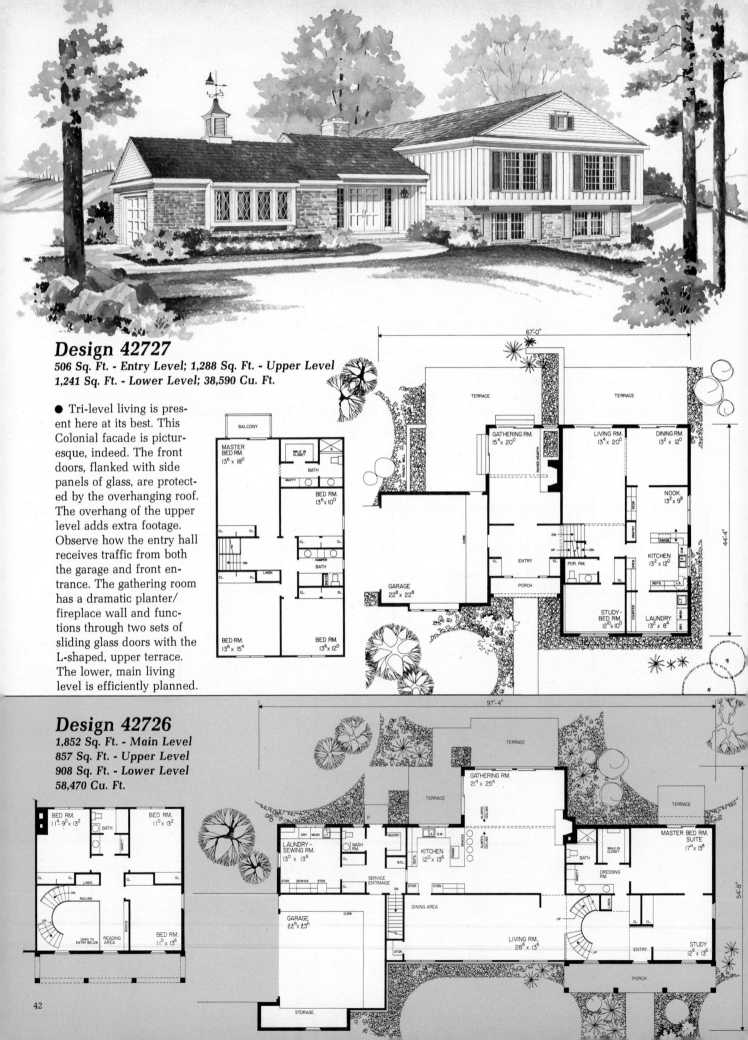

Design 42727

506 Sq. Ft. - Entry Level; 1,288 Sq. Ft. - Upper Level
1,241 Sq. Ft. - Lower Level; 38,590 Cu. Ft.

● Tri-level living is present here at its best. This Colonial facade is picturesque, indeed. The front doors, flanked with side panels of glass, are protected by the overhanging roof. The overhang of the upper level adds extra footage. Observe how the entry hall receives traffic from both the garage and front entrance. The gathering room has a dramatic planter/ fireplace wall and functions through two sets of sliding glass doors with the L-shaped, upper terrace. The lower, main living level is efficiently planned.

Design 42726

1,852 Sq. Ft. - Main Level
857 Sq. Ft. - Upper Level
908 Sq. Ft. - Lower Level
58,470 Cu. Ft.

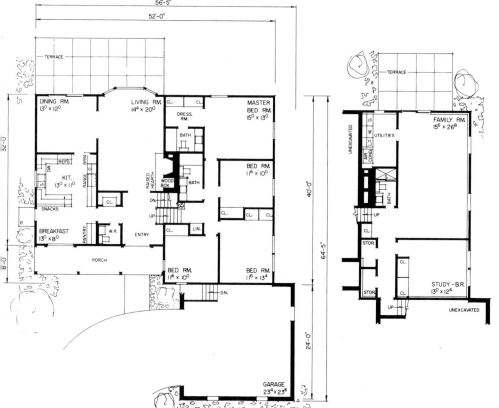

Design 41721

896 Sq. Ft. - Main Level
960 Sq. Ft. - Upper Level
960 Sq. Ft. - Lower Level
32,595 Cu. Ft.

● Ideal for a relatively narrow site, this L-shaped tri-level will serve the large family wonderfully. The double doors of the front entry are sheltered by the long, covered porch and lead to the spacious hall which routes traffic efficiently to all areas. The kitchen, flanked by the informal breakfast room and the separate dining room, has an abundance of counter and cupboard space. Four bedrooms and two baths comprise the quiet, upper level sleeping area. An abundance of dual-use space is found on the lower level, accessible from the garage. Note utility room, bath with stall shower, study/bedroom, large, family room and two storage closets which are all features of the lower level.

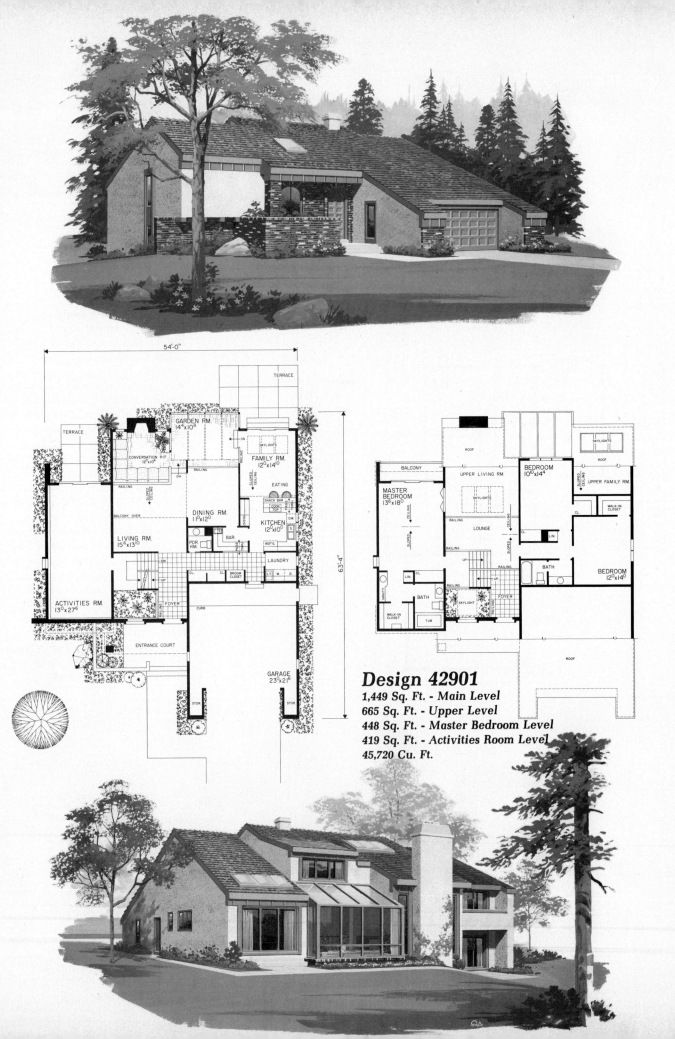

Design 42901

1,449 Sq. Ft. - Main Level
665 Sq. Ft. - Upper Level
448 Sq. Ft. - Master Bedroom Level
419 Sq. Ft. - Activities Room Level
45,720 Cu. Ft.

CONTEMPORARY SPLIT-LEVELS . . .

like their traditional counterparts offer the feature of a separation of functions and their location on the main (living) level, upper (sleeping) level & lower (recreation) level. However, because of the unconventional configurations of many contemporary designs, variations of the popular tri-level arrangement come into existence. Examples of both the straight forward, popularly accepted split-level & the uniquely designed, less conventional split-level are featured. Note indoor & outdoor balconies, functional terraces, sloping ceilings & dramatic glass areas. Along with offering different living patterns from the one or two-story home, the contemporary split-level puts a refreshing, new face on them.

Design 42893

1,297 Sq. Ft. - Main Level
1,256 Sq. Ft. - Upper Level
654 Sq. Ft. - Lower Level
49,198 Cu. Ft.

● Here is a contemporary split-level with a lot of appeal. To the right of the foyer and up a few steps you will find three bedrooms and a bath. Also, a master bedroom suite with an over-sized tub, shower, walk-in closet and sliding glass doors to a balcony. (One of the front bedrooms also has a balcony.) A sunken living room is on the main level. It has a wet bar and shares with the dining room a thru-fireplace, sloped ceiling and a skylight. A spacious kitchen and breakfast room are nearby. They offer easy access to the covered porch - ideal for summer meals. The lower level has a large family room with sliding glass doors to the lower terrace, another wet bar and a fireplace. The laundry, full bath, large closet and garage access are just steps away.

Design 42393 392 Sq. Ft. - Entry Level; 841 Sq. Ft. - Upper Level; 848 Sq. Ft. - Lower Level; 24,980 Cu. Ft.

● For those with a flair for something refreshingly contemporary both inside and out. This modest sized multi-level has a unique exterior and an equally interesting interior. The low-pitched, wide-overhanging roof protects the inviting double front doors and the large picture window. The raised planter and the side balcony add an extra measure of appeal. Inside, the living patterns will be delightful! The formal living room will look down into the dining room. Like the front entry, the living room has direct access to the lower level. The kitchen is efficient and spacious enough to accommodate an informal breakfast eating area. The laundry room is nearby. The all-purpose family room has beamed ceiling, fireplace and sliding glass doors to rear terrace. The angular, open stairwell to the upper level is dramatic, indeed. Notice how each bedroom has direct access to an outdoor balcony.

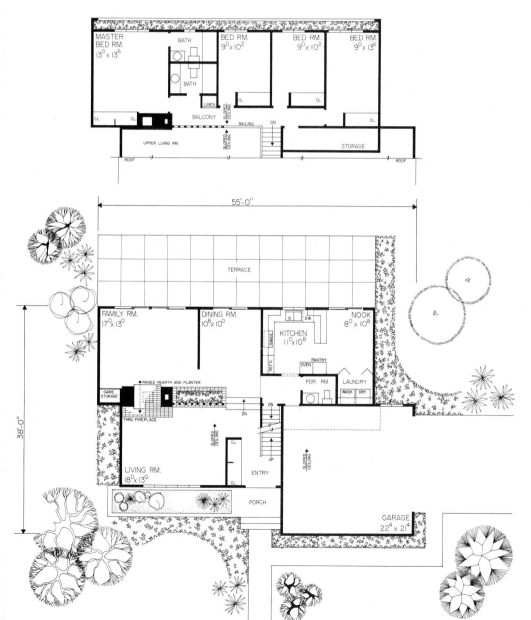

MASTER BED RM. 13⁰ x 13⁶

BATH

BATH

BED RM. 9⁰ x 10²

BED RM. 9⁰ x 10²

BED RM. 9⁰ x 13⁶

LINEN

CL.

CL.

CL.

CL.

CL.

BALCONY

SLOPED CEILING

RAILING

DN.

CL.

UPPER LIVING RM.

SLOPED CEILING

STORAGE

ROOF

ROOF

55'-0"

TERRACE

38'-0"

FAMILY RM. 17⁰ x 13⁰

DINING RM. 10⁸ x 10⁰

KITCHEN 11⁰ x 10⁶

NOOK 8⁰ x 10⁸

RANGE

REF'G.

S.

D.W.

PANTRY

OVEN

POR. RM.

LAUNDRY

WASH.

DRY.

RAISED HEARTH AND PLANTER

GAME STORAGE

THRU FIREPLACE

DN.

SLOPED CEILING

CL.

CL.

ENTRY

UP

SLOPED CEILING

DN.

LIVING RM. 18⁰ x 13⁰

PORCH

GARAGE 22⁴ x 21⁴

Design 42377

388 Sq. Ft. - Living Room Level
782 Sq. Ft. - Main Level
815 Sq. Ft. - Upper Level
22,477 Cu. Ft.

● What an impressive up-to-date multi-level home this is. Its refreshing configuration will command a full measure of attention. Separating the living and slightly lower levels is a thru-fireplace which has a raised hearth in the family room. An adjacent planter with vertical members provides additional interest and beauty. The rear terrace is accessible from nook, family and dining rooms. Notice the powder room, the convenient laundry area and the basement stairs. Four bedrooms serviced by two full baths comprise the upper level which looks down into the living room. A large walk-in storage closet will be ideal for those seasonal items. An attractive outdoor planter extends across the rear just outside the bedroom windows. This will surely be a house that will be fun in which to live.

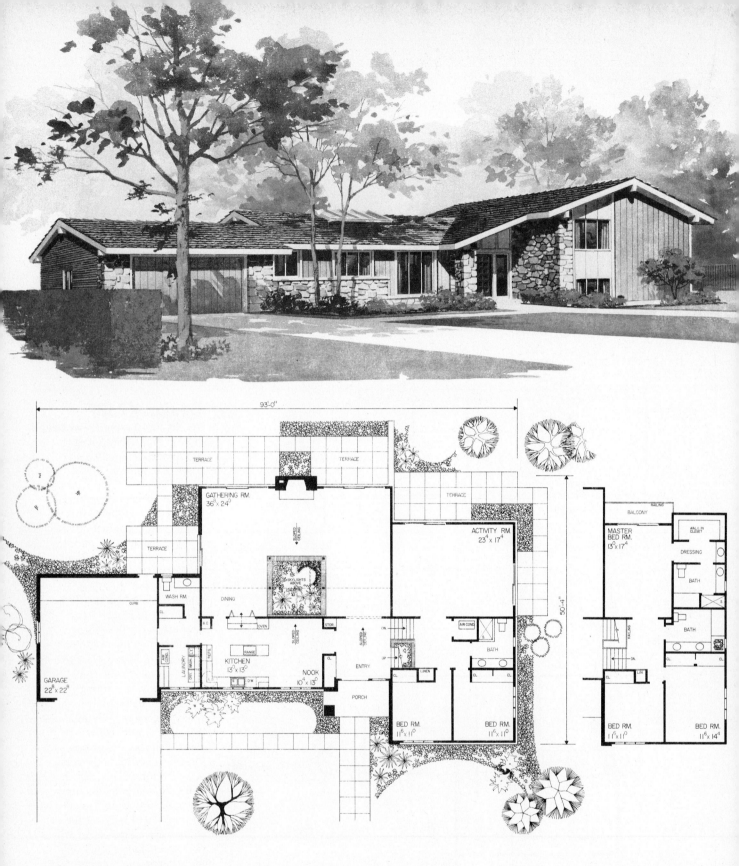

Design 42584 1,604 Sq. Ft. - Main Level; 1,018 Sq. Ft. - Upper Level; 1,026 Sq. Ft. - Lower Level; 39,200 Cu. Ft.

● Imagine an indoor garden with a skylight above in the huge gathering room plus a planter beside the lower level stairs. The gathering room also has a sloped ceiling, fireplace and two sets of sliding glass doors leading to the rear terrace and one set to the side terrace. That sure is luxury. But the appeal does not stop there. There are sloped ceilings in the foyer and breakfast nook. The kitchen has an island range, built-in oven and pass-thru to the dining room. Plus a large activities room. A great place for those informal activities. Five bedrooms in all to serve the large family. Including a master suite with a private balcony, dressing room, walk-in closet and bath.

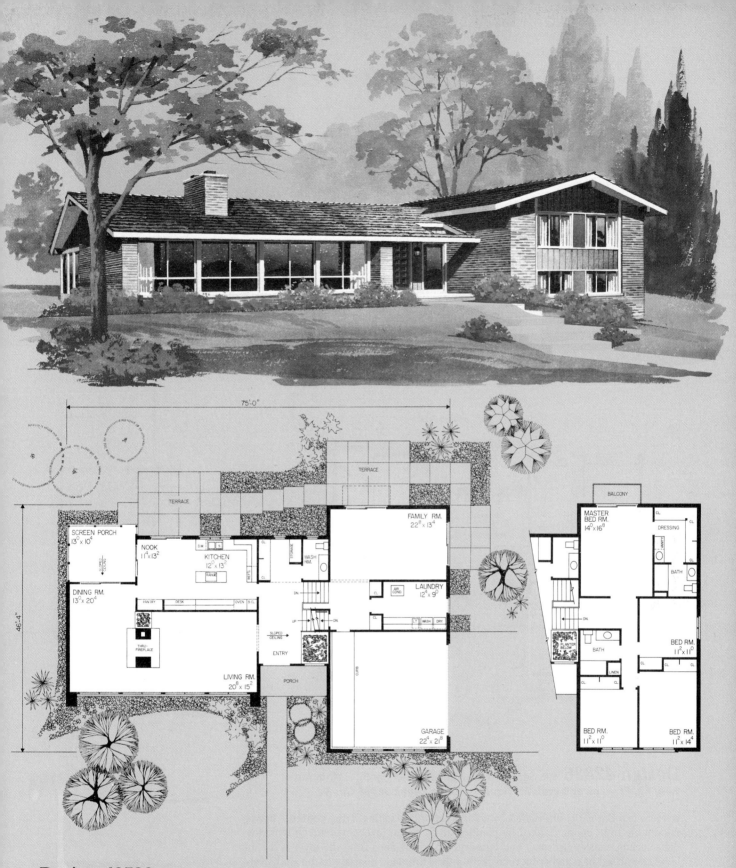

Design 42588 1,354 Sq. Ft. - Main Level; 1,112 Sq. Ft. - Upper Level; 562 Sq. Ft. - Lower Level; 46,925 Cu. Ft.

● A thru-fireplace with an accompa- nying planter for the formal dining room and living room. That's old- fashioned good cheer in a contempo- rary home. The dining room has an ad- jacent screened-in porch for outdoor dining in the summertime. There are companions for these two formal areas, an informal breakfast nook and a fami- ly room. Each having sliding glass doors to separate rear terraces. Built-in desk, pantry, ample work space and is- land range are features of the L- shaped kitchen. The large laundry on the lower level houses the heating and cooling equipment. Three family bed- rooms, bath and master bedroom suite are on the upper level.

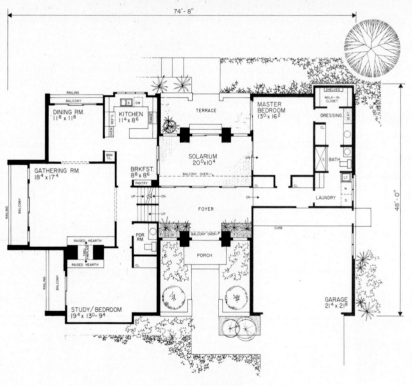

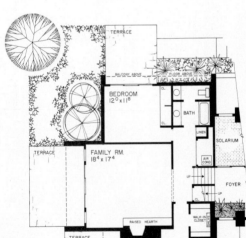

Design 42836 *998 Sq. Ft. - Foyer Level; 1,146 Sq. Ft. - Main Level*
1,090 Sq. Ft. - Lower Level; 241 Sq. Ft. - Studio Level; 39,705 Cu. Ft.

● Here is a dramatic, hip-roofed contemporary with exciting living patterns. Inside the double front doors, flanked by planting areas, is the foyer level which includes the solarium, master bedroom and laundry. Up seven steps from the foyer is the main level comprised of a gathering room with a thru-fireplace opening to the study, formal dining and informal breakfast rooms and an efficient, U-shaped kitchen. Across from the gathering room is the short flight of stairs to the upper level studio. Like the breakfast room immediately below, the studio looks down into the solarium. The skylight provides both studio and solarium with an abundance of natural light. Heat is absorbed and stored in the thermal brick floor of this centrally located solarium. The floor will then radiate heat into the living areas to stabilize the temperature when necessary. The lower sleeping level is down a few steps from the foyer. It functions well with its terrace and the children's bedrooms. Don't miss the three main level balconies and the three lower level terraces. They will create wonderful indoor-outdoor living relationships for the entire family to enjoy.

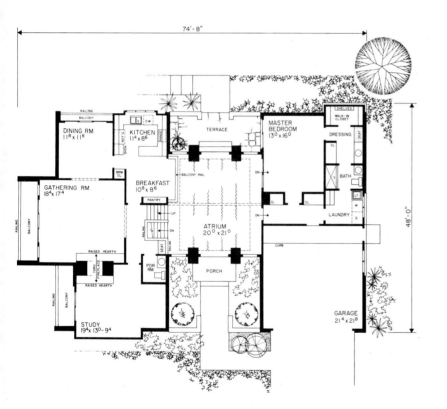

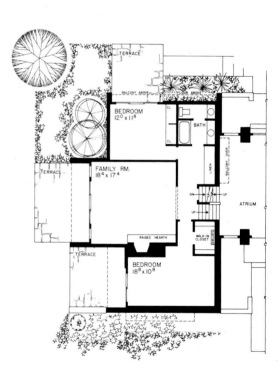

Design *42837* 1,165 Sq. Ft. - Main Level; 998 Sq. Ft. - Atrium Level; 1,090 Sq. Ft. - Lower Level; 43,760 Cu. Ft.

● This atrium plan is housed in the same dramatic exterior as the solarium plan on the opposite page. The exterior remains exactly the same but the floor plan has been altered to house an atrium. Enclosed in glass, the atrium admits daytime solar warmth, which radiates into the other rooms for direct-gain heating. Seeing that this plan includes a basement underneath the atrium, it lacks the thick, heat-storing thermal floor which is featured in the solarium version. For this reason, the plan calls for a furnace in the basement as the primary heat source. The floor plan of this atrium version is similar to its solarium counterpart except that the studio level has been omitted. As a result it has three living levels instead of four, plus a basement.

The master suite is outstanding. It is complete with dressing room, two large closets, bathroom and access to the laundry. The rear terrace is accessible by way of sliding glass doors. Fireplaces can be enjoyed in three rooms, gathering, study and lower level family room. Continue to study this unique design and its solarium counterpart for their many features.

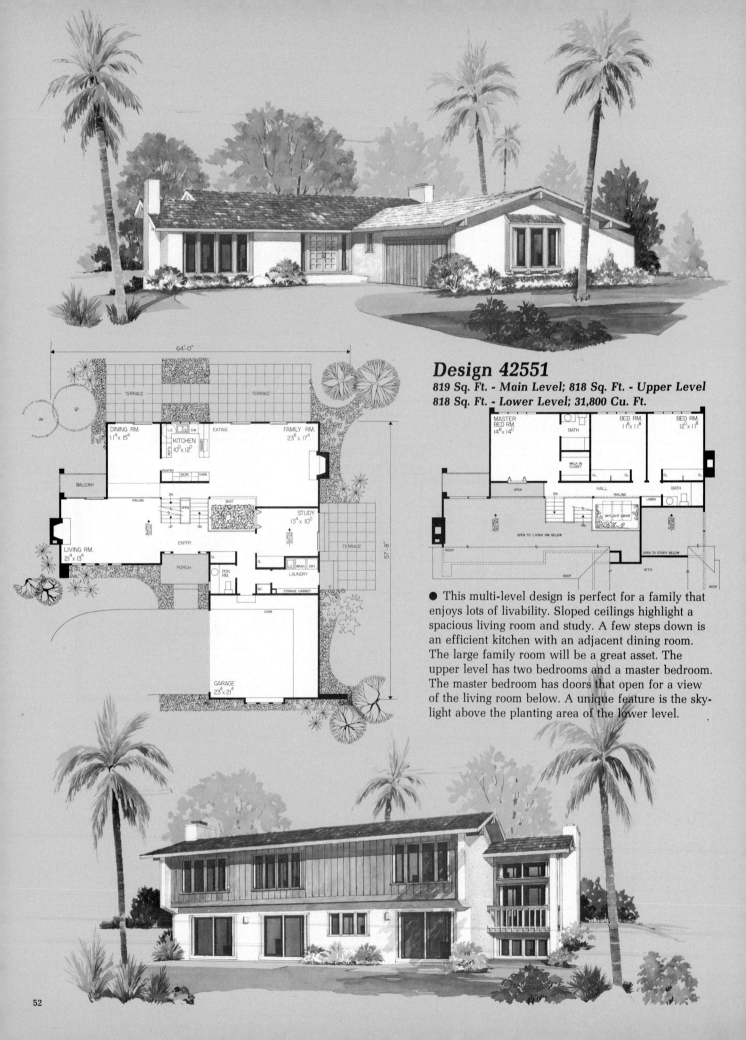

Design 42551

819 Sq. Ft. - Main Level; 818 Sq. Ft. - Upper Level
818 Sq. Ft. - Lower Level; 31,800 Cu. Ft.

● This multi-level design is perfect for a family that enjoys lots of livability. Sloped ceilings highlight a spacious living room and study. A few steps down is an efficient kitchen with an adjacent dining room. The large family room will be a great asset. The upper level has two bedrooms and a master bedroom. The master bedroom has doors that open for a view of the living room below. A unique feature is the skylight above the planting area of the lower level.

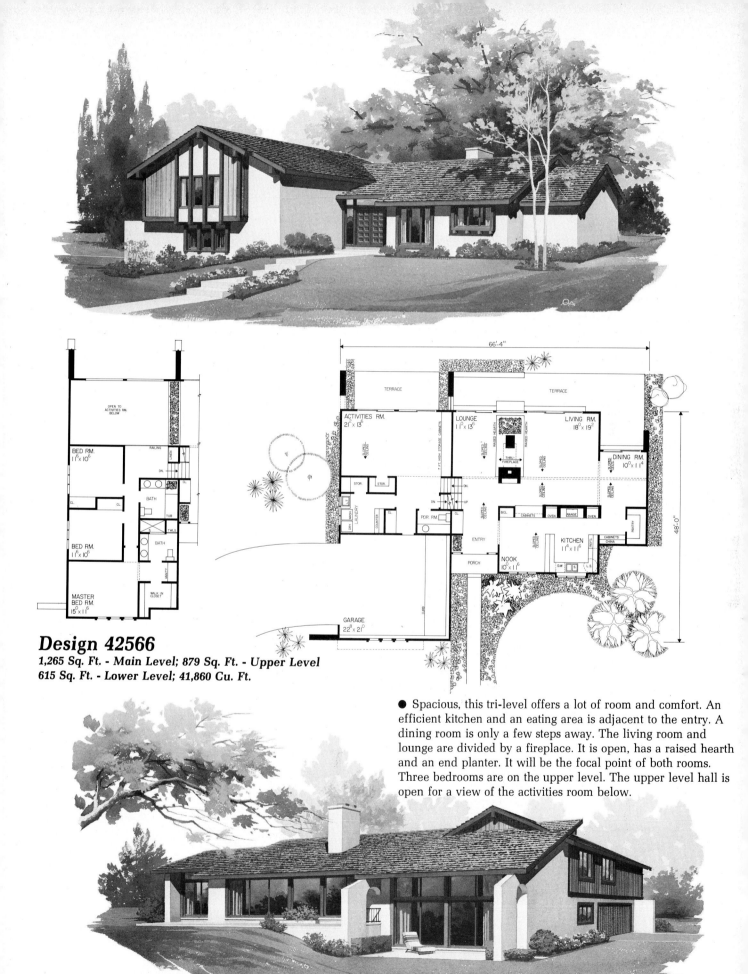

Design 42566

1,265 Sq. Ft. - Main Level; 879 Sq. Ft. - Upper Level
615 Sq. Ft. - Lower Level; 41,860 Cu. Ft.

● Spacious, this tri-level offers a lot of room and comfort. An efficient kitchen and an eating area is adjacent to the entry. A dining room is only a few steps away. The living room and lounge are divided by a fireplace. It is open, has a raised hearth and an end planter. It will be the focal point of both rooms. Three bedrooms are on the upper level. The upper level hall is open for a view of the activities room below.

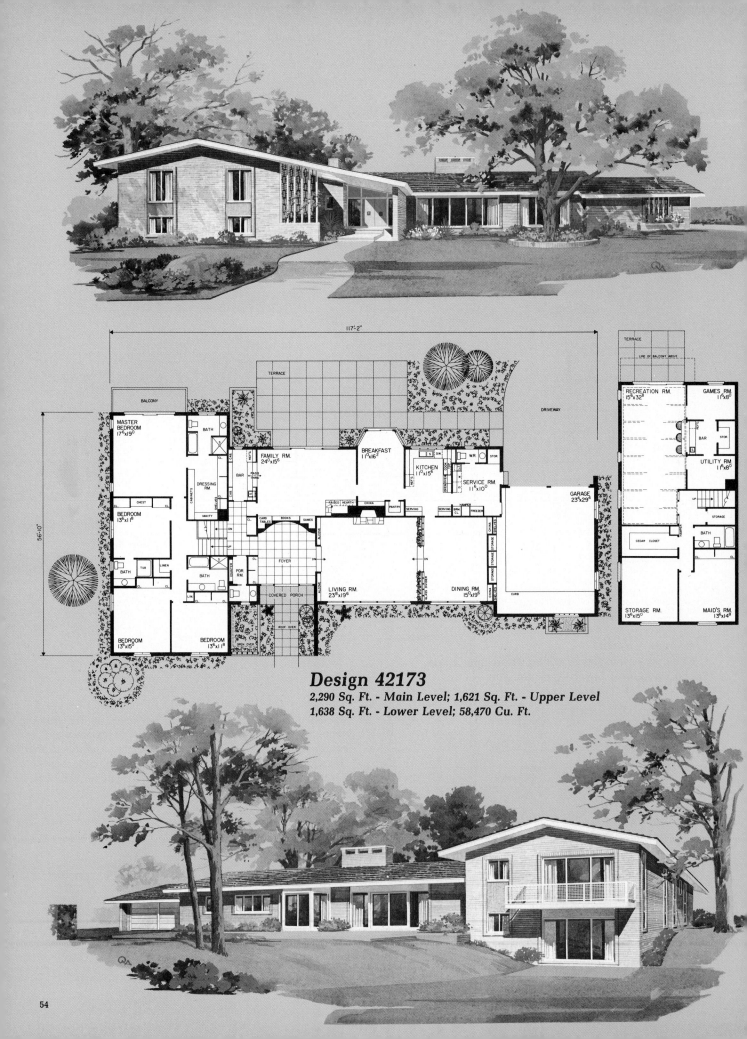

Design 42173
2,290 Sq. Ft. - Main Level; 1,621 Sq. Ft. - Upper Level
1,638 Sq. Ft. - Lower Level; 58,470 Cu. Ft.

Main Level floor plan labels:
117'-2"
56'-10"
BALCONY
MASTER BEDROOM 17⁶x19⁰
BATH
TERRACE
FAMILY RM. 24⁰x15⁶
BREAKFAST 11⁶x16²
KITCHEN 11⁰x15⁶
W.R.
STOR.
SERVICE RM. 11⁶x10⁰
DRIVEWAY
DRESSING RM.
CABINETS
BAR
PASS THRU
BEDROOM 13⁶x11⁸
VANITY
CARD TABLES
BOOKS
GAMES
ALCOVE
CHINA
PANTRY
SERVING
HAMPER
FREEZER
GARAGE 23⁶x29⁴
CHEST
CL.
RAISED HEARTH
SERVING
BRM.
CL.
BATH
TUB
LINEN
BATH
PDR. RM.
LIN
FOYER
LIVING RM. 23⁶x19⁶
DINING RM. 15⁰x19⁶
STORAGE
CURB
BEDROOM 13⁶x15⁰
BEDROOM 13⁶x11⁸
COVERED PORCH
ROOF OVER
OPEN OVER

Lower/Upper Level floor plan labels:
TERRACE
LINE OF BALCONY ABOVE
RECREATION RM. 15⁶x32⁶
GAMES RM. 11⁶x8⁰
BAR
STOR.
UTILITY RM. 11⁶x8⁰
UP
STORAGE
CEDAR CLOSET
BATH
STORAGE RM. 13⁶x15⁰
MAID'S RM. 13⁶x14⁸

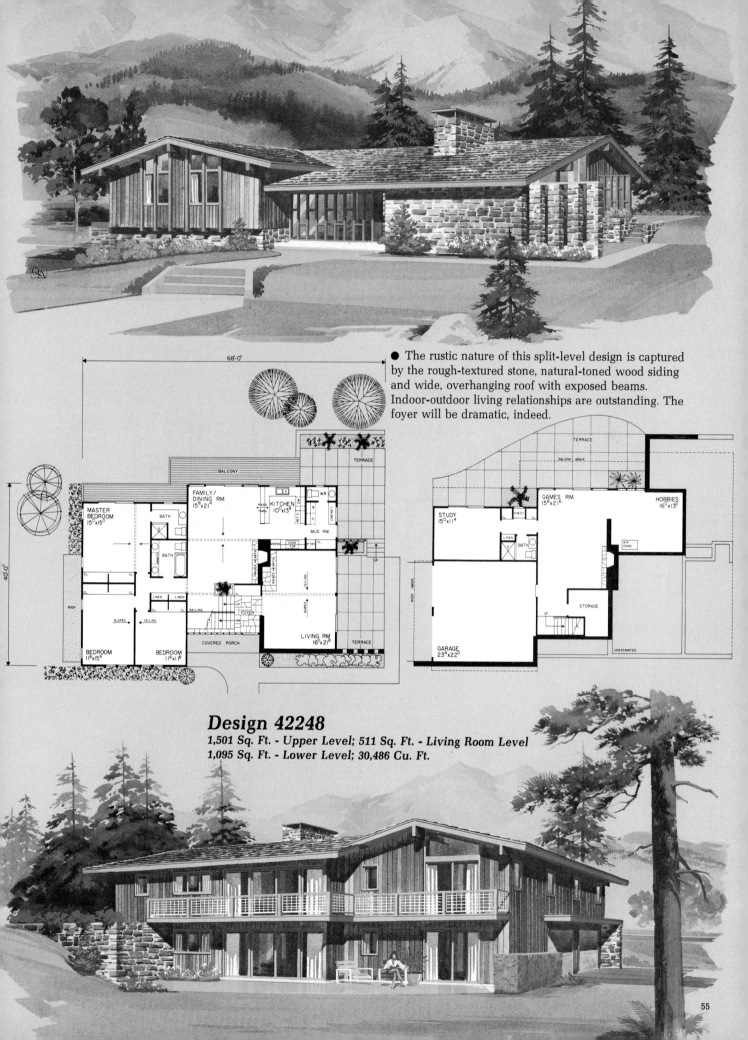

● The rustic nature of this split-level design is captured by the rough-textured stone, natural-toned wood siding and wide, overhanging roof with exposed beams. Indoor-outdoor living relationships are outstanding. The foyer will be dramatic, indeed.

Design 42248

1,501 Sq. Ft. - Upper Level; 511 Sq. Ft. - Living Room Level
1,095 Sq. Ft. - Lower Level; 30,486 Cu. Ft.

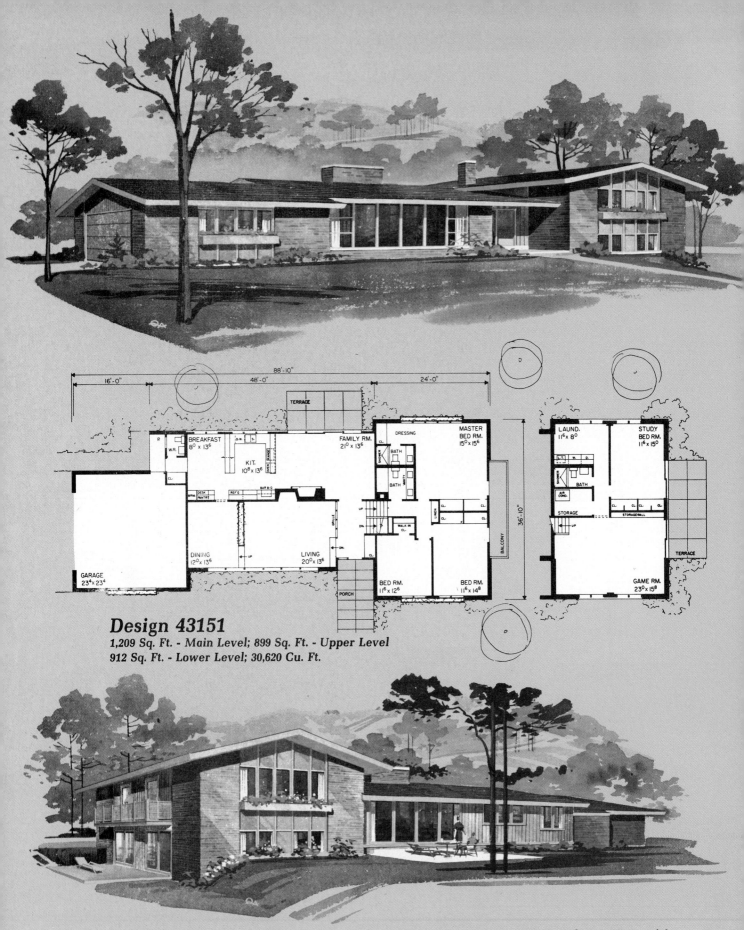

Design 43151
1,209 Sq. Ft. - Main Level; 899 Sq. Ft. - Upper Level
912 Sq. Ft. - Lower Level; 30,620 Cu. Ft.

● Split-level living can be great fun. And it certainly will be for the occupants of this impressive house. First and fore-most, you and your family will appreciate the practical zoning. The upper level is the quiet sleeping level. List the fea-tures. They are many. The main level is zoned for both formal and informal living. Don't miss the sunken living room or the twin fireplaces. The lower level provides that extra measure of livability for all to enjoy.

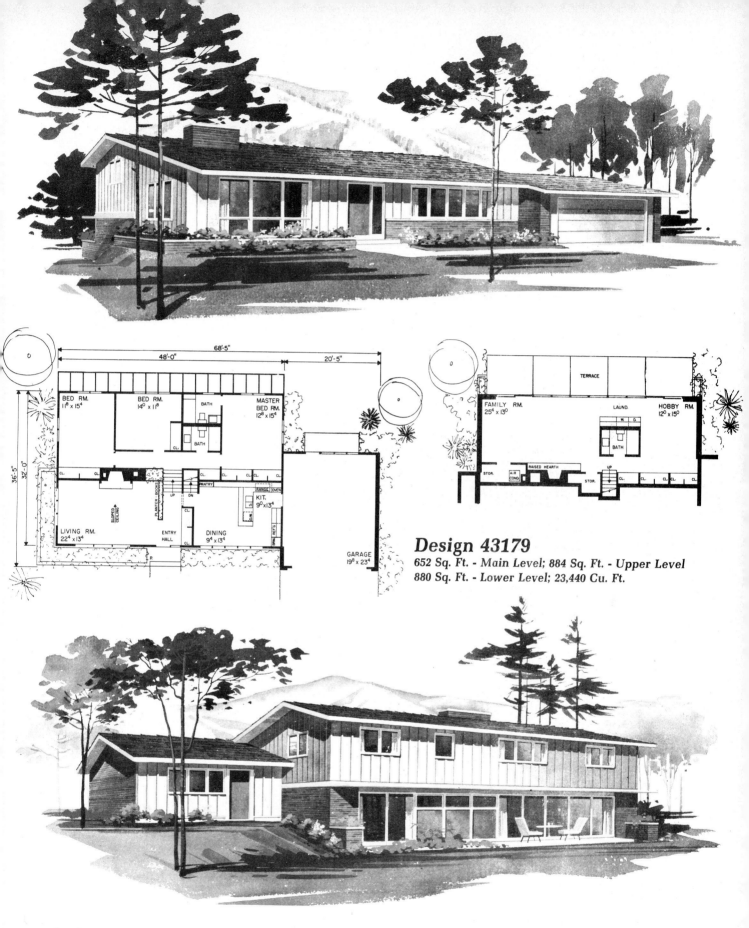

Design 43179
652 Sq. Ft. - Main Level; 884 Sq. Ft. - Upper Level
880 Sq. Ft. - Lower Level; 23,440 Cu. Ft.

● This tri-level home has four distinct areas, each performing its function to perfection. The sleeping area has two full baths, three big bedrooms and plenty of closets. The living area of the main level is spacious, has good light and is free of cross-room traffic. The dining-kitchen is efficient and lends itself to formal and informal dining. The lower level is bright, cheerful, has plenty of space and functions with the outdoors. Note extra full bath.

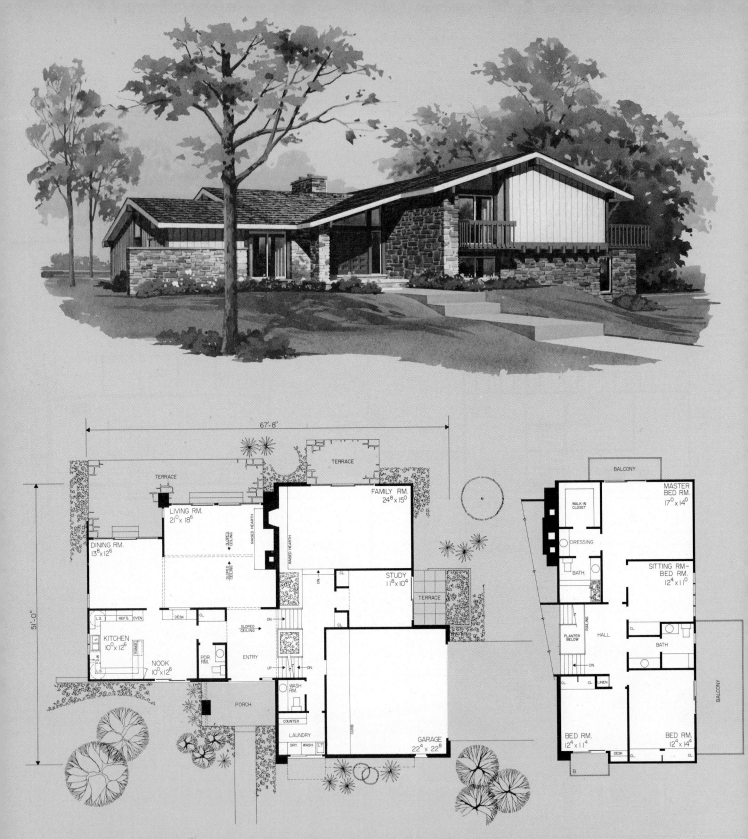

Design 42536 1,077 Sq. Ft. - Main Level; 1,319 Sq. Ft. - Upper Level; 914 Sq. Ft. - Lower Level; 31,266 Cu. Ft.

● Here are three levels of outstanding livability all packed in a delightfully contemporary exterior. The low pitched roof has a wide overhang with exposed rafter tails. The stone masses contrast effectively with the vertical siding and the glass areas. The extension of the sloping roof provides the recessed feature of the front entrance with the patterned double doors. The homemaker's favorite highlight will be the layout of the kitchen. No crossroom traffic here. Only a few steps from the formal and informal eating areas, it is the epitome of efficiency. A sloping beamed ceiling, sliding glass doors and a raised hearth fireplace enhance the appeal of the living room. The upper level offers the option of a fourth bedroom or a sitting room functioning with the master bedroom. Note the three balconies. On the lower level, the big family room, quiet study, laundry and extra washroom are present.

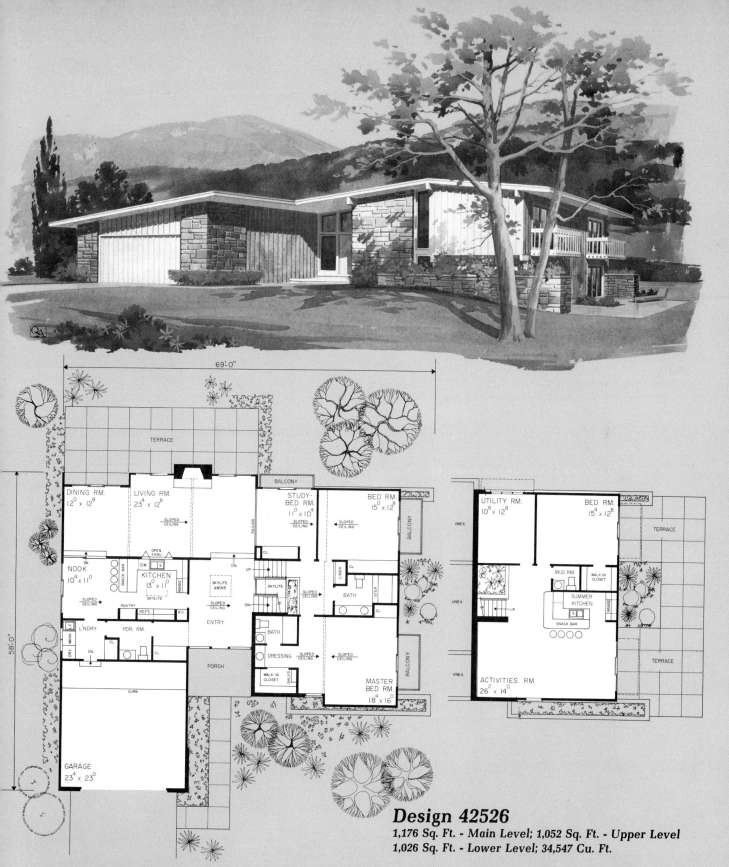

Design 42526

1,176 Sq. Ft. - Main Level; 1,052 Sq. Ft. - Upper Level
1,026 Sq. Ft. - Lower Level; 34,547 Cu. Ft.

● Here is an eye-catching multi-level which offers living patterns that will surely please the whole family. Flanking the front door, and above as well, are large glass panels which provide with the help of the skylite, plenty of natural light to the spacious entry. From this generous area traffic flows conveniently. To the left is the well-planned kitchen area. The breakfast nook, laundry, powder room and plenty of storage are nearby. Straight ahead is the sunken living room with the adjacent dining room. Having a sloping beamed ceiling and an abundance of glass, this will be another cheerful area. To the right, stairs lead to the upper level. Here two bedrooms, study and two baths are housed. Note the exceptional features including a planter, balcony and sunken tub. Also from the hall, there is access to the featured-packed lower level. How do you like that huge activities room?

Design 42111 1,036 Sq. Ft. - Main Level
1,339 Sq. Ft. - Upper Level; 306 Sq. Ft. - Study Level; 1,419 Sq. Ft. - Lower Level; 45,224 Cu. Ft.

● If you have a sloping site, you'd better give this dramatic contemporary a second, or even a third, look. Should your property have a view worth enjoying from the main level living areas, the large expanses of glass would undoubtedly be your most favorite feature. Notice how the glass wall is pushed outward like the bow of a ship.

Design 42247

979 Sq. Ft. - Main Level
1,049 Sq. Ft. - Upper Level
915 Sq. Ft. - Lower Level
29,880 Cu. Ft.

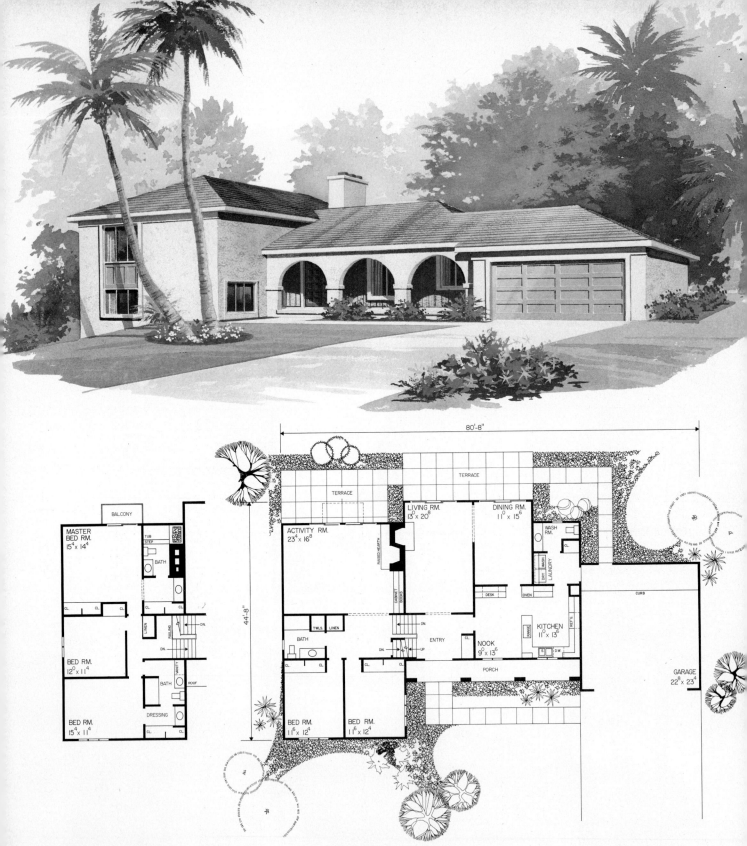

Design 42574 *984 Sq. Ft. - Main Level; 968 Sq. Ft. - Upper Level; 976 Sq. Ft. - Lower Level; 43,440 Cu. Ft.*

● Spanish flair! This home has four bedrooms plus a master suite with a private balcony, dressing room, a luxury bath with a step-up tub and four closets. Also featuring extravagant living space. The activity room is more than 23' by 16' and offers a raised hearth fireplace and a built-in bookcase. Double sliding glass doors open onto the terrace. The main level houses the formal living room with another fireplace and a formal dining room. Both with sliding glass doors that open onto a second terrace. Plus an exceptional kitchen! U-shaped for convenience, it features a built-in desk as well as an oven and range. A separate breakfast nook gaurantees to make every meal something special. Steps away, a first floor laundry to keep all your work in one area.

Floor plan labels (upper level):
BALCONY
STORAGE | BATH | CHEST | CL | BED RM. 12⁶ x 11⁸ | MASTER BED RM. 17⁰ x 15⁴
LINEN | DN.
STORAGE | WALK-IN CL.
BED RM. 12⁰ x 11⁸ | CL | BED RM. 12⁰ x 11⁸ | CL | BATH

Design 42300
1,579 Sq. Ft. - Main Level
1,176 Sq. Ft. - Upper Level
321 Sq. Ft. - Lower Level
34,820 Cu. Ft.

● A T-shaped contemporary with just loads of livability. You may enter this house on the lower level through the garage, or by ascending the steps to the delightful terrace which leads to the main level front entry. Zoning of the interior is wonderful. Projecting to the front and functioning with the formal dining room is the living room. Projecting to the rear and functioning with the kitchen is the family room. Each of these two living areas features a fireplace, beamed ceiling and sliding glass doors to the outside. Also notice the nook, the laundry and the closet space. On the upper level there are four large bedrooms, two full baths, two storage rooms and an outdoor balcony. The lower level offers that fifth bedroom with a full bath nearby. Don't miss the storage facilities of the garage. Truly fine livability.

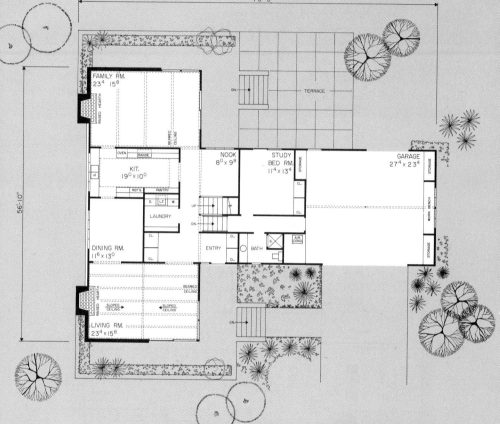

Floor plan labels (main level):
76'-5"
56'-10"
FAMILY RM. 23⁴ x 15⁸ | RAISED HEARTH | BEAMED CEILING
TERRACE | DN.
OVEN | RANGE | KIT. 19⁰ x 10⁰ | REFG. | PANTRY | NOOK 8⁰ x 9⁸ | STUDY BED RM. 11⁴ x 13⁴ | STORAGE | GARAGE 27⁴ x 23⁴ | WORK BENCH | STORAGE
D. | LT. | W.
LAUNDRY | UP | CL
DN.
DINING RM. 11⁶ x 13⁰ | ENTRY | BATH | AIR COND.
RAISED HEARTH | SLOPED CEILING | BEAMED CEILING | SLOPED CEILING
LIVING RM. 23⁴ x 15⁸ | DN.

Design 42734 1,626 Sq. Ft. - Main Level; 1,033 Sq. Ft. - Upper Level; 1,273 Sq. Ft. - Lower Level; 47,095 Cu. Ft.

● If you have a desire for something delightfully different that offers unique, yet practical and enjoyable living patterns, then this house deserves careful study by all the members of your family. Having three bedrooms and a study on the upper level and a guest (or hobby) room on the lower level; it offers sleeping flexibility for the growing family. Notice how the living area looks down on the delightful planting area of the lower level. Also it shares a thru-fireplace with the study. Other features of the study include a 7 foot high book shelve, private balcony and separate stairs to the master bedroom. The outstanding U-shaped kitchen is flanked by the family and dining room. In addition to the living room, there is the huge, 32 foot activity room on the lower level. An abundance of storage space will be found in the three-car garage and the basement.

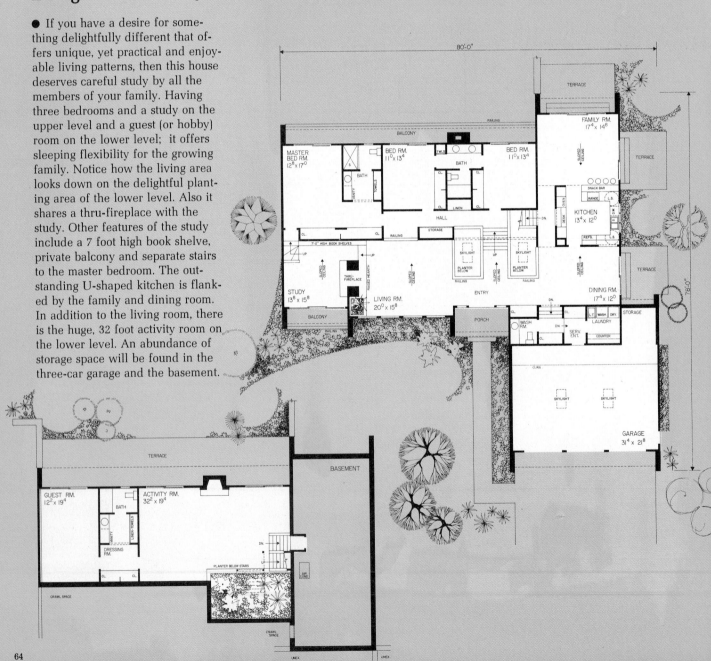

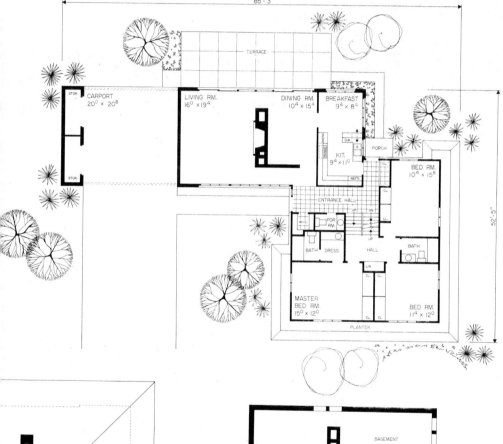

TERRACE

CARPORT
20⁰ x 20⁸

LIVING RM.
16⁰ x 19⁴

DINING RM.
10⁴ x 15⁴

BREAKFAST
9⁴ x 8⁴

KIT.
9⁴ x 11⁰

PORCH

BED RM.
10⁴ x 15⁸

ENTRANCE HALL

POR. RM.

BATH   DRESS

HALL

BATH

MASTER BED RM.
15⁰ x 12⁰

BED RM.
11⁴ x 12⁰

PLANTER

85'-3"

52'-5"

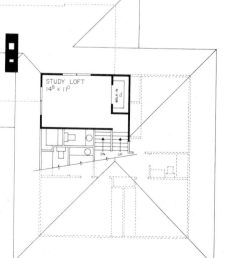

ROOF

STUDY LOFT
14⁸ x 11⁰

WALK-IN CL.

ROOF

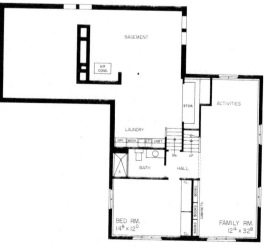

BASEMENT

AIR COND.

STOR.

ACTIVITIES

LAUNDRY

DRY. WASH. CAB'T.

BATH

HALL

BED RM.
14⁸ x 12⁰

FAMILY RM.
12⁴ x 32⁸

Design 42296

993 Sq. Ft. - Main Level
810 Sq. Ft. - Upper Level
842 Sq. Ft. - Lower Level
255 Sq. Ft. - Study Level
38,788 Cu. Ft.

● Here is real multi-level living with each level making a fine contribution to convenient living for the whole family. Including the basement, there are five distinct levels. The L-shaped plan gives birth to the distinctive contemporary exterior. The hip-roof has a wide, pleasing overhang. Just below is the unique, overhanging planter. If desired, this refreshing design could function wonderfully as a five bedroom home. The formal dining room and the breakfast room provide excellent eating facilities. The 32 foot lower level family room provides all the space necessary for multi-purpose activities. The basement offers an extra area for hobbies. Don't miss the laundry, three full baths and the powder room.

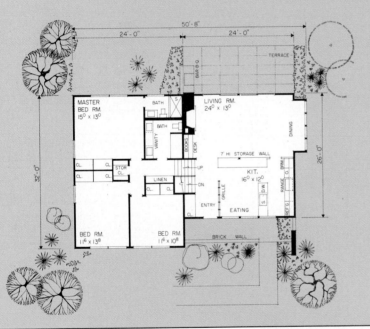

Design 41093
654 Sq. Ft. - Main Level; 768 Sq. Ft. - Upper Level
492 Sq. Ft. - Lower Level; 18,762 Cu. Ft.

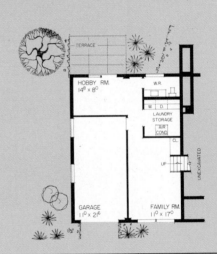

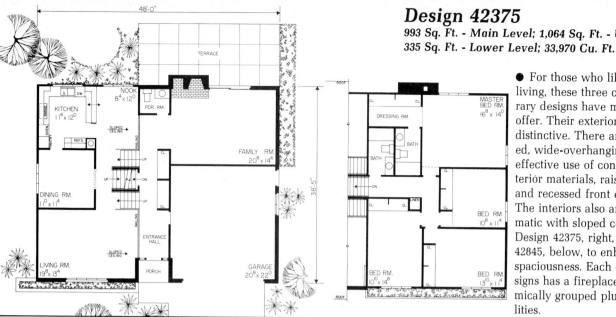

Design 42375
993 Sq. Ft. - Main Level; 1,064 Sq. Ft. - Upper Level
335 Sq. Ft. - Lower Level; 33,970 Cu. Ft.

● For those who like tri-level living, these three contemporary designs have much to offer. Their exteriors are most-distinctive. There are low-pitched, wide-overhanging roofs, effective use of contrasting exterior materials, raised planters and recessed front entrances. The interiors also are quite dramatic with sloped ceilings in Design 42375, right, and Design 42845, below, to enhance the spaciousness. Each of the designs has a fireplace and economically grouped plumbing facilities.

Design 42845
804 Sq. Ft. - Main Level; 1,089 Sq. Ft. - Upper Level
619 Sq. Ft. - Foyer and Lower Level; 36,030 Cu. Ft.

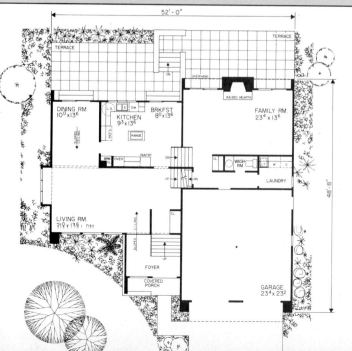

● This multi-level design will be ideal on a sloping site, both in the front and the rear of the house. The contemporary exterior is made up of vertical wood siding. The sloping roofline adds to the exterior appeal and creates a sloped ceiling in the formal living and dining rooms. An attractive bay window highlights the living room as will sliding glass doors in the dining room. The U-shaped kitchen and breakfast room also are located on this main level.

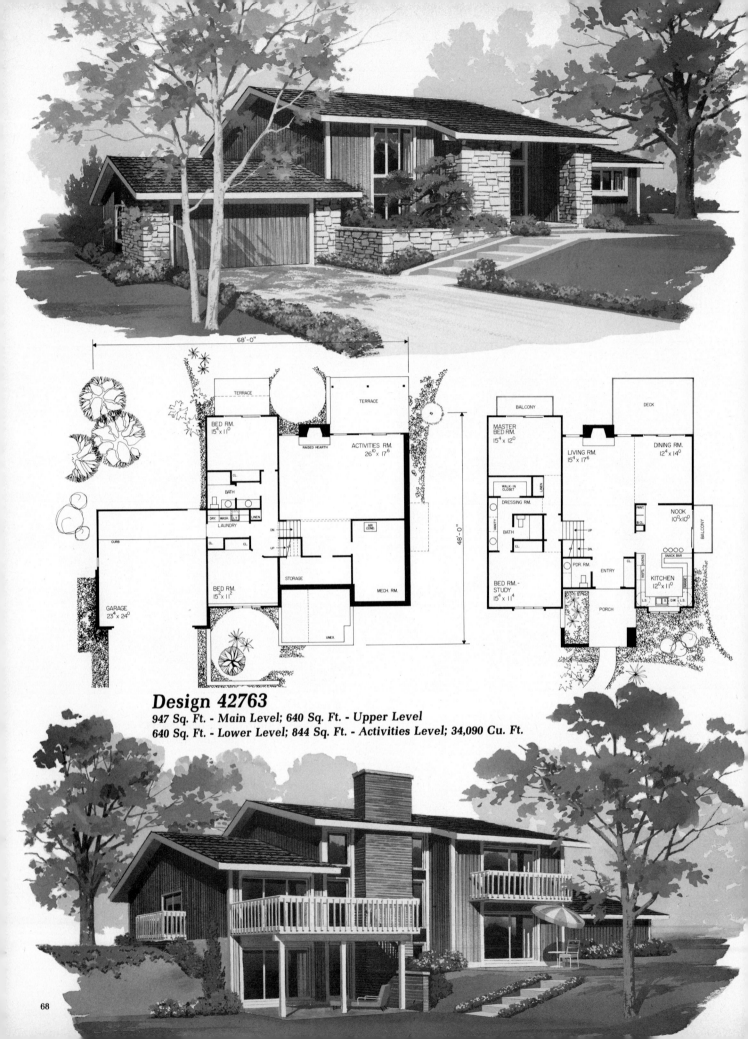

BED RM.
15⁴ x 11⁰

CL.

BATH

DRY. WASH. LT. LINEN

LAUNDRY

CL. CL.

DN

UP

STORAGE

BED RM.
15² x 11⁰

TERRACE

RAISED HEARTH

ACTIVITIES RM.
26¹⁰ x 17⁶

AIR COND.

MECH. RM.

TERRACE

UNEX.

GARAGE
23⁴ x 24⁰

CURB

68'-0"

48'-0"

BALCONY

MASTER BED RM.
15⁴ x 12⁰

WALK-IN CLOSET

LINEN

DRESSING RM.

VANITY

BATH

CL.

BED RM.- STUDY
15⁴ x 11⁴

UP

DN

PDR. RM.

ENTRY

CL.

PORCH

LIVING RM.
15⁴ x 17⁶

DECK

DINING RM.
12⁴ x 14⁰

PANT.

B. CL.

NOOK
10⁰ x 10⁰

BALCONY

SNACK BAR

OVENS

REFG.

KITCHEN
12⁰ x 11⁰

RANGE

L.S. D.W. L.S.

Design 42763

947 Sq. Ft. - Main Level; 640 Sq. Ft. - Upper Level
640 Sq. Ft. - Lower Level; 844 Sq. Ft. - Activities Level; 34,090 Cu. Ft.

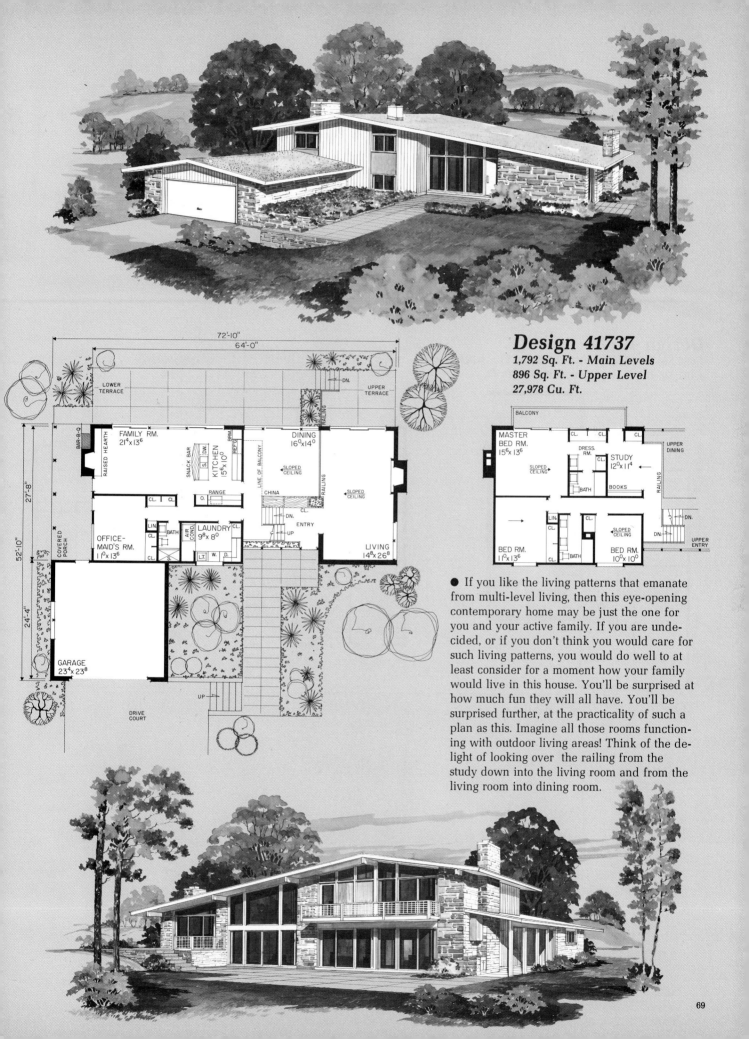

Design 41737

1,792 Sq. Ft. - Main Levels
896 Sq. Ft. - Upper Level
27,978 Cu. Ft.

Main Level Floor Plan Labels

72'-10"
64'-0"
27'-8"
52'-10"
24'-4"

LOWER TERRACE

UPPER TERRACE

DN.

BAR-B-Q

RAISED HEARTH

FAMILY RM. 21⁴x13⁶

SNACK BAR

KITCHEN 15⁶x10⁰

REF'G

DINING 16⁰x14⁰

RAILING

SLOPED CEILING

SLOPED CEILING

LINE OF BALCONY

RANGE

O.

CHINA

CL.

CL.

COVERED PORCH

OFFICE-MAID'S RM. 11⁰x13⁶

LIN.

CL.

BATH

AIR COND.

LAUNDRY 9⁸x8⁰

CL.

S.

LT.

W.

D.

DN.

UP

ENTRY

LIVING 14⁸x26⁸

GARAGE 23⁴x23⁸

UP

DRIVE COURT

Upper Level Floor Plan Labels

BALCONY

MASTER BED RM. 15⁶x13⁶

DRESS. RM.

CL.

CL.

CL.

STUDY 12⁰x11⁴

UPPER DINING

SLOPED CEILING

BATH

BOOKS

RAILING

BED RM. 11⁰x13⁶

LIN.

CL.

CL.

CL.

CL.

BATH

SLOPED CEILING

BED RM. 10⁰x10⁰

DN.

DN.

UPPER ENTRY

● If you like the living patterns that emanate from multi-level living, then this eye-opening contemporary home may be just the one for you and your active family. If you are undecided, or if you don't think you would care for such living patterns, you would do well to at least consider for a moment how your family would live in this house. You'll be surprised at how much fun they will all have. You'll be surprised further, at the practicality of such a plan as this. Imagine all those rooms functioning with outdoor living areas! Think of the delight of looking over the railing from the study down into the living room and from the living room into dining room.

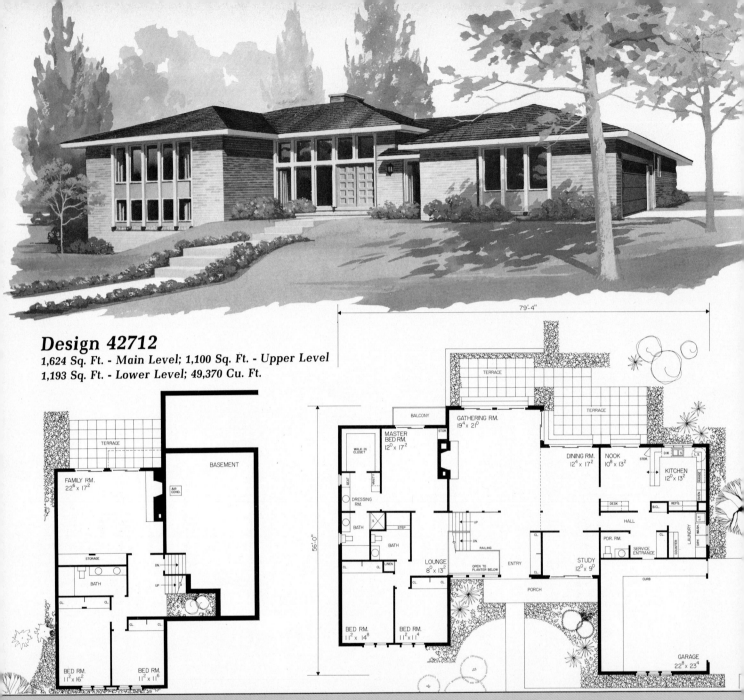

Design 42712
1,624 Sq. Ft. - Main Level; 1,100 Sq. Ft. - Upper Level
1,193 Sq. Ft. - Lower Level; 49,370 Cu. Ft.

79'-4"

56'-0"

TERRACE

FAMILY RM.
$22^6 \times 17^2$

BASEMENT

AIR COND.

STORAGE

BATH

DN.

UP

CL.

CL.

CL.

BED RM.
$11^2 \times 16^2$

BED RM.
$11^2 \times 11^6$

TERRACE

BALCONY

GATHERING RM.
$19^4 \times 21^0$

TERRACE

WALK-IN CLOSET

MASTER BED RM.
$12^0 \times 17^2$

STOR.

DINING RM.
$12^4 \times 17^2$

NOOK
$10^8 \times 13^2$

STOR.

D.W.

S

KITCHEN
$12^0 \times 13^2$

SEAT

VANITY

DESK

B.CL.

REFG.

OVEN

RANGE

DRESSING RM.

S

BATH

STEP

UP

DN

RAILING

CL.

WASH

DRY

LAUNDRY

BATH

LINEN

CL.

CL.

LOUNGE
$8^0 \times 13^2$

OPEN TO PLANTER BELOW

ENTRY

CL.

HALL

DESK

PDR. RM.

COUNTER

CURB

STUDY
$12^0 \times 9^0$

SERVICE ENTRANCE

PORCH

BED RM.
$11^2 \times 14^8$

BED RM.
$11^2 \times 11^4$

GARAGE
$22^8 \times 23^4$

Design 41789 1,486 Sq. Ft. - Main Level; 1,200 Sq. Ft. - Upper Level; 1,200 Sq. Ft. - Lower Level; 39,516 Cu. Ft.

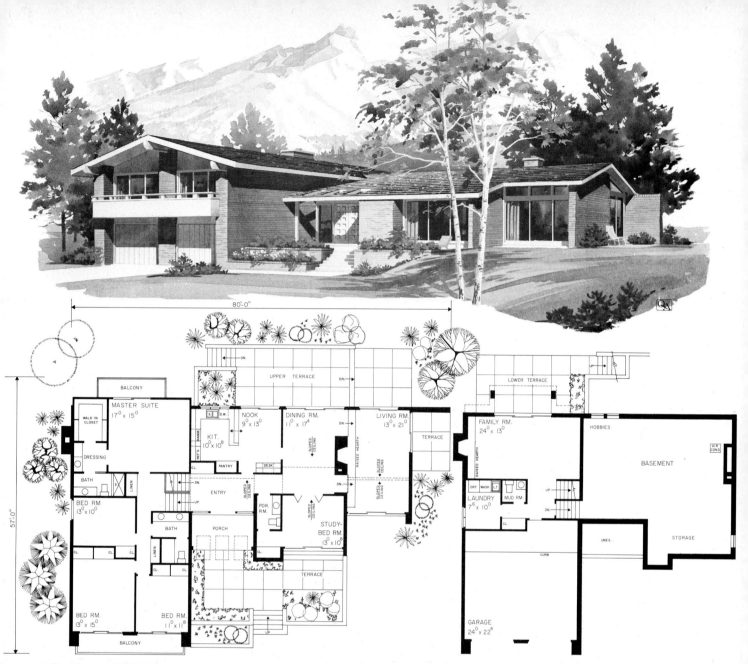

80'-0"

57'-0"

BALCONY

MASTER SUITE 17⁰ x 15⁰

WALK-IN CLOSET

DRESSING

BATH

LINEN

BED RM. 13⁰ x 10⁰

CL. CL. CL.

BED RM. 13⁰ x 15⁰

BALCONY

BED RM. 11⁰ x 11⁸

UPPER TERRACE

DN.

DN.

NOOK 9⁰ x 13⁰

KIT. 10⁰ x 10⁸

REF'G RANGE

S. D.W.

PANTRY

CL.

DESK

DN.

UP

ENTRY

BATH

LINEN

CL.

PORCH

DINING RM. 11⁰ x 17⁴

SLOPED CEILING

PDR. RM.

SLOPED CEILING

LIVING RM. 13⁰ x 21⁰

RAISED HEARTH

SLOPED CEILING

TERRACE

DN.

STUDY-BED RM. 13⁰ x 10⁸

TERRACE

UP

LOWER TERRACE

DN.

FAMILY RM. 24⁰ x 13⁰

HOBBIES

RAISED HEARTH

AIR COND.

BASEMENT

DRY WASH

L.T.

LAUNDRY 7⁶ x 10⁰

MUD. RM.

UP

DN.

UNEX.

STORAGE

CURB

GARAGE 24⁰ x 22⁴

Design 42516 1,183 Sq. Ft. - Main Level; 1,248 Sq. Ft. - Upper Level; 607 Sq. Ft. - Lower Level; 41,775 Cu. Ft.

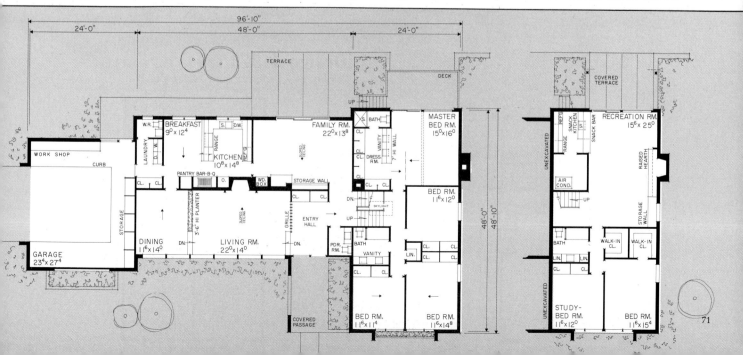

96'-10"

24'-0" **48'-0"** **24'-0"**

48'-0"

48'-10"

TERRACE

DECK

COVERED TERRACE

UP

WORK SHOP

CURB

W.R.

BREAKFAST 9⁰ x 12⁴

LAUNDRY

D. W.

RANGE

S. D.W.

REF'G

KITCHEN 10⁸ x 14⁸

FAMILY RM. 22⁰ x 13⁸

SLOPED CEILING

BATH

S.

CL.

VANITY

7' HI WALL

MASTER BED RM. 15⁰ x 16⁰

DRESS. RM.

CL.

RANGE

SNACK KITCHEN

REF'G

SNACK BAR

RECREATION RM. 15⁶ x 25⁰

UNEXCAVATED

STORAGE

CL. CL.

PANTRY BAR-B-Q

3-6 HI PLANTER

O.

WD. BOX

STORAGE WALL

CL. CL.

GRILLE

STORAGE WALL

DN.

SKYLIGHT

CL. CL.

BED RM. 11⁶ x 12⁰

AIR COND.

UP

RAISED HEARTH

GARAGE 23⁴ x 27⁴

STORAGE

DINING 11⁶ x 14⁰

DN.

LIVING RM. 22⁰ x 14⁰

SLOPED CEILING

ENTRY HALL

UP

PDR. RM.

VANITY

BATH

LIN.

CL. CL.

BATH

LIN. LIN.

WALK-IN CL.

WALK-IN CL.

COVERED PASSAGE

BED RM. 11⁶ x 11⁴

BED RM. 11⁶ x 14⁸

UNEXCAVATED

STUDY-BED RM. 11⁶ x 12⁰

BED RM. 11⁶ x 15⁴

71

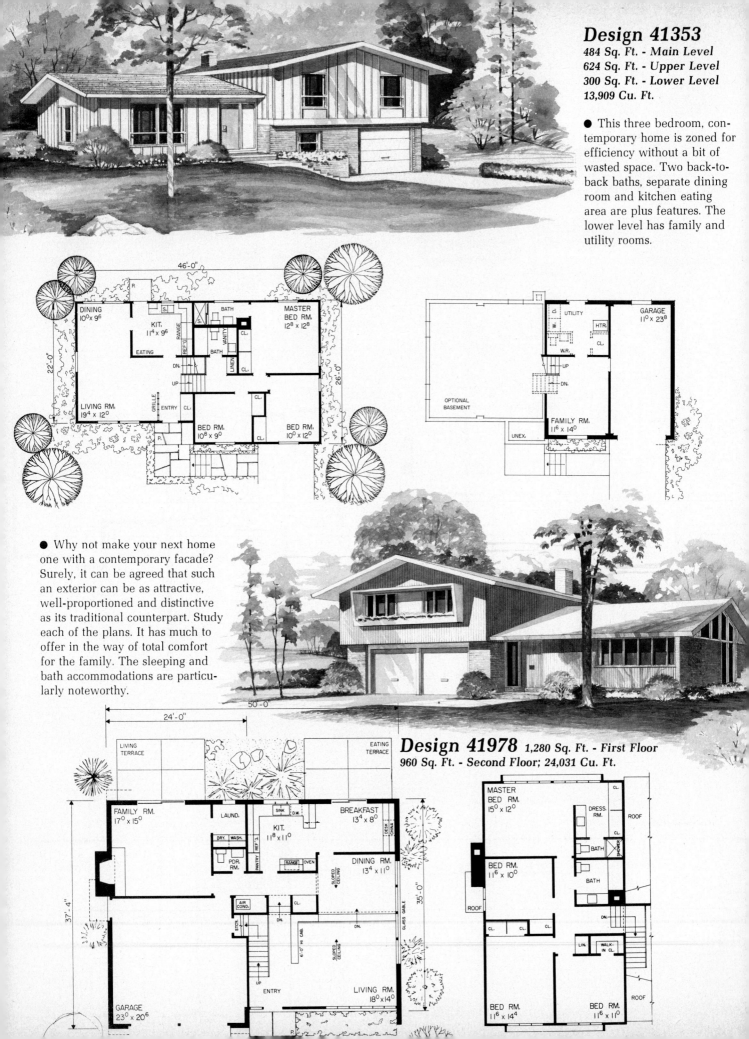

Design 41353
484 Sq. Ft. - Main Level
624 Sq. Ft. - Upper Level
300 Sq. Ft. - Lower Level
13,909 Cu. Ft.

● This three bedroom, contemporary home is zoned for efficiency without a bit of wasted space. Two back-to-back baths, separate dining room and kitchen eating area are plus features. The lower level has family and utility rooms.

46'-0"

DINING 10⁰ x 9⁶
KIT. 11⁴ x 9⁶
EATING
BATH
MASTER BED RM. 12⁸ x 12⁸
S. RANGE REF'G. DN. UP
VANITY BATH LINEN CL. CL.
LIVING RM. 19⁴ x 12⁰
GRILLE ENTRY CL.
P.
BED RM. 10⁸ x 9⁰
CL.
BED RM. 10⁰ x 12⁰
22'-0"   26'-0"

UTILITY
W. HTR. CL.
W.R. UP DN.
GARAGE 11⁰ x 23⁸
OPTIONAL BASEMENT
FAMILY RM. 11⁶ x 14⁰
UNEX.

● Why not make your next home one with a contemporary facade? Surely, it can be agreed that such an exterior can be as attractive, well-proportioned and distinctive as its traditional counterpart. Study each of the plans. It has much to offer in the way of total comfort for the family. The sleeping and bath accommodations are particularly noteworthy.

Design 41978 1,280 Sq. Ft. - First Floor
960 Sq. Ft. - Second Floor; 24,031 Cu. Ft.

50'-0"
24'-0"
37'-4"
35'-0"

LIVING TERRACE
EATING TERRACE
FAMILY RM. 17⁰ x 15⁰
LAUND.
SINK D.W.
KIT. 11⁸ x 11⁰
BREAKFAST 13⁴ x 8⁰
DESK
DRY. WASH.
PDR. RM.
PANTRY
REF'G
RANGE OVEN
DINING RM. 13⁴ x 11⁰
SLOPED CEILING
AIR COND.
CL.
DN.
6'-0" HI. CAB.
DN.
SLOPED CEILING
GLASS GABLE
STOR.
UP
LIVING RM. 18⁰ x 14⁰
GARAGE 23⁰ x 20⁶
ENTRY
P.

MASTER BED RM. 15⁰ x 12⁰
DRESS. RM.
BATH
SHOWER
ROOF
BED RM. 11⁶ x 10⁰
BATH
ROOF
CL. CL.
DN.
LIN. WALK-IN CL.
BED RM. 11⁶ x 14⁴
BED RM. 11⁶ x 11⁰
ROOF

BI-LEVEL DESIGNS . . .

can have many different forms. These designs highlight the split-foyer and lower entry variations. Like so many floor plan types, the bi-level adapts well to a variety of exterior styles. Note the pleasing proportions of the Contemporary, Early American, Spanish, Tudor and French adaptations. Bi-levels adapt well to either flat or sloping sites. In many cases minimal grading of a flat site can permit the utilization of a gently sloping site design. Frequently referred to as a "raised ranch", the bi-level in essence raises the basement out of the ground and provides it with enough natural light to be livable area.

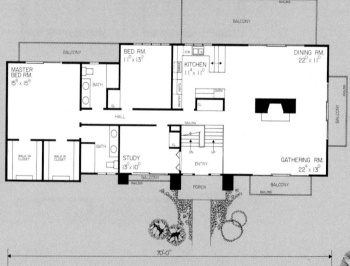

Design 42580

1,852 Sq. Ft. - Upper Level
1,297 Sq. Ft. - Lower Level
32,805 Cu. Ft.

● Indoor-outdoor living hardly could ask for more! And here's why. Imagine, five balconies and three terraces! These unique balconies add great beauty to the exterior while adding pleasure to those who utilize them from the interior. And there's more. This home has enough space for all to appreciate. Take note of the size of the gathering room, family room and activity room. There's also a large dining room. Four bedrooms too, for the large or growing family. Or three plus a study. Two fireplaces, one to service each of the two levels in this bi-level design. The rear terrace is accessible thru sliding glass doors from the lower level bedroom and activity room. The side terrace functions with the activity/family room area. The master suite has two walk-in closets and a private bath.

Design 42842

156 Sq. Ft. - Entrance Level; 1,038 Sq. Ft. - Upper Level
1,022 Sq. Ft. - Lower Level; 25,630 Cu. Ft.

● This narrow, 42 foot width, house can be built on a narrow lot to cut down overall costs. Yet its dramatic appeal surely is worth a million. The projecting front garage creates a pleasing curved drive. One enters this house through the covered porch to the entrance level foyer. At this point the stairs lead down to the living area consisting of formal living room, family room, kitchen and dining area then up the stairs to the four bedroom-two bath sleeping area. The indoor-outdoor living relationship at the rear is outstanding.

Design 42843
1,861 Sq. Ft. - Upper Level
1,181 Sq. Ft. - Lower Level; 32,485 Cu. Ft.

● Bi-level living will be enjoyed to its fullest in this Spanish styled design. There is a lot of room for the various family activities. Informal living will take place on the lower level in the family room and lounge. The formal living and dining rooms, sharing a thru-fireplace, are located on the upper level.

● This attractive, contemporary bi-level will overwhelm you with its features: two balconies, an open staircase with planter below, two lower level bedrooms, six sets of sliding glass doors and an outstanding master suite loaded with features. The occupants of this house will love the large exercise room. After a tough workout, you can relax in the whirlpool or the sauna or simply take a shower!

Design 42856 1,801 Sq. Ft. - Upper Level
2,170 Sq. Ft. - Lower Level; 44,935 Cu. Ft.

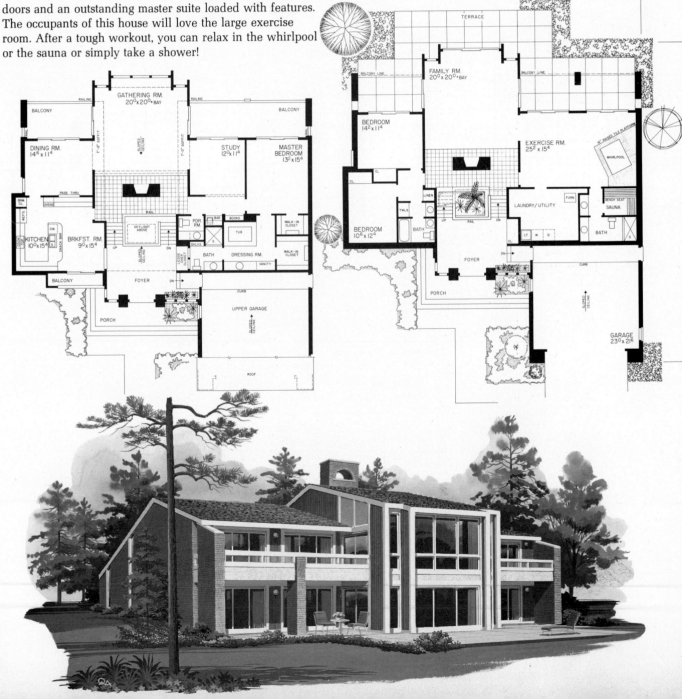

Design 42844 1,882 Sq. Ft. - Upper Level
1,168 Sq. Ft. - Lower Level; 37,860 Cu. Ft.

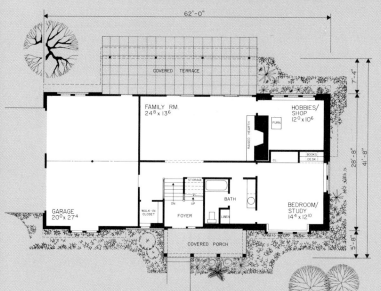

● Bi-level living will be enjoyed to the fullest in this Tudor design. The split-foyer type design will be very efficient for the active family. Three bedrooms are on the upper level, a fourth on the lower level.

Design 42868

1,203 Sq. Ft. - Upper Level
1,317 Sq. Ft. - Lower Level; 29,595 Cu. Ft.

Common Living Areas –
Sleeping Privacy

● Two couples sharing the expense of a house has got to be ideal and, of course, economical. The occupants of this house could do just that. The lower level, housing the kitchen, dining room, family and living rooms and the laundry facilities, is the common area to be shared by both couples. Centrally located, the kitchen and dining room act as a space divider to the living and family rooms so both couples can enjoy privacy.

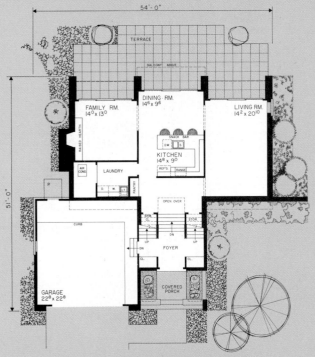

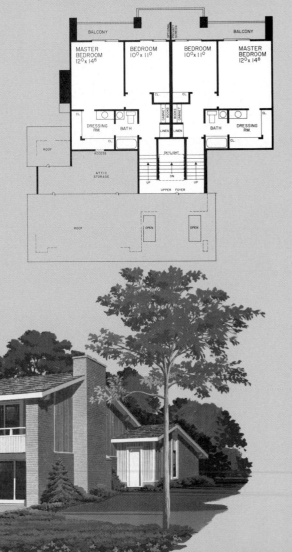

Separate stairways lead to the upper level from the skylit foyer. Each private area has two bedrooms, a dressing room and a full bath. Individual entrances can be locked for additional privacy. Sliding glass doors are in each of the rear rooms on both levels so the outdoors can be enjoyed to its fullest.

Design 42827 1,618 Sq. Ft. - Upper Level
1,458 Sq. Ft. - Lower Level; 41,370 Cu. Ft.

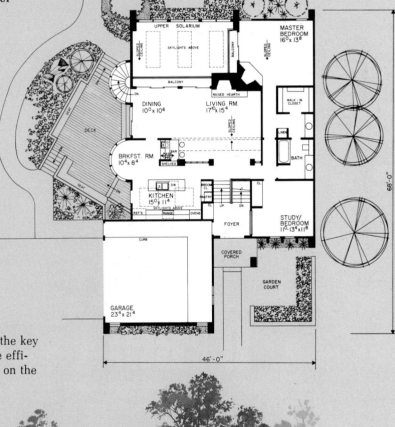

● The two-story solarium with skylights above is the key to energy savings to this bi-level design. Study the efficiency of this floor plan. The conversation lounge on the lower level is a unique focal point.

Design 42715
2,299 Sq. Ft. - Upper Level
1,524 Sq. Ft. - Lower Level; 40,700 Cu. Ft.

66'-0"

39'-4"

TERRACE

ACTIVITES RM.
21⁸ x 26⁸

SNACK BAR

SUMMER KIT.
10⁴ x 11²

REFG.

STORAGE

CL.

DRY. WASH. LT.

LAUNDRY
9⁰ x 9¹⁰

AIR COND.

LINEN

BATH

TWLS.

CL.

GUEST BED RM.
12⁰ x 13²

THRU-FIREPLACE

RAISED HEARTH

GAMES
10⁰ x 8⁴

DN.

CUPS.

UP   DN

ENTRY

PLANTER

PORCH

GARAGE
23⁰ x 23⁶

DN

DECK

RAILING

BALCONY

DINING RM.
12⁰ x 13⁶

NOOK
9⁸ x 13⁶

D.W.

KITCHEN
10⁴ x 13⁶

REFG.

PANTRY   PANTRY   OVEN

SLOPED CEILING

B.CL.

STUDY
11⁰ x 13⁶

CL.

BATH

TWLS.

CL.

CL.

LINEN

BED RM.
11⁰ x 17⁸

SLOPED CEILING

GATHERING RM.
19⁸ x 15⁶

RAISED HEARTH

THRU-FIREPLACE

LOUNGE
10⁰ x 9⁰

BENCH SEAT

RAILING

RAILING

UP   DN

ENTRY

PLANTER

S

BATH

VANITY

CL.

DRESSING RM.

MASTER BED RM.
21⁰ x 13⁰

PORCH

BALCONY

● A lounge with built-in seating and a thru-fireplace to the gathering room highlights this upper level. A delightful attraction to view upon entrance of this home. A formal dining room, study and U-shaped kitchen with breakfast nook are present, too. That is a lot of room. There's more! A huge activities room has a fireplace, snack bar and adjacent summer kitchen. This is the perfect set-up for teenage parties or family cook-outs on the terrace. The entire family certainly will enjoy the convenience of this area. All this, plus three bedrooms (optional four without the study), including a luxury master suite with its own outdoor balcony. The upper level, outdoor deck provides partial cover for the lower level terrace. This home offers outdoor living potential on both levels.

Design 42579
2,383 Sq. Ft. - Upper level
1,716 Sq. Ft. - Lower Level
43,842 Cu. Ft.

● A huge gathering room, almost 27' with a raised hearth fireplace in the center, sloped ceilings and separate areas for dining and games. Plus balconies on two sides and a deck on the third. A family room on the lower level of equal size to the gathering room with its own center fireplace and adjoining terrace. An activities room to enjoy more living space. A room both youngsters along with adults can utilize. There is an efficient kitchen and dining nook with a built-in desk. Four bedrooms, including a master suite with private bath, two walk-in closets and a private balcony. In fact, every room in the house opens onto a terrace, a deck or a balcony. Sometimes more than one! Indoor-outdoor living will be enjoyed to the maximum. With a total of over 4,000 square feet, there are truly years of gracious living ahead.

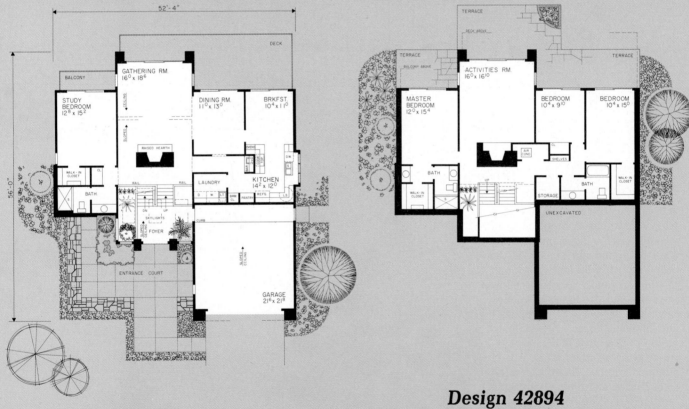

Design 42894

1,490 Sq. Ft. - Main Level
1,357 Sq. Ft. - Lower Level; 38,450 Cu. Ft.

● Contemporary, bi-level living will be enjoyed by all members of the family. Upon entering the foyer, complimented by skylights, stairs will lead you to the upper and lower levels. Up a few steps, you will find yourself in the large gathering room. The fireplace, sloped ceiling and the size of this room will make this a favorite spot. To the left is a study/bedroom with a full bath and walk-in closet. Notice the efficient kitchen and breakfast room with nearby wet bar. The lower level houses two bedrooms and a bath to one side; and a master bedroom suite to the other. Centered is a large activity room with raised-hearth fireplace. It will be enjoyed by all. Note - all of the rear rooms on both levels have easy access to the outdoors for excellent indoor-outdoor livability.

Design 42759

1,747 Sq. Ft. - Upper Level
1,513 Sq. Ft. - Lower Level; 34,540 Cu. Ft.

● A contemporary bi-level with a large bonus room on a third level over the garage. This studio will serve as a great room to be creative in or just to sit back in. The design also provides great indoor/outdoor living relationships with terraces and decks. The for-mal living/dining area has a sloped ceiling and built-in wet bar. The dra-matic beauty of a raised hearth fire-place and built-in planter will be en-joyed by those in the living room. Both have sliding glass doors to the rear deck. The breakfast area will serve as a pleasant eating room with ample space for a table plus the built-in snack bar. The lower level houses the recreation room, laundry and an out-standing master suite. This master suite includes a thru-fireplace, sitting room, tub and shower and more.

Design 42723

1,748 Sq. Ft. - Main Level
294 Sq. Ft. - Entry Level
743 Sq. Ft. - Upper Level
45,400 Cu. Ft.

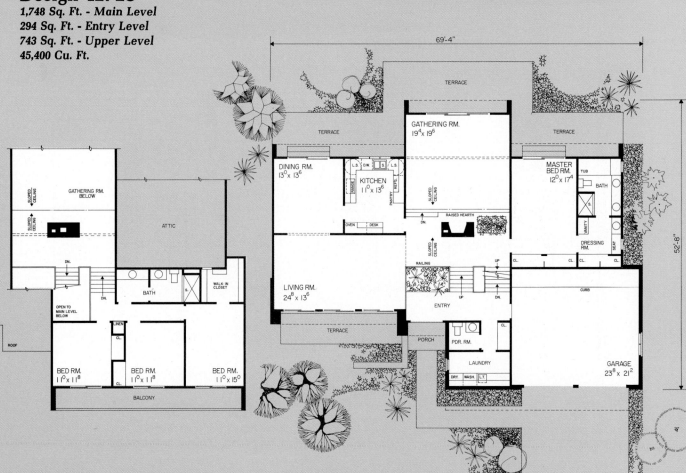

● Bi-level living that begins with a front entry level which houses a powder room and a laundry. The main level has a sunken gathering room! This area has a sloped ceiling, raised hearth fireplace, built-in planter and sliding glass doors to the rear terrace. Also a living room with an adjacent formal dining room. The U-shaped kitchen is a convenient work center with easy access to all areas. The master bedroom's occupants will enjoy their private bath, dressing room and sliding glass doors to another section of the rear terrace. The upper level is an entire sleeping zone. Three bedrooms and a bath will further serve the family. View the gathering room from the upper level.

Design 42735

1,545 Sq. Ft. – Upper Level
1,633 Sq. Ft. – Lower Level
33,295 Cu. Ft.

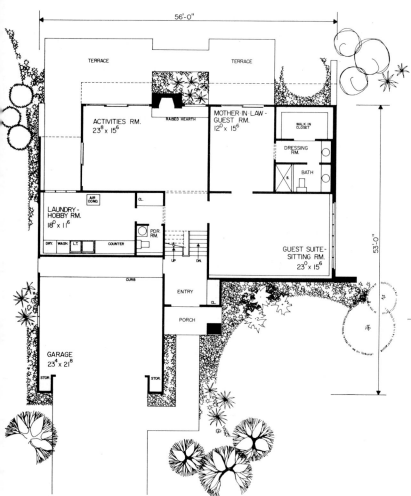

● Whether entering this house through the double front doors, or from the garage, access is gained to the lower level by descending seven stairs. Here, there is a bonus of livability. If desired, this level could be used to accommodate a live-in relative while still providing the family with a fine informal activities room and a separate laundry/hobby room and extra powder room. Up seven risers from the entry is the main living level. It has a large gathering room; a sizable nook which could be called upon to function as a separate dining room; an efficient kitchen with pass-thru to a formal dining area and a two bedroom, two bath and study sleeping zone. Don't miss the balconies and deck.

Design 42788
1,795 Sq. Ft. - Upper Level
866 Sq. Ft. - Lower Level
34,230 Cu. Ft.

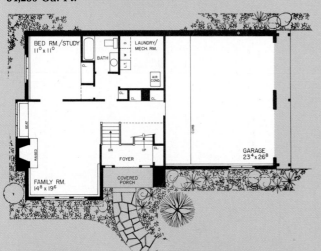

Design 42589
1,801 Sq. Ft. - Upper Level
1,061 Sq. Ft. - Lower Level
32,770 Cu. Ft.

STORAGE

TERRACE

LAUNDRY RM.
13⁴ x 11¹⁰

FAMILY RM.
21⁰ x 15⁶

AIR COND.

CL.

HALL

BATH

STORAGE

CL.

RAISED HEARTH

CABINET
BOOKS

GARAGE
22⁸ x 27⁴

ENTRY

DESK

BED RM.-
STUDY
18⁸ x 11²

PORCH

59'-0"

RAILING

BALCONY

RAILING

BALCONY

MASTER
BED RM.
11⁰ x 15⁶

BATH

KITCHEN
11⁰ x 12²

NOOK
9⁰ x 12²

DINING RM.
12⁰ x 15⁶

DRESSING RM.

BATH

OVEN   DESK   PANTRY

32'-0"

CL.

CL.

LIN.

CL.

RAILING

CHINA
BOOKS

BED RM.
14⁴ x 11²

BED RM.
11⁴ x 13⁶

ENTRY

SLOPED
CEILING

SLOPED
CEILING

LIVING RM.
21⁴ x 13²

Design 41267
1,114 Sq. Ft. - Upper Level
1,194 Sq. Ft. - Lower Level
23,351 Cu. Ft.

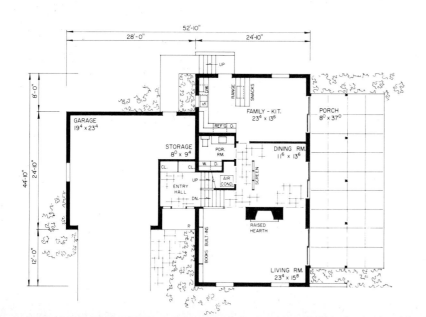

52'-10"

28'-0"

24'-10"

8'-0"

44'-10"

24'-0"

12'-0"

UP

GARAGE
19⁴ x 23⁴

DW.

RANGE   SNACKS

FAMILY - KIT.
23⁴ x 13⁶

PORCH
8⁰ x 37⁰

REF'G.

STORAGE
8⁰ x 9⁴

PDR.
RM.

DINING RM.
11⁶ x 13⁶

W. D.

CL.   CL.

AIR
COND.

SCREEN

ENTRY
HALL

UP

DN.

RAISED
HEARTH

BOOKS   BUILT-INS

LIVING RM.
23⁴ x 15⁸

CL.

DRESS.
RM.

MASTER
BED RM.
15⁰ x 13⁶

CL.

BATH

S.

LIN.   CL.   CHEST   CL.

BATH

VANITY

DN.

BED RM.
11⁶ x 11⁰

ROOF

WALK
IN
CL.

STOR.

CL.   CL.

ROOF

BED RM.
11⁶ x 10⁰

BED RM.
11⁶ x 13⁴

87

Your Choice Of Contemporary - Plus Your 2 Floor Plans

● The bi-level, or split foyer design has become increasingly popular. Here are six alternate elevations – three Traditional and three Contemporary – which may be built with either of two basic floor plans. One plan contains 960 square feet on each level and is 24 feet in depth; the other contains 1,040 square feet on each level and is 26 feet in depth. Plans for traditional and contemporary series include each of the three optional elevations.

Design 41377 Traditional Exteriors
24 Foot Depth Plan (18,960 Cu. Ft.)

Design 41375 Traditional Exteriors
26 Foot Depth Plan (20,778 Cu. Ft.)

960 Sq. Ft. - Upper Level; 960 Sq. Ft. - Lower Level

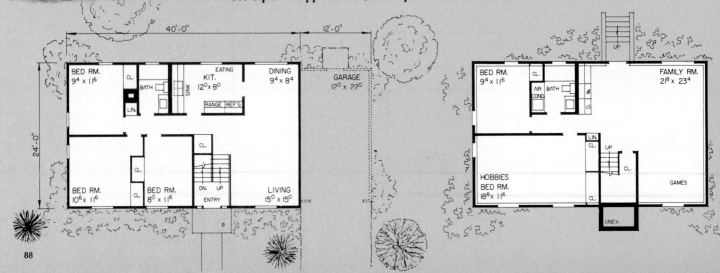

Traditional or Exterior Styling - Choice of For Each Style

● The popularity of the bi-level design can be traced to the tremendous amount of the livable space that such a design provides per construction dollar. While the lower level is partially below grade, it enjoys plenty of natural light and, hence, provides a bright, cheerful atmosphere for total livability. While these two basic floor plans are essentially the same, it is important to note that the larger of the two features a private bath for the master bedroom. Study the plans.

Design 41376 Contemporary Exteriors
24 Foot Depth Plan (18,000 Cu. Ft.)

Design 41378 Contemporary Exteriors
26 Foot Depth Plan (19,624 Cu. Ft.)

1,040 Sq. Ft. - Upper Level; 1,040 Sq. Ft. - Lower Level

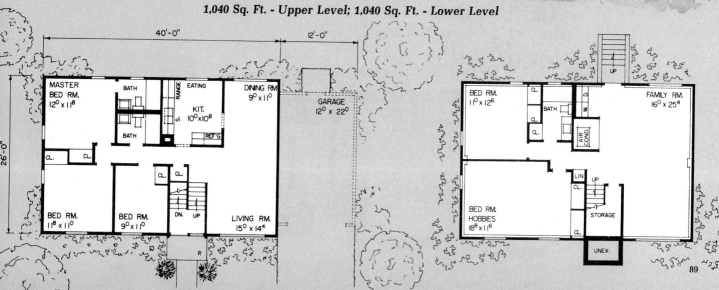

Design 41850 1,456 Sq. Ft. - Upper Level
728 Sq. Ft. - Lower Level; 23,850 Cu. Ft.

● This attractive, traditional bi-level house surely will prove to be an outstanding investment. While it is a perfect rectangle - which leads to economical construction - it has a full measure of eye-appeal. Setting the character of the exterior is the effective window treatment, plus the unique design of the recessed front entrance.

Design 41386 880 Sq. Ft. - Upper Level
596 Sq. Ft. - Lower Level; 14,043 Cu. Ft.

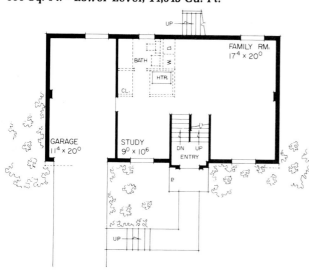

● These three designs feature traditional exterior styling with a split-foyer, bi-level living interior. Owners of a bi-level design achieve a great amount of livability from an economical plan without sacrificing any of the fine qualities of a much larger and more expensive plan.

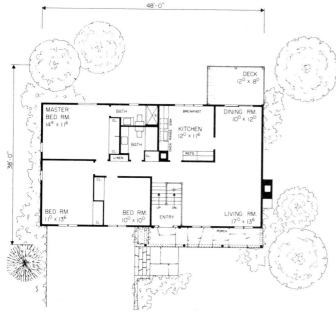

Design 41210 1,248 Sq. Ft. - Upper Level
676 Sq. Ft. - Lower Level; 19,812 Cu. Ft.

Design 43198

1,040 Sq. Ft. - Upper Level
986 Sq. Ft. - Lower Level; 20,368 Cu. Ft.

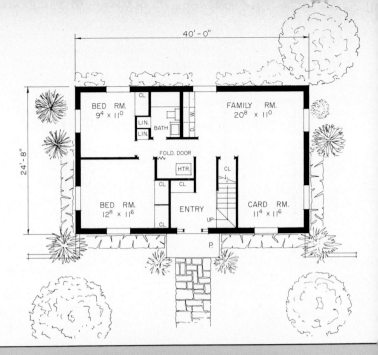

Design 42334

1,694 Sq. Ft. - Upper Level
1,020 Sq. Ft. - Lower Level; 34,259 Cu. Ft.

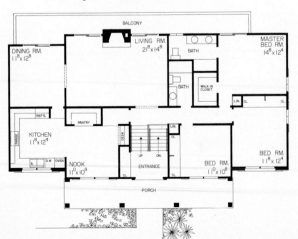

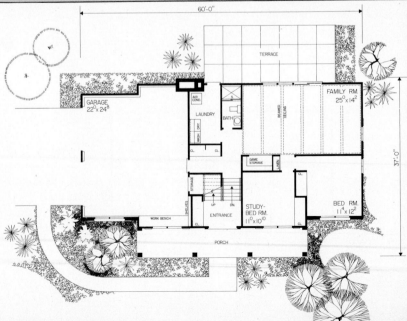

Design 41341 1,248 Sq. Ft. - Upper Level; 676 Sq. Ft. - Lower Level; 19,812 Cu. Ft.

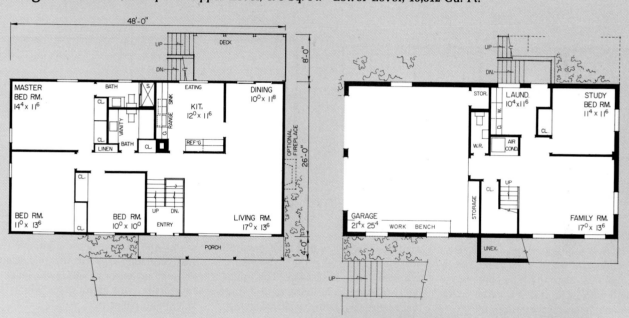

MASTER BED RM. 14⁴ x 11⁶

BATH

EATING

DINING 10⁰ x 11⁸

KIT. 12⁰ x 11⁶

LINEN BATH

REF'G

OPTIONAL FIREPLACE

BED RM. 11⁰ x 13⁶

BED RM. 10⁰ x 10⁰

UP DN. ENTRY

LIVING RM. 17⁰ x 13⁶

PORCH

48'-0"

8'-0"

26'-0"

4'-0"

UP DN. DECK

VANITY RANGE SINK

UP DN.

STOR. LAUND. 10⁴ x 11⁶

STUDY BED RM. 11⁴ x 11⁶

W.R. AIR COND.

STORAGE UP

GARAGE 21⁴ x 25⁴ WORK BENCH

FAMILY RM. 17⁰ x 13⁶

UNEX.

UP

Design 42514
1,713 Sq. Ft. - Upper Level
916 Sq. Ft. - Lower Level; 32,000 Cu. Ft.

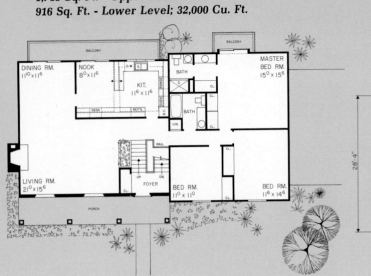

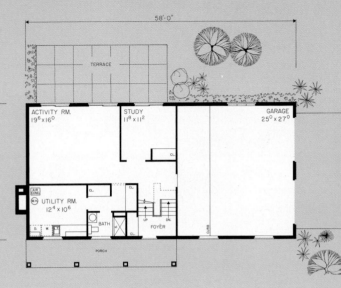

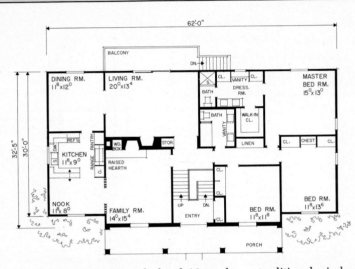

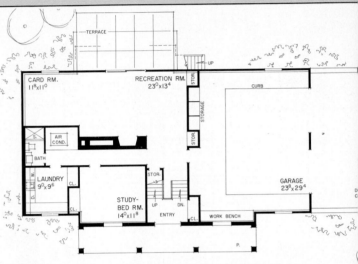

● Here is a unique bi-level. Not only in its delightful exterior appeal, but in its practical planning. The covered porch with its impressive columns, the contrasting use of materials and the traditional window and door detailing are all features which will provoke comment from passers-by. The upper level is a complete living unit of three bedrooms, two baths, separate living, dining and family rooms, a kitchen with an eating area, two fireplaces and an outdoor balcony. The lower level represents extra living space which is bright and cheerful.

Design 42547
1,946 Sq. Ft. - Upper Level
1,340 Sq. Ft. - Lower Level; 40,166 Cu. Ft.

Design 41822 1,836 Sq. Ft. - Upper Level; 1,150 Sq. Ft. - Lower Level; 33,280 Cu. Ft.

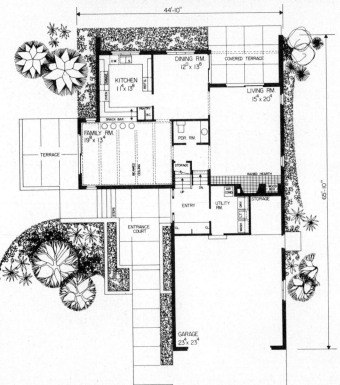

Design 42394

180 Sq. Ft. - Entry Level; 1,145 Sq. Ft. - Upper Level
1,098 Sq. Ft. - Lower Level; 24,660 Cu. Ft.

● This handsome traditional adaptation with a Mansard roof is dramatic. Its appeal is to be found in its straight forward simplicity. The inviting entrance court with its raised planters ties in with the side terrace. Other outdoor living areas include the covered terrace for the large living room and the sweeping balcony overlooking the rear yard for upstairs bedrooms. Certainly, fine indoor-outdoor living relationships.

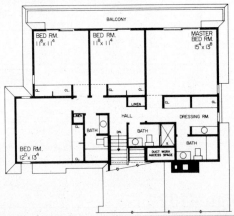

Design 41743 1,580 Sq. Ft. - Upper Level
950 Sq. Ft. - Lower Level; 25,888 Cu. Ft.

● Stately, and a delight to behold. A tailored hip roof and pleasing cornice work cap an exterior whose graciousness emanates from the contrast of the masses of brick and the delightfully delicate detailing of the windows.

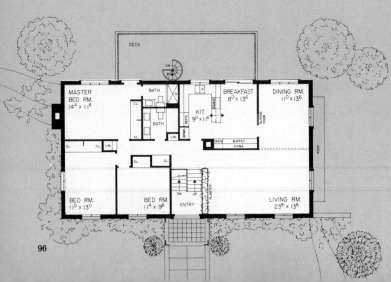

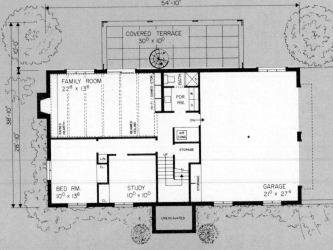

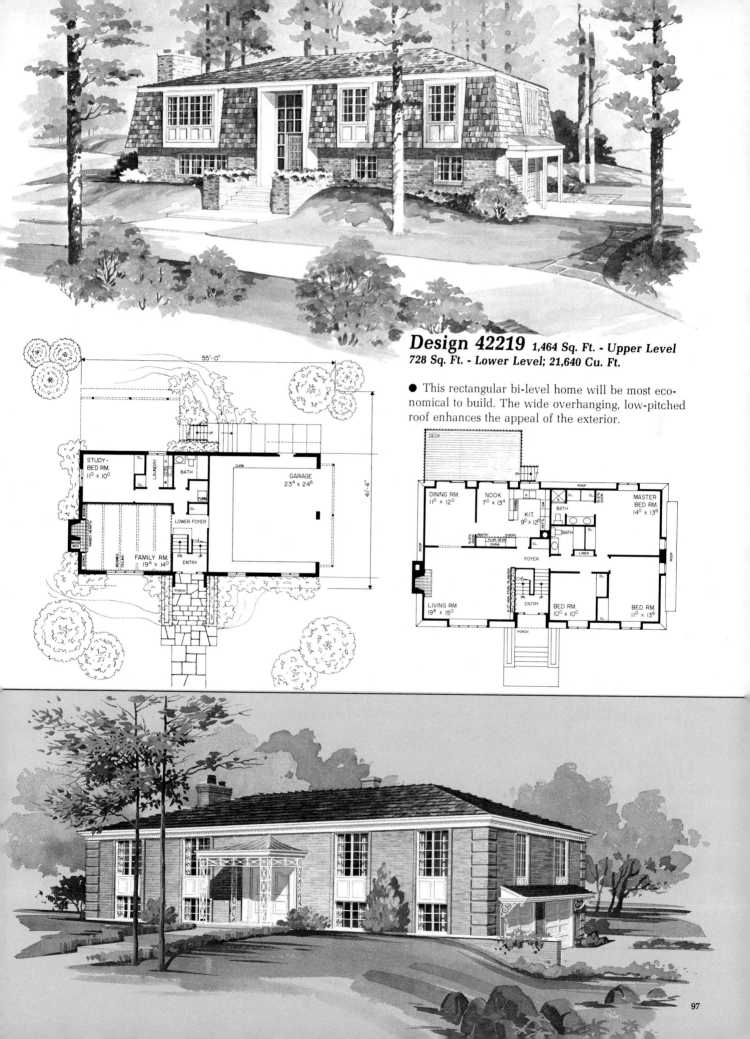

Design 42219 1,464 Sq. Ft. - Upper Level
728 Sq. Ft. - Lower Level; 21,640 Cu. Ft.

● This rectangular bi-level home will be most economical to build. The wide overhanging, low-pitched roof enhances the appeal of the exterior.

Design 42319 1,343 Sq. Ft. - Upper Level
980 Sq. Ft. - Lower Level; 23,290 Cu. Ft.

● This rectangular, bi-level home will be economical to build. The wide overhanging, low-pitched roof enhances the appeal of the exterior. Inside, there are four bedrooms, two on each level, a family activities area, plus a more formal, living room with an adjacent dining room and an efficient kitchen opening into the breakfast room.

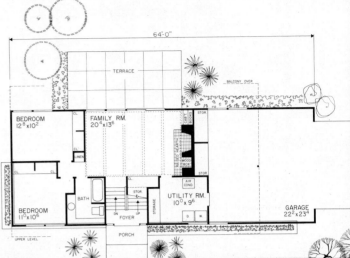

Design 42567 1,773 Sq. Ft. - Upper Level; 1,356 Sq. Ft. - Lower Level; 35,750 Cu. Ft.

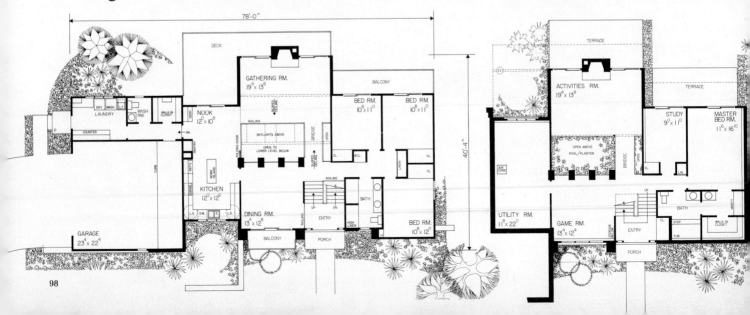

Design 41220
1,456 Sq. Ft. - Upper Level
862 Sq. Ft. - Lower Level; 22,563 Cu. Ft.

● This fresh, contemporary exterior sets the stage for exceptional livability. Measuring only 52 across the front, this bi-level home offers the large family outstanding features. Whether called upon to function as a four or five bedroom home, there is plenty of space in which to move around.

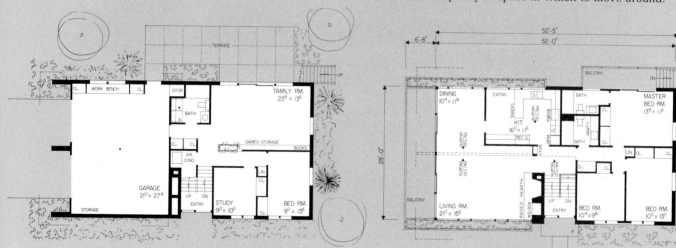

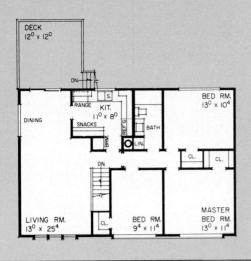

DECK
12⁰ x 12⁰

DN.

DINING

RANGE KIT.
11⁰ x 8⁰

SNACKS

S

REF'G

BRM.

LIN.

BATH

BED RM.
13⁰ x 10⁴

CL. CL.

DN.

LIVING RM.
13⁰ x 25⁴

CL.

BED RM.
9⁴ x 11⁴

MASTER
BED RM.
13⁰ x 11⁴

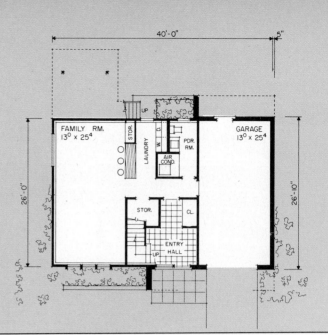

40'-0" 5"

FAMILY RM.
13⁰ x 25⁴

UP

STOR.

LAUNDRY

W. D.

AIR COND.

PDR. RM.

GARAGE
13⁰ x 25⁴

26'-0"

26'-10"

STOR.

CL.

ENTRY HALL

UP

● The gathering room is separated from the dining room by a stone wall and a short flight of stairs. Dining and breakfast rooms both have sliding glass doors leading to a rear terrace and are within convenient reach of the U-shaped kitchen. Two bedrooms and two baths are in a separate wing. The master suite opens to the terrace.

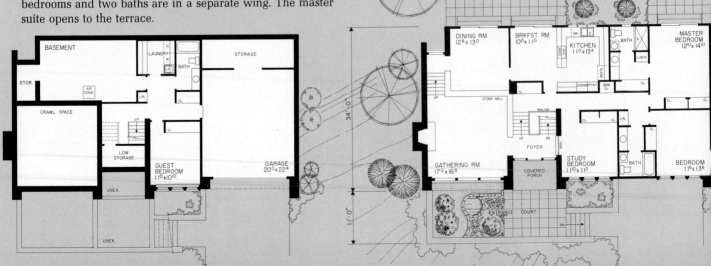

BASEMENT

LAUNDRY

BATH

STORAGE

STOR.

AIR COND.

LIN.

CL.

CRAWL SPACE

UP

LOW STORAGE

CL.

GUEST BEDROOM
11⁰ x 10¹⁰

GARAGE
20⁰ x 22⁴

UNEX.

UNEX.

62'-0"

TERRACE

DINING RM.
12⁸ x 13⁰

BRKFST RM.
10⁰ x 11⁰

KITCHEN
11⁰ x 13⁴

DW S

COOK TOP

REF'G

OVEN/DRY

BRM

CL.

BATH

LINEN

MASTER BEDROOM
12¹⁰ x 14¹⁰

CL. CL.

UP

STONE WALL

34'-0"

RAILING

FOYER

DN

CL. LIN.

GATHERING RM.
17⁰ x 16⁸

COVERED PORCH

STUDY BEDROOM
11¹⁰ x 11²

BATH

BEDROOM
11⁶ x 13⁶

11'-0"

ENTRANCE COURT

DN

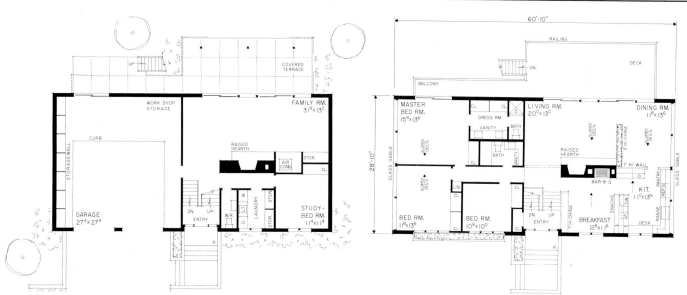

Design 41842 1,747 Sq. Ft. - Upper Level; 937 Sq. Ft. - Lower Level; 27,212 Cu. Ft.

Design 42885 1,922 Sq. Ft. Upper Level
492 Sq. Ft. - Lower Level; 34,640 Cu. Ft.

Design 41778
1,344 Sq. Ft. - Upper Level
768 Sq. Ft. - Lower Level
22,266 Cu. Ft.

● Interesting? You bet it is. The low-pitched, wide overhanging roof, the vertical siding and the dramatic glass areas give the facade of this contemporary bi-level house an appearance all its own.

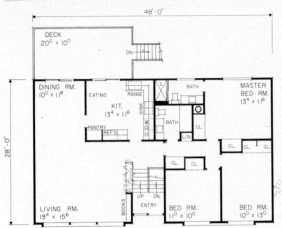

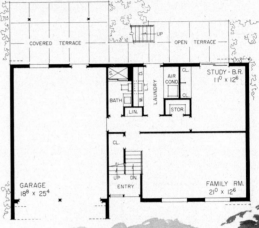

Design 41704
1,498 Sq. Ft. - Upper Level
870 Sq. Ft. - Lower Level
23,882 Cu. Ft.

● The bi-level concept of living has become popular. This is understandable, for it represents a fine way in which to gain a maximum amount of extra livable area beneath the basic floor plan.

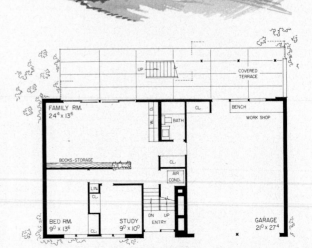

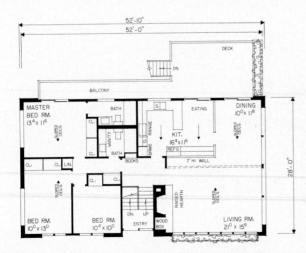

LEISURE LIVING MULTI-LEVELS . . .

offer interesting living patterns. This is the result of the informal, easy-going lifestyle generally sought and associated with vacation living. Open planning, dual use space, large glass areas, sloping ceilings, interior and exterior balconies, decks, etc. are among the features which adapt to multi-level living and can help make that home away from home a refreshing living experience. Common to each of these designs is the outstanding sleeping potential - a must where weekend entertaining and family get-togethers are to be considered a frequent occurrence. Each of these leisure living designs adapts well to year 'round use.

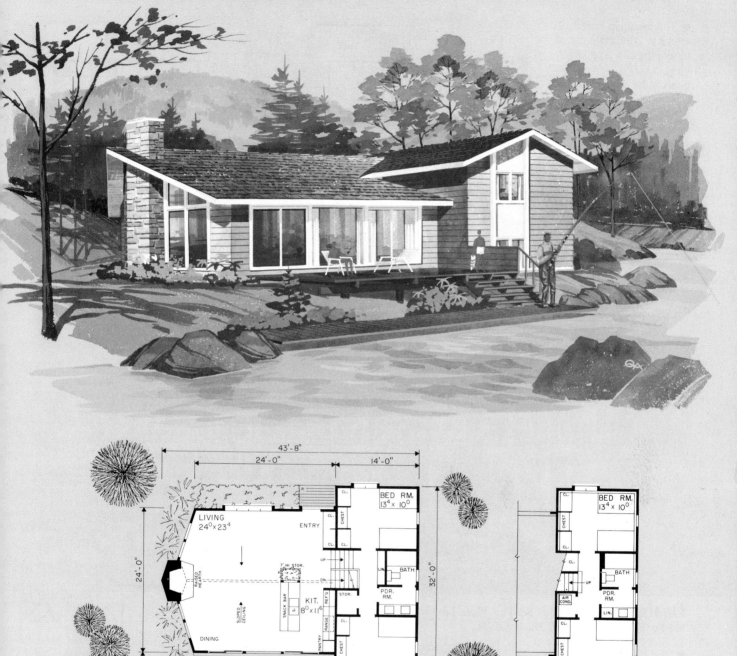

Design 42463
624 Sq. Ft. - Main Level; 448 Sq. Ft. - Upper Level
448 Sq. Ft. - Lower Level; 16,232 Cu. Ft.

● If you like split-level living there is no reason why your second home can't provide you with those living patterns. If you haven't ever lived in a split-level home, here is your opportunity to do so. The one-story portion of this plan houses the living areas. The two-story section comprises the sleeping zones. Open planning results in a gloriously spacious living, dining and kitchen area. The raised hearth fireplace is strategically located and will be enjoyed from the main living area and even the kitchen. Each of the two sleeping levels features two very good sized bedrooms, a compartmented bath and excellent storage facilities. The use of double bunks will really enable you to entertain a crowd on those glorious holiday weekends. Note built-in chests.

Design 41457
640 Sq. Ft. - Upper Level
640 Sq. Ft. - Lower Level
11,712 Cu. Ft.

● This vacation home seems to grow right out of its sloping site. The street view of this design appears to be a one-story. It, therefore, is putting its site to the best possible use. As a result of being able to expose the lower level, the total livable floor area of the house is doubled. This is the most practical and economical manner to increase livability so dramatically.

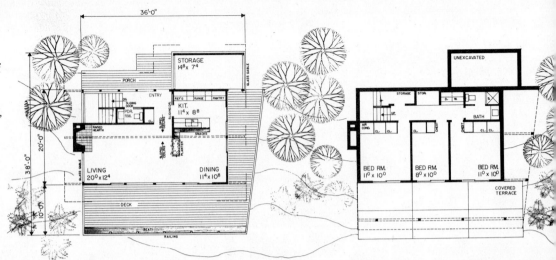

Design 42485 1,108 Sq. Ft. - Main Level
983 Sq. Ft. - Lower Level; 21,530 Cu. Ft.

● The rear exterior of this design is a full two-story; while from the road it has the appearance of a one-story. Notice the projecting deck and how it shelters the terrace. Each of the generous glass areas is protected from the summer sun by the overhangs and the extended walls. The clerestory windows of the front exterior provide natural light to the center of the plan.

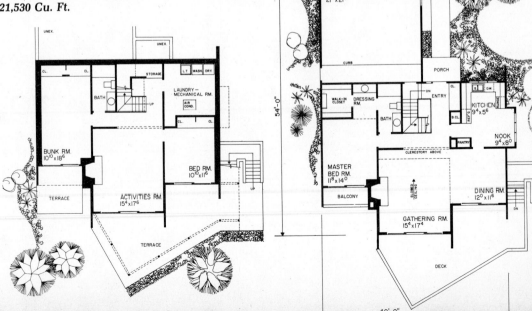

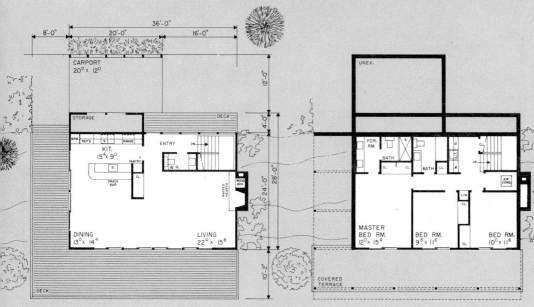

Design 42455
864 Sq. Ft. - Upper Level
864 Sq. Ft. - Lower Level
16,934 Cu. Ft.

● Delightful vacation living experiences will be in store for the owners and guests of this second home. Designed for a sloping site, the lakeside elevation has both the upper and lower levels completely exposed for the fullest enjoyment of indoor-outdoor living. The deck, which runs the full length of two sides of the house, is but a step from the upper level living areas. A covered terrace is accessible from the lower level bedrooms. Note the size of the living-dining area.

Design 42482
960 Sq. Ft. - Upper Level
622 Sq. Ft. - Lower Level
17,352 Cu. Ft.

● This home has a sunny deck. It is accessible from the living room by two sets of sliding glass doors. The dining room plus an informal snack bar are available for eating. Three bedrooms and two full baths will serve the family for sleeping arrangements. The deck acts as a cover for the carport/terrace. A great area when hiding away from the weather is necessary.

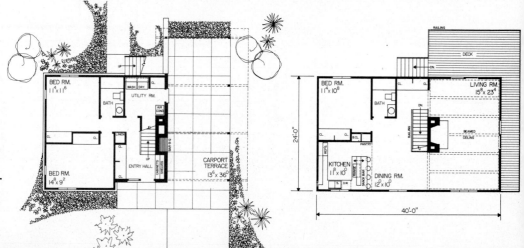

Design 42435 *960 Sq. Ft. - Upper Level; 312 Sq. Ft. - Lower Level; 14,026 Cu. Ft.*

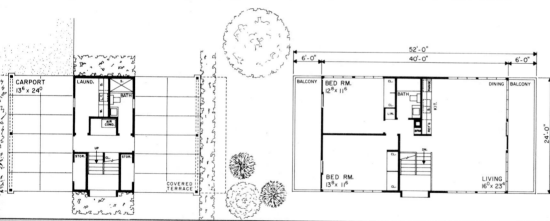

● Make your second home or retirement home, one that has a distinctive flair. This modified, T-shaped design will be great fun. You'll not have any difficulty enjoying the surrounding countryside from the vantage points offered here. The projecting bedroom and living wings have their own outdoor balconies. In addition, they cleverly provide the shelter for the carport and the terrace.

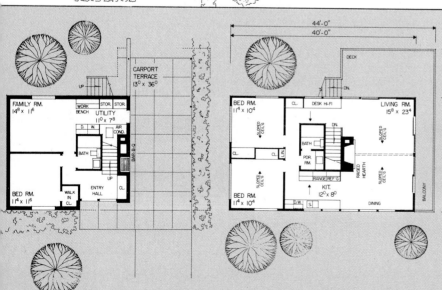

Design 41445
960 Sq. Ft. - Upper Level
628 Sq. Ft. - Lower Level; 15,304 Cu. Ft.

● Why not give two-level living a try and make your leisure-time home something delightfully different? If there is plenty of countryside or water around, you'll love viewing it from the upper level. And the best seat in the house will not be inside at all, but one on the balcony or deck. While the upper level is a complete living unit with its two bedrooms, bath, kitchen and spacious living area; the lower level with its one bedroom, bath, utility room (make it a kitchen) and family room could be a complete living unit, too.

Design 42465

1,144 Sq. Ft. - Upper Level
1,144 Sq. Ft. - Lower Level
22,651 Cu. Ft.

● Here is a ski or hunting lodge which will cater successfully to a crowd. Or, here is a summer home which will be ideal for your own family and an occasional weekend guest. Whatever its purpose, this bi-level design will be appreciated. There is plenty of space as illustrated by the 29 foot living-dining area, 15 foot kitchen, three full baths, four sizable bedrooms and bunk room. The list continues. List your favorite features.

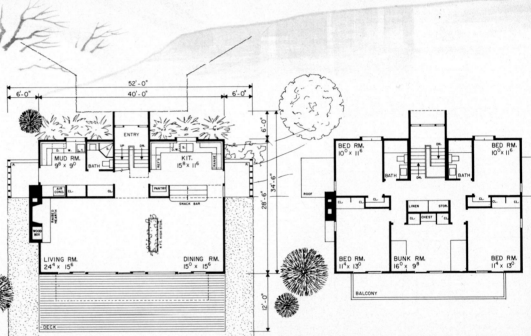

Design 41498 768 Sq. Ft. - Main Level; 546 Sq. Ft. - Upper Level; 768 Sq. Ft. - Lower Level; 18,811 Cu. Ft.

● If it is space you need in your leisure living home, you should give a lot of thought to this multi-level design. It has just about everything to assure a pleasant visit. There are spacious sleeping facilities, fine recreational areas, 2½ baths, an excellent kitchen and good storage potential. The large deck and covered terrace will be popular outdoor spots.

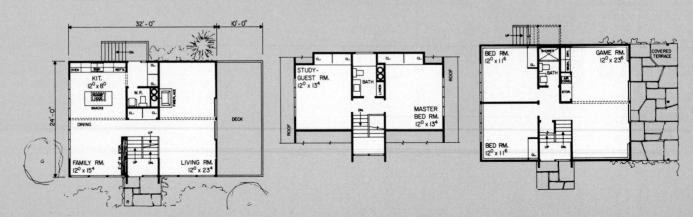

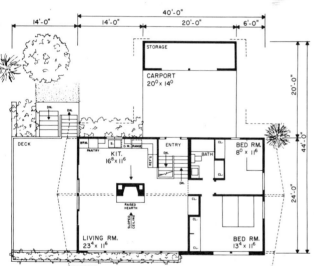

14'-0" 14'-0" 40'-0" 20'-0" 6'-0"

STORAGE

CARPORT
20⁰ x 14⁰

20'-0"

44'-0"

24'-0"

DECK

DN. DN.

BR'K.
S

D.W.
RANGE

PANTRY

REF'G.

KIT.
16⁸ x 11⁶

ENTRY

DN.

BATH

CL.

BED RM.
8⁰ x 11⁶

CL.

RAISED
HEARTH

SLOPED CEILING

DN.

CL.

CL.

LIVING RM.
23⁴ x 11⁶

BED RM.
13⁴ x 11⁶

Design 42438 977 Sq. Ft. - Upper Level
987 Sq. Ft. - Lower Level; 19,129 Cu. Ft.

● A great bi-level that easily could be adapted to either a flat or sloping site. As you walk into the main entry, you will either go up a short stairway to the upper, main level, or down a few stairs to the lower, recreation level.

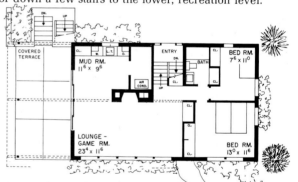

DN. UP

COVERED
TERRACE

CL.

L.T.
D

MUD RM.
11⁶ x 9⁶

AIR COND.

ENTRY

DN.

UP

CL.

BATH

CL.

BED RM.
7⁶ x 11⁰

CL.

LOUNGE -
GAME RM.
23⁰ x 11⁶

CL.

BED RM.
13⁰ x 11⁶

Design 41460 1,035 Sq. Ft. - Upper Level; 1,067 Sq. Ft. - Lower Level; 21,125 Cu. Ft.

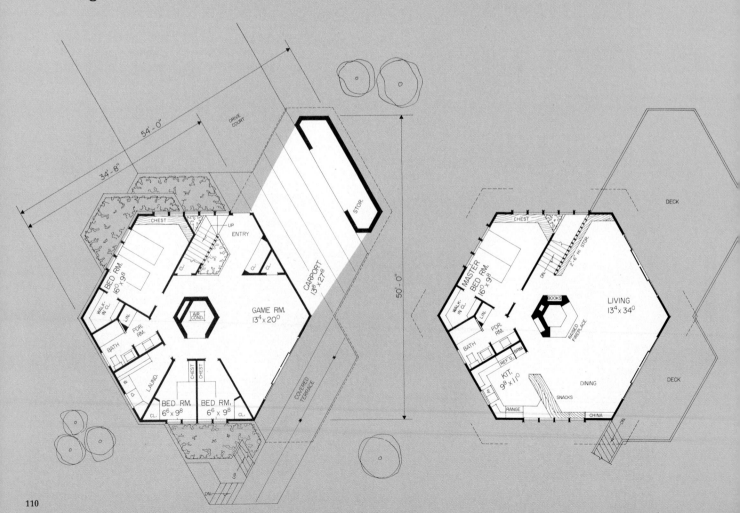

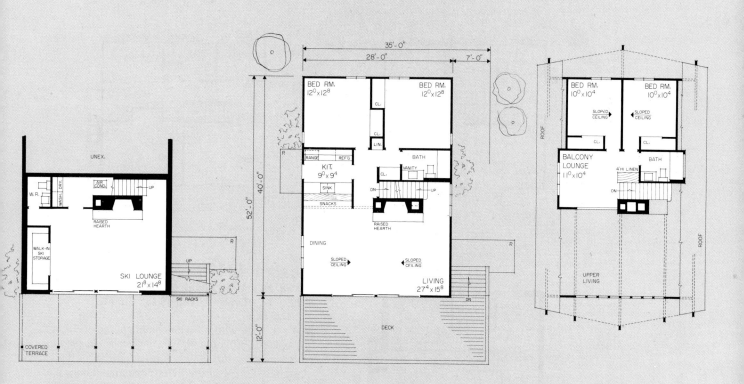

Design 41475 1,120 Sq. Ft. - Main Level; 522 Sq. Ft. - Upper Level; 616 Sq. Ft. - Lower Level; 24,406 Cu. Ft.

● Skiers take notice! This vacation home tells an exciting story of activity - and people. Whether you build this design to function as your ski lodge, or to serve your family and friends during the summer months, it will perform ideally. It would take little imagination to envision this second home overlooking your lakeshore site with the grown-ups sunning themselves on the deck while the children play on the terrace. Whatever the season or the location, visualize how your family will enjoy the many hours spent in this delightful chalet adaptation.

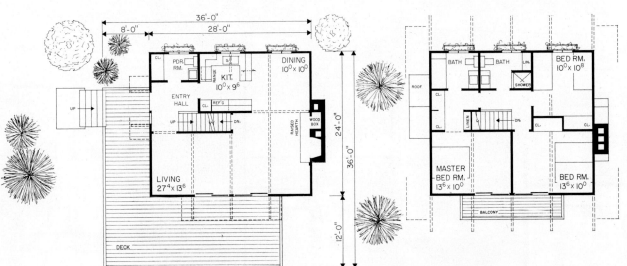

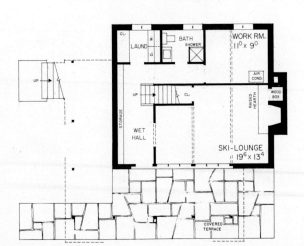

Design 42429

672 Sq. Ft. - Main Level; 672 Sq. Ft. - Upper Level
672 Sq. Ft. - Lower Level; 19,152 Cu. Ft.

● A ski lodge with a Swiss chalet character. If you are a skier, you know that all the fun is not restricted to schussing the slopes. A great portion of the pleasure is found in the living accommodations and the pursuant merriment fostered by good fellowship. As for the specific features which will surely contribute to everyone's off-the-slopes fun consider: the outdoor deck, balcony and covered terrace; the ski lounge; the two fireplaces; and the huge L-shaped living and dining room area. The three bedrooms are of good size and with bunk beds will sleep quite a crew. Note the wet hall for skis, the all important work room and the laundry.

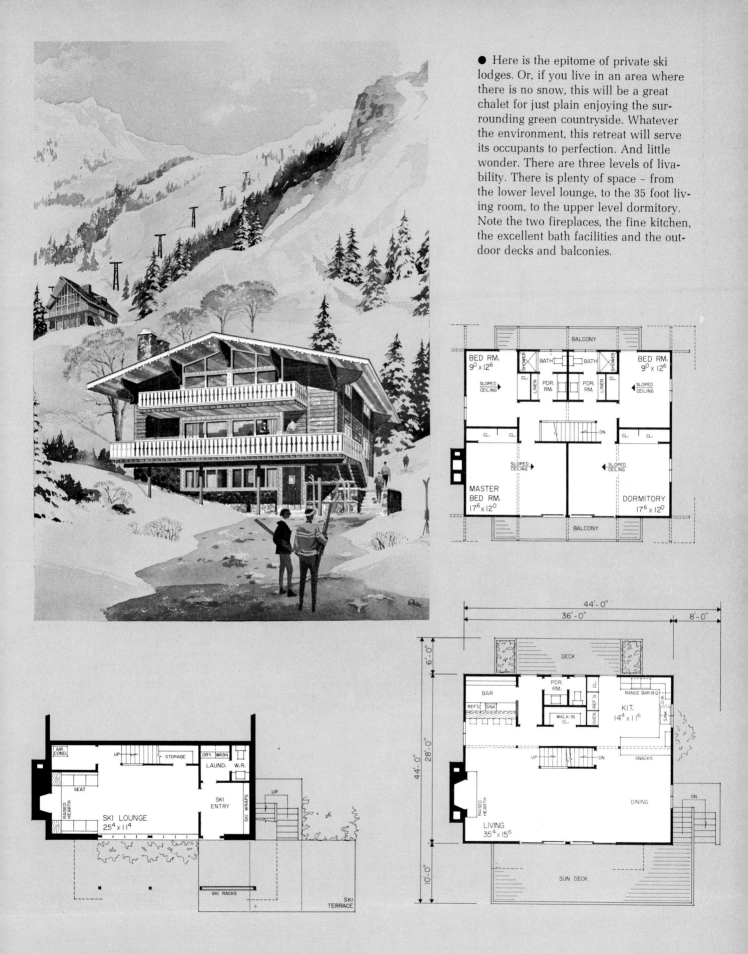

● Here is the epitome of private ski lodges. Or, if you live in an area where there is no snow, this will be a great chalet for just plain enjoying the surrounding green countryside. Whatever the environment, this retreat will serve its occupants to perfection. And little wonder. There are three levels of livability. There is plenty of space – from the lower level lounge, to the 35 foot living room, to the upper level dormitory. Note the two fireplaces, the fine kitchen, the excellent bath facilities and the outdoor decks and balconies.

Design 41474 1,008 Sq. Ft. - Main Level; 1,008 Sq. Ft. - Upper Level; 594 Sq. Ft. - Lower Level; 23,803 Cu. Ft.

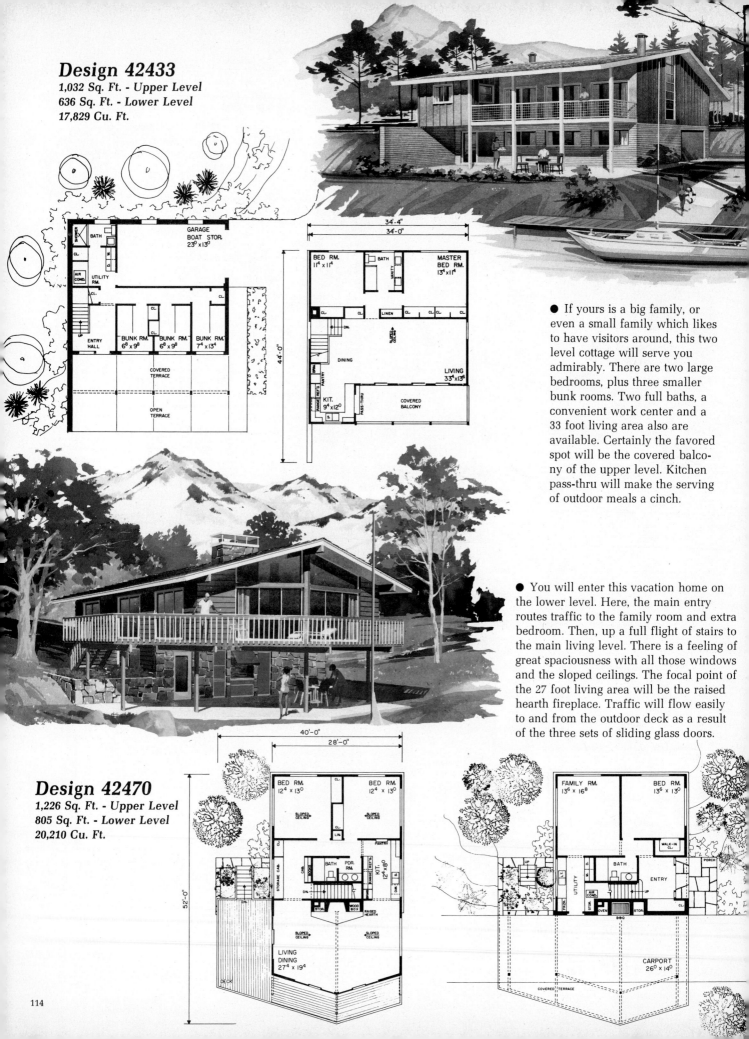

Design 42433

1,032 Sq. Ft. - Upper Level
636 Sq. Ft. - Lower Level
17,829 Cu. Ft.

GARAGE BOAT STOR. 23⁰ x 13⁰

SHOWER / BATH / CL. / AIR COND. / UTILITY RM. / CL.

ENTRY HALL / UP

BUNK RM. 6⁸ x 9⁸ / BUNK RM. 6⁸ x 9⁸ / BUNK RM. 7⁴ x 13⁴ / CL.

COVERED TERRACE

OPEN TERRACE

34'-4"
34'-0"
44'-0"

BED RM. 11⁴ x 11⁴ / BATH / VANITY / MASTER BED RM. 13⁴ x 11⁴

CL. / LINEN / CL. / CL. / CL.

DN. / SLOPED CEILING

DINING

BMA / PANTRY / RANGE / REF'G / PASS-THRU

KIT. 9⁴ x 12⁰

LIVING 33⁴ x 13⁶

COVERED BALCONY

● If yours is a big family, or even a small family which likes to have visitors around, this two level cottage will serve you admirably. There are two large bedrooms, plus three smaller bunk rooms. Two full baths, a convenient work center and a 33 foot living area also are available. Certainly the favored spot will be the covered balcony of the upper level. Kitchen pass-thru will make the serving of outdoor meals a cinch.

● You will enter this vacation home on the lower level. Here, the main entry routes traffic to the family room and extra bedroom. Then, up a full flight of stairs to the main living level. There is a feeling of great spaciousness with all those windows and the sloped ceilings. The focal point of the 27 foot living area will be the raised hearth fireplace. Traffic will flow easily to and from the outdoor deck as a result of the three sets of sliding glass doors.

Design 42470

1,226 Sq. Ft. - Upper Level
805 Sq. Ft. - Lower Level
20,210 Cu. Ft.

40'-0"
28'-0"
52'-0"

BED RM. 12⁴ x 13⁰ / CL. / BED RM. 12⁴ x 13⁰

SLOPED CEILING / CL. / LIN. / SLOPED CEILING

STORAGE CAB. / CAB / BATH / PDR. RM. / PANTRY / KIT. 12⁴ x 8⁰

DN. / STOR. / WOOD BOX / RAISED HEARTH

SLOPED CEILING / SLOPED CEILING

LIVING DINING 27⁴ x 19⁴

DECK

FAMILY RM. 13⁶ x 16⁸ / BED RM. 13⁶ x 13⁰

WALK-IN CL.

UP / UTILITY / BATH / ENTRY / PORCH

AIR COND. / FR'S / OVEN / STOR. / B-B-Q / STOR. / UP / CL.

CARPORT 26⁰ x 14⁰

COVERED TERRACE

LOWER LEVEL UTILITY....

can make a great contribution to the value as well at to the daily living patterns of the family. The designs in this section illustrate just how well the basement level (partial or full) can be made to function with the main living level of the house. In each design the highly developed lower level is more than just a dark, damp basement. It is, instead, a bright, cheerful area which can even have a major design impact on the ambience of the main living level. In some houses the addition and development of this lower level also impacts, and pleasingly so, on the exterior design.

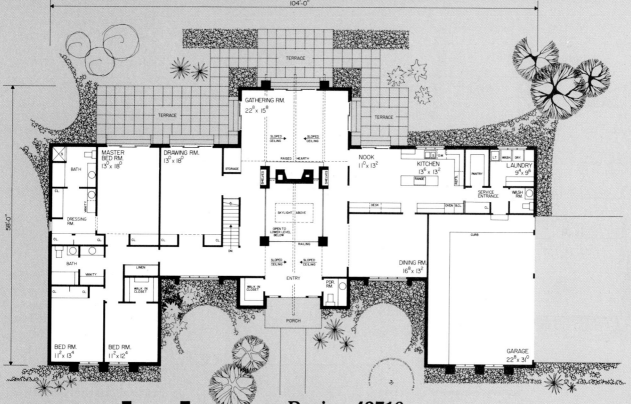

Design 42710 3,296 Sq. Ft.; 57,500 Cu. Ft.

● Artful design! In the skylight foyer, a balcony overlooks the lower level conversation pit. The gathering room features sloped ceilings, a raised hearth fireplace and triple sliding glass doors leading to the terrace. A drawing room and activities room (an additional 1,135 sq. ft. of livability on lower level) provide even more living space. Check out the kitchen carefully! Its size alone is unusual but there's also a built-in desk, island range and walk-in pantry. A luxury master suite with four closets, a dressing room, private bath and entry to the terrace. Two more large bedrooms. This is a glamourous home. Its unique design makes you proud when guests arrive. And its spacious qualities make family life a joy. The storage facilities in this plan are particularly noteworthy.

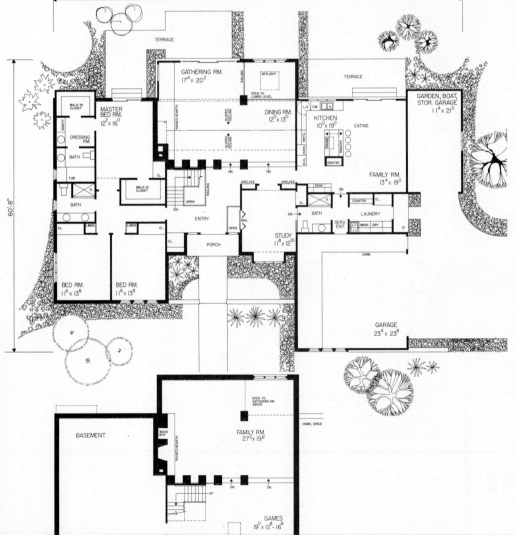

Design 42721
2,667 Sq. Ft. - Main Level
1,153 Sq. Ft. - Lower Level
53,150 Cu. Ft.

● Visually exciting! A sunken gathering room with a sloped ceiling, raised hearth fireplace, corner balcony and skylight . . . the last two features shared by the formal dining room. There's more. Two family rooms . . . one on the lower level (1,153 sq. ft.) with a raised hearth fireplace, another adjacent to the kitchen with a snack bar! Plus a study and game room. A lavish master suite and two large bedrooms. A first floor laundry and reams of storage space, including a special garage for a boat, sports equipment, garden tools etc. There's plenty of space for family activities in this home. From chic dinner parties for friends to birthday gatherings for kids, there's always the right setting . . . and so much room that adults and children can entertain at the same time.

Design 42730

2,490 Sq. Ft. - Main Level
1,086 Sq. Ft. - Lower Level
50,340 Cu. Ft.

● Here is a basic one-story home that is really loaded with livability on the first floor and has a bonus of an extra 1,086 sq. ft. of planned livability on a lower level. What makes this so livable is that the first floor, adjacent to the stairs leading below, is open and forms a balcony looking down into a dramatic planting area. The first floor traffic patterns flow around this impressive and distinctive feature. In addition to the gathering room, study and family room, there is the lounge and activity room. Notice the second balcony open to the activity room below. The master bedroom is outstanding with two baths and two walk-in closets. The attached three-car garage has a bulk storage area and is accessible through the service area.

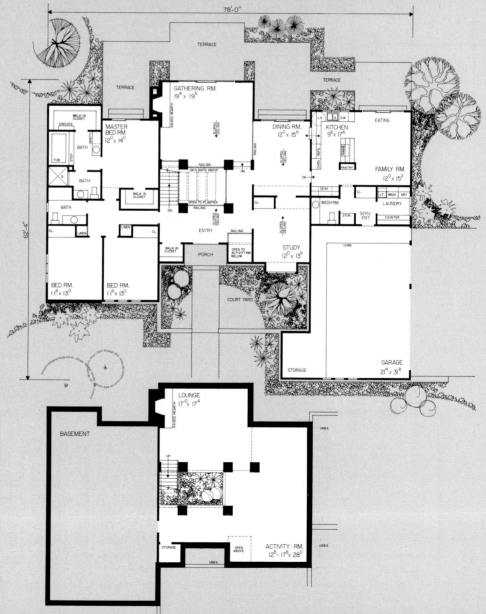

Design 42562

2,884 Sq. Ft. - First Floor
864 Sq. Ft. - Second Floor
73,625 Cu. Ft.

● Here is an exciting contemporary design for the large, active family. It can be called upon to function as either a four or five bedroom home. As a four bedroom home the parents will enjoy a wonderful suite with study and exceptional bath facilities. Note stall shower, plus sunken tub. The upstairs features the children's bedrooms and a spacious balcony lounge which looks down to the floor below. The sunken gathering room will be just that with its sloped beamed ceiling, dramatic raised hearth fireplace and direct access to the rear terrace.

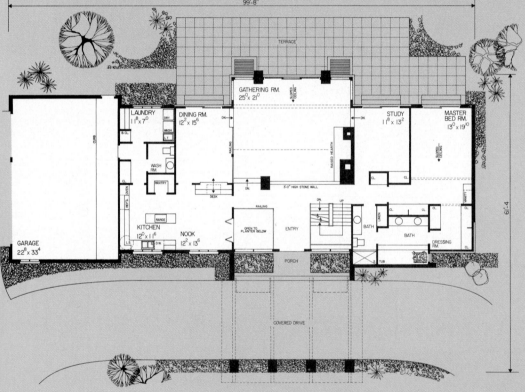

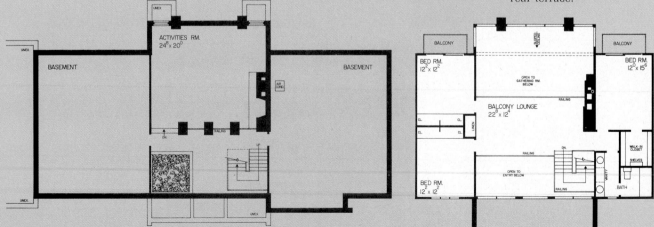

Design 42709

2,471 Sq. Ft. - Main Level
2,038 Sq. Ft. - Upper Level
1,435 Sq. Ft. - Lower Level
73,125 Cu. Ft.

● A lower-level conversation pit! Above, a skylight. And on the first and second floors, open balconies. . . .offering a view of both the conversation pit and skylight. That's just the beginning. Develop the basement area around the conversation pit and add 1,435 square feet to your informal living area. The gathering room features a balcony overlooking an indoor garden . . . part of the scenery in the family room. Fireplace in both those rooms. An enormous kitchen with a walk-in pantry, island range, built-in desk. Four large bedrooms, including a luxury master suite. Observe the storage potential.

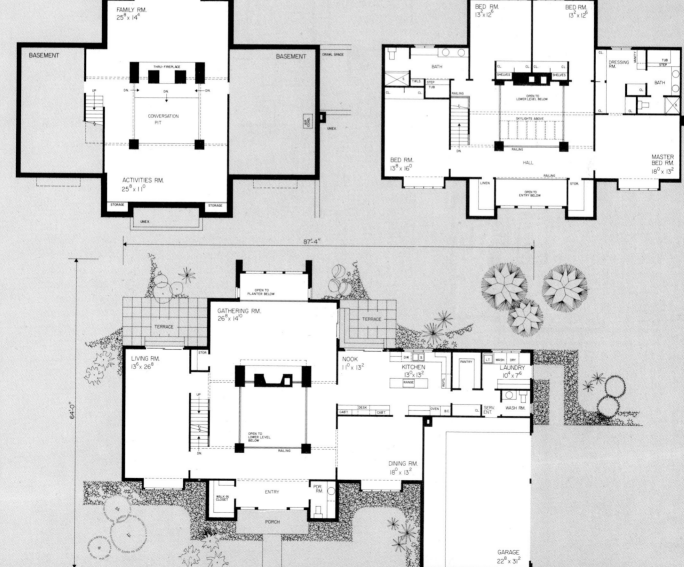

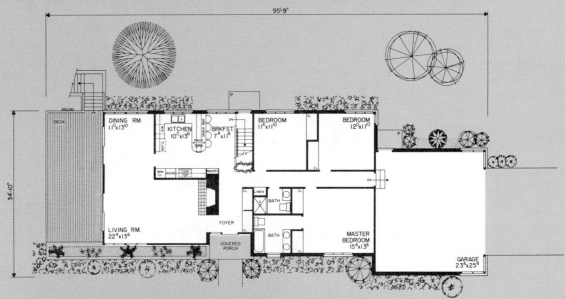

Design 42272
1,731 Sq. Ft. - Main Level
672 Sq. Ft. - Lower Level; 27,802 Cu. Ft.

● Certainly not a huge house. But one, nevertheless, that is long on livability and one that surely will be fun to live in. With its wide-overhanging hip roof, this unadorned facade is the picture of simplicity. As such, it has a quiet appeal all its own. The living-dining area is one of the focal points of the plan. It is wonderfully spacious. The large glass areas and the accessibility, through sliding glass doors, of the outdoor balcony are fine features. For recreation, there is the lower level area which opens onto a large terrace covered by the balcony above.

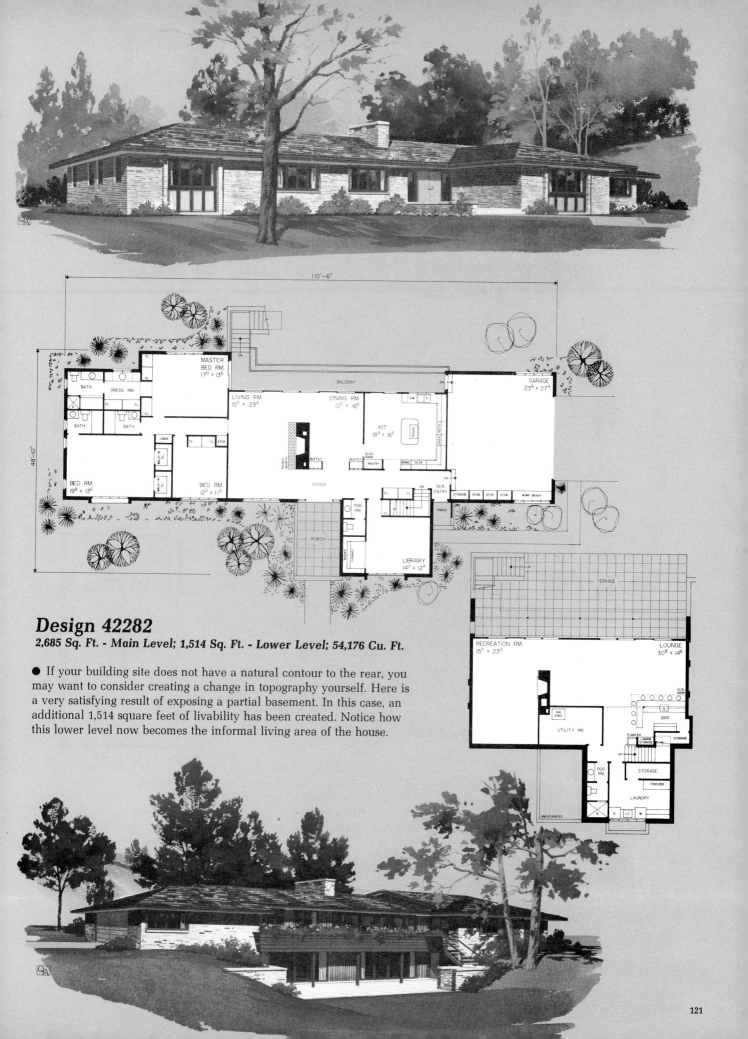

Design 42282

2,685 Sq. Ft. - Main Level; 1,514 Sq. Ft. - Lower Level; 54,176 Cu. Ft.

● If your building site does not have a natural contour to the rear, you may want to consider creating a change in topography yourself. Here is a very satisfying result of exposing a partial basement. In this case, an additional 1,514 square feet of livability has been created. Notice how this lower level now becomes the informal living area of the house.

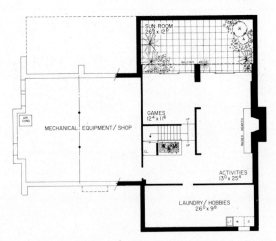

Design 42834

1,775 Sq. Ft. - First Floor; 1,041 Sq. Ft. - Second Floor
1,128 Sq. Ft. - Lower Level; 55,690 Cu. Ft.

● This passive solar design offers 4,200 square feet of livability situated on three levels. The primary passive element will be the lower level sun room which admits sunlight for direct-gain heating. The solar warmth collected in the sun room will radiate into the rest of the house after it passes the sliding glass doors. During the warm summer months, shades are put over the skylight to protect it from direct sunlight. This design has the option of incorporating active solar heating panels to the roof. The collectors would be installed on the south-facing portion of the roof. They would absorb the sun's warmth for both domestic water and supplementary space heating. An attic fan exhausts any hot air out of the house in the summer and circulates air in the winter. With or without the active solar panels, this is a marvelous two-story contemporary.

Design 42830 1,795 Sq. Ft. - Main Level; 1,546 Sq. Ft. - Lower Level; 49,900 Cu. Ft.

● Outstanding contemporary design! This home has been created with the advantages of passive solar heating in mind. For optimum energy savings, this delightful design combines passive solar devices, the solarium, with optional active collectors. Included with the purchase of this design are four plot plans to assure that the solar collectors will face the south. The garage in each plan acts as a buffer against cold northern winds. Schematic details for solar application also are included. Along with being energy-efficient, this design has excellent living patterns. Three bedrooms, the master bedroom on the main level and two others on the lower level at each side of the solarium. The living area of the main level will be able to enjoy the delightful view of the solarium and sunken garden.

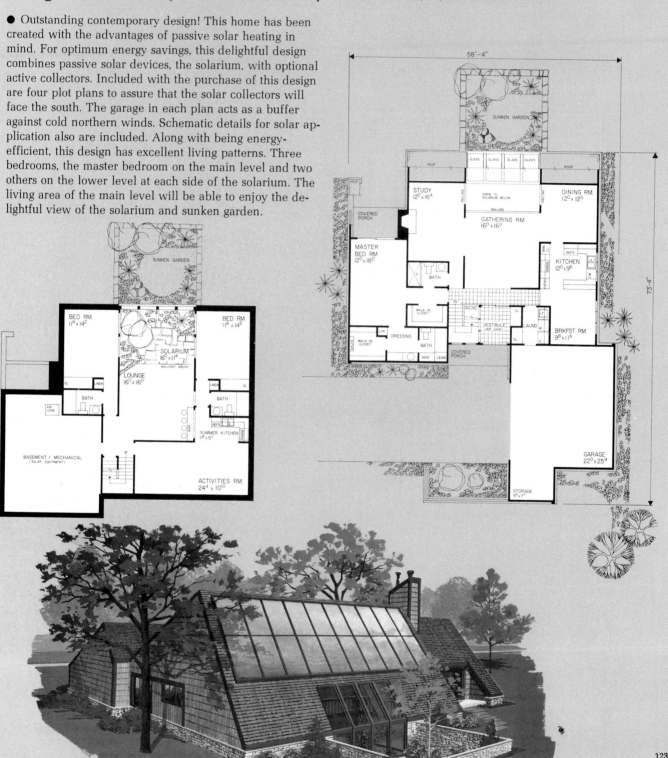

MASTER BED RM. 15⁰ x 16⁰
BATH
BATH
BED RM. 11⁴ x 12⁰
BED RM. 12⁰ x 16⁰
LINEN
HALL
CL. CL. CL. CL. LINEN CL. CL.
DN.
ROOF
ROOF
ROOF
ATTIC STORAGE

Design 42273

1,357 Sq. Ft. - First Floor
1,065 Sq. Ft. - Second Floor
630 Sq. Ft. - Lower Level
38,303 Cu. Ft.

● Picture this charming, traditional design as your new home. Its exterior appeal is loaded with distinction and warmth. The floor plan of this design offers lots of livability on the three floors. On the left side of the entrance hall, the spacious living room will be found. It has a fireplace and sliding glass doors leading onto the porch. Straight ahead, the formal dining room will efficiently serve those formal occasions. It, too, has access to the rear porch. The adjacent nook and kitchen will prove to be an excellent work place. A second porch is between the kitchen and the garage. To your right of the entrance hall you will find the stairs to the second floor, a full bath and a library/bedroom, contingent upon your needs. Upstairs you will find lots of closet space, two bedrooms, a full bath and a master bedroom with a full bath. The lower level also has been planned. You will enjoy a spacious recreation room with fireplace, a washroom and the usual basement storage area.

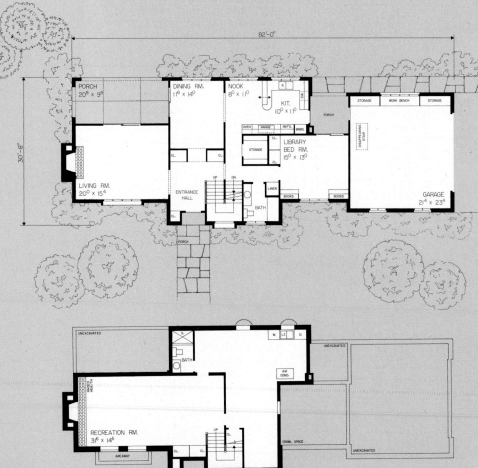

82'-0"
30'-8"
PORCH 20⁸ x 9⁸
DINING RM. 11⁶ x 14⁰
NOOK 8⁰ x 11⁰
KIT. 10⁰ x 11⁰
OVEN RANGE REF'S DRMS
STORAGE WORK BENCH STORAGE
PORCH
DISAPPEARING STAIR
STORAGE
LIBRARY BED RM. 15⁰ x 13⁰
LIVING RM. 20⁰ x 15⁴
ENTRANCE HALL
UP DN
BATH
LINEN
BOOKS
BOOKS
GARAGE 21⁴ x 23⁴
PORCH

UNEXCAVATED
BATH
AIR COND.
UNEXCAVATED
RECREATION RM. 31⁶ x 14⁶
UP
CRAWL SPACE
AREAWAY
UNEXCAVATED

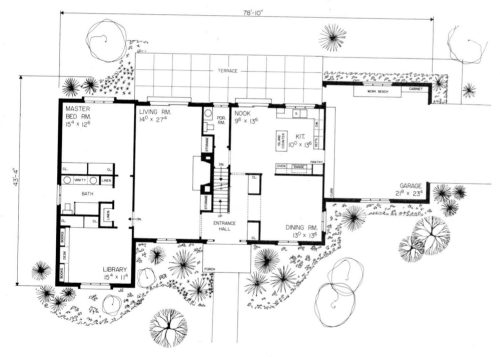

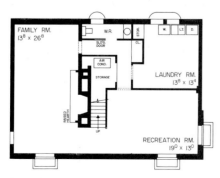

Design 42279

1,797 Sq. Ft. - First Floor
867 Sq. Ft. - Second Floor
735 Sq. Ft. - Lower Level
37,884 Ct. Ft.

● The appeal of this traditional, story-and-a-half home can be traced to a variety of features. However, its most important feature is its fine proportion. Heightening the interest of the exterior, there are front and side projecting wings. Window, door cornice and chimney design are noteworthy features, along with the side opening garage. Inside, there is space galore to serve every family function. Each of the three bedrooms is large and has fine storage facilities. Adjacent to the master bedroom, the library will be a quiet haven for the pursuit of numerous activities. Extending from front to rear, the 27 foot living room will have the fireplace as its focal point. The kitchen has an island counter and is open to the informal eating area. But a step or two away is the separate, formal dining room. It will serve those very formal occasions. Development of the basement results in family, recreation and laundry rooms. There is also a second fireplace and an extra washroom to serve your growing family.

Design 42887   1,338 Sq. Ft. - First Floor; 661 Sq. Ft. - Second Floor; 36,307 Cu. Ft.

● This attractive, contemporary one-and-a-half story will be the envy of many. First, examine the efficient kitchen. Not only does it offer a snack bar for those quick meals but also a large dining room. Notice the adjacent dining porch. The laundry and garage access are also adjacent to the kitchen.

An exciting feature is the gathering room with fireplace. The first floor also offers a study with a wet bar and sliding glass doors that open to a private porch. This will make those quiet times cherishable. Adjacent to the study is a full bath followed by a bedroom. Upstairs a large master bedroom suite oc-

cupies the entire floor. It features a bath with an oversized tub and shower, a large walk-in closet with built-ins and an open lounge with fireplace. Both the lounge and master bedroom, along with the gathering room, have sloped ceilings. Develop the lower level for additional space.

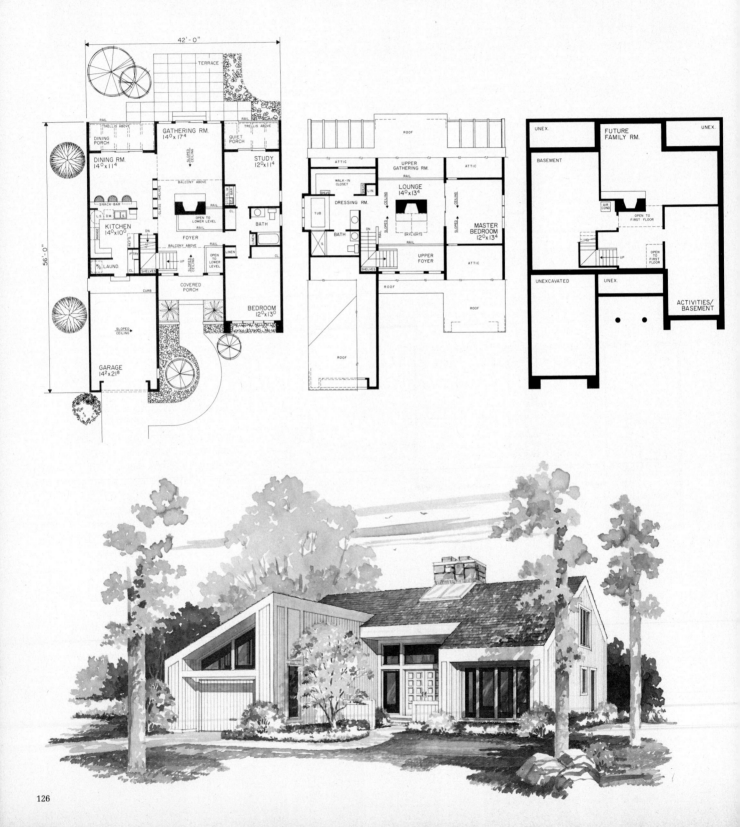

SUNKEN LIVING AREAS . . .

are one more aspect of multi-level living and, therefore, deserve recognition. While not as obvious as varied levels in split and bi-level houses, sunken living areas can make a dramatic and appealing contribution to the interior environment. As shown on the following pages the sunken areas can be the living, sleeping or kitchen zones. Of further interest is the sunken garage. Examples of this reveal its impact on the exterior design. They further indicate how well a house, whether a one or two- story, can adapt to a gently sloping site and, hence, become almost a part of it.

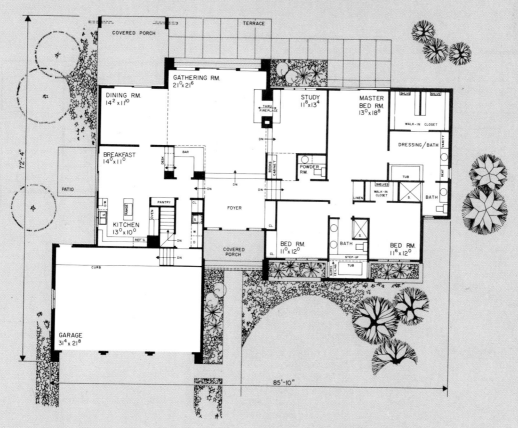

Design 42789 2,732 Sq. Ft.; 54,935 Cu. Ft.

● An attached three car garage! What a fantastic feature of this three bedroom contemporary design. And there's more. As one walks up the steps to the covered porch and through the double front doors the charm of this design will be overwhelming. Inside, a large foyer greets all visitors and leads them to each of the three areas, each down a few steps. The living area has a large gathering room with fireplace and a study adjacent on one side and the formal dining room on the other. The work center has an efficient kitchen with island range, breakfast room, laundry and built-in desk and bar. Then there is the sleeping area. Note the raised tub with sloped ceiling.

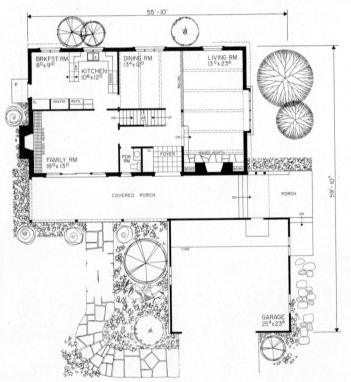

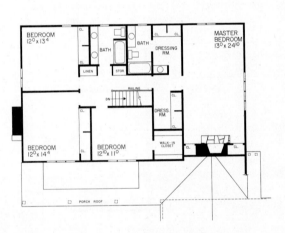

Design 42324

1,256 Sq. Ft. - First Floor
1,351 Sq. Ft. - Second Floor
37,603 Cu. Ft.

● Here is an economically built, rectangular shaped, two-story design. This unique, Tudor design offers tremendous livability in an atmosphere of warmth and coziness. The end living room is sunken and features a beamed ceiling and a commanding fireplace. A railing divides the living room from the dining room. Informal living will be enjoyed in the family room. It has a second fireplace and functions through sliding glass doors with the covered porch. Efficient and U-shaped, the kitchen is but a couple of steps from the breakfast room. The third fireplace is to be found upstairs in the spacious master bedroom. Note the dressing rooms and the private bath. A second bath serves the three children's bedrooms. Don't miss the stairs to the full basement or the covered front porch.

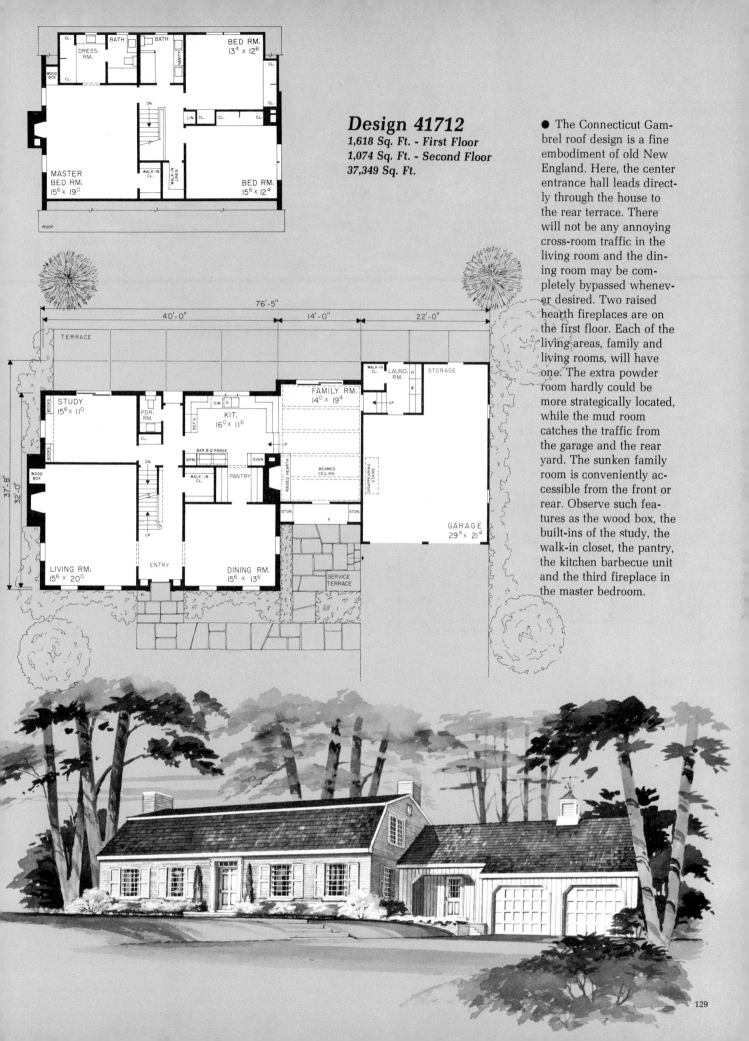

Second Floor:

- CL.
- BATH
- BATH
- DRESS. RM.
- CL.
- WOOD BOX
- VANITY
- PNTRY.
- BED RM. 13⁴ x 12⁶ → $13^4 \times 12^6$
- CL.
- DN.
- CL.
- LIN.
- CL.
- CL.
- WALK-IN CL.
- WALK-IN LINEN
- MASTER BED RM. 15⁶ x 19⁰ → $15^6 \times 19^0$
- BED RM. 15⁶ x 12⁴ → $15^6 \times 12^4$
- ROOF

Design 41712

1,618 Sq. Ft. - First Floor
1,074 Sq. Ft. - Second Floor
37,349 Sq. Ft.

● The Connecticut Gambrel roof design is a fine embodiment of old New England. Here, the center entrance hall leads directly through the house to the rear terrace. There will not be any annoying cross-room traffic in the living room and the dining room may be completely bypassed whenever desired. Two raised hearth fireplaces are on the first floor. Each of the living areas, family and living rooms, will have one. The extra powder room hardly could be more strategically located, while the mud room catches the traffic from the garage and the rear yard. The sunken family room is conveniently accessible from the front or rear. Observe such features as the wood box, the built-ins of the study, the walk-in closet, the pantry, the kitchen barbecue unit and the third fireplace in the master bedroom.

First Floor dimensions:

- 76'-5"
- 40'-0"
- 14'-0"
- 22'-0"
- 32'-0"
- 37'-8"

First Floor labels:

- TERRACE
- STUDY 15⁶ x 11⁰ → $15^6 \times 11^0$
- BOOKS
- PDR. RM.
- CL.
- D.W.
- S.
- REF'G
- KIT. 16⁰ x 11⁶ → $16^0 \times 11^6$
- WALK-IN CL.
- FAMILY RM. 14⁰ x 19⁴ → $14^0 \times 19^4$
- WALK-IN CL.
- LAUND. RM.
- D.
- W.
- STORAGE
- UP
- BEAMED CEILING
- RAISED HEARTH
- DISAPPEARING STAIRS
- BAR B-Q RANGE
- BRM.
- OVEN
- PANTRY
- STOR.
- R
- STOR.
- GARAGE 29⁴ x 21⁴ → $29^4 \times 21^4$
- WOOD BOX
- LIVING RM. 15⁶ x 20⁰ → $15^6 \times 20^0$
- DN.
- UP
- ENTRY
- DINING RM. 15⁶ x 13⁶ → $15^6 \times 13^6$
- SERVICE TERRACE

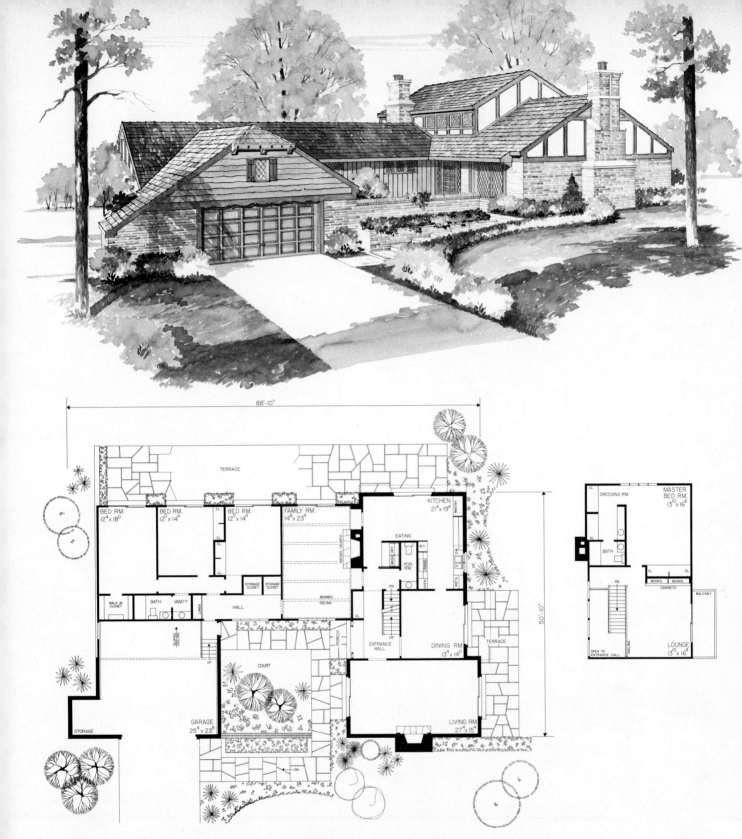

Design 42372 *2,634 Sq. Ft. - First Floor; 819 Sq. Ft. - Second Floor; 47,867 Cu. Ft.*

● What a wonderfully different and imposing two-story design this is! The Tudor styling and the varying roof planes, along with its U-shape, add to the air of distinction. From the driveway, steps lead past a big raised planter up to the enclosed entrance court. A wide overhanging roof shelters the massive patterned double doors flanked by diamond paned sidelites. The living room is outstanding. It is located a distance from other living areas and is quite spacious. The centered fireplace is the dominant feature, while sliding-glass doors open from each end onto outdoor terraces. The kitchen, too, is spacious and functions well. Two eating areas are nearby. It is worth noting that each of the major first floor rooms have direct access to the outdoor terraces. Note second floor suite which includes a lounge with built-in book cabinets.

Design 41783 2,412 Sq. Ft. - First Floor; 640 Sq. Ft. - Second Floor; 36,026 Cu. Ft.

● Large families, take notice! Here is an impressive contemporary that is not only going to be fun to live in, but to look at, as well. Contributing to the appeal of this design, interesting roof levels, exposed rafters and wide over-hangs will be noticed immediately. An entrance court, screened from the street heightens the drama of the front exterior. The 27 foot living room is captivating, indeed. It can function, through sliding glass doors, with either the front court or the side terrace. Eating patterns can be quite flexible with the extra space in the kitchen, a formal dining room and a dining terrace. Don't miss sloping ceilings, featured in many of the rooms.

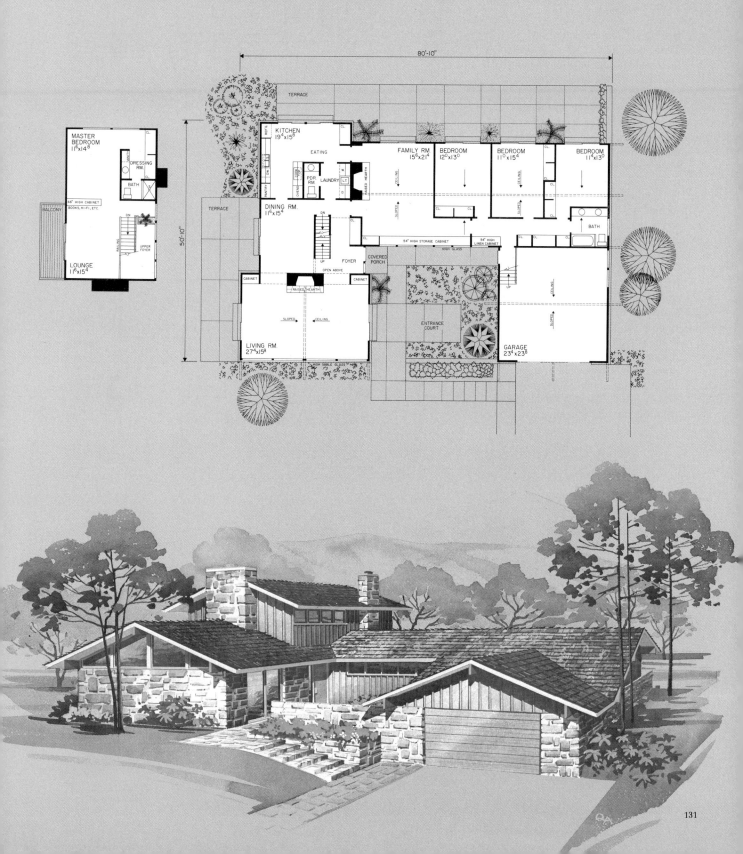

Design 42794

1,680 Sq. Ft. - First Floor
1,165 Sq. Ft. - Second Floor
867 Sq. Ft. - Apartment
55,900 Cu. Ft.

● This exceptionally pleasing Tudor design has a great deal of interior livability to offer its occupants. Use the main entrance, enter into the foyer and begin your journey throughout this design. To the left of the foyer is the study, to the right, the formal living room. The living room leads to the rear, formal dining room. This room has access to the outdoors and is conveniently located adjacent to the kitchen. A snack bar divides the kitchen from the family room which also has access to outdoors plus it has a fireplace as does the living room. The second floor houses the family's four bedrooms. Down six steps from the mud room is the laundry and entrance to the garage, up six steps from this area is a complete apartment. This is an excellent room for a live-in relative. It is completely private by gaining access from the outdoor balcony.

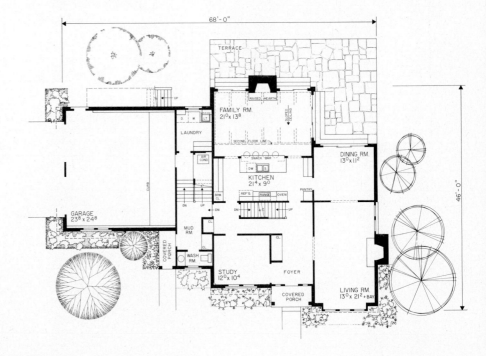

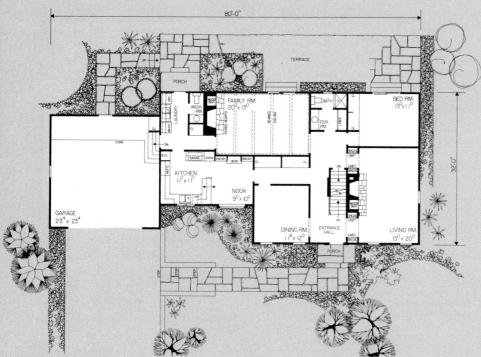

Design 42625 *1,640 Sq. Ft. - First Floor; 1,072 Sq. Ft. - Second Floor; 39,360 Cu. Ft.*

● A 19th-Century farmhouse! So it might seem. But it is one with contemporary features like the U-shaped kitchen with a built-in desk and appliances as well as a separate dining nook. Adjacent is the 20' by 13' family room. There, a beamed ceiling and raised hearth fireplace add traditional warmth to a modern convention. A

sliding glass door opens onto the terrace, too. Around the corner is another modern convenience, the first-floor laundry. Formal rooms, too. A living room has a traditional fireplace and attached wood box. Plus four sets of built-in shelves, perfect for books or displaying a collection. And a formal dining room. Four bedrooms! Including

a master suite with a dressing room, walk-in wardrobe, two closets and a private bath. Or there could be three bedrooms, plus a study. Since the first-floor bedroom easily could be converted to that purpose. Here's a home with traditional charm and modern convenience all housed under one roof. Study this plan thoroughly.

133

Design 41713
2,374 Sq. Ft.; 33,852 Cu. Ft.

● Are you among those who enjoy informal living, but prefer to keep pots and pans, dirty laundry and youngsters, just learning to feed themselves, in the background? Then study this plan carefully. Kitchen and eating area are neatly tucked behind the garage, along with an adequately sized laundry and washroom. The family room is located to serve as a transition between the work areas and the more formal living space. The dining room is beautifully planned to overlook the courtyard garden. Three spacious bedrooms and two baths are in the sleeping wing.

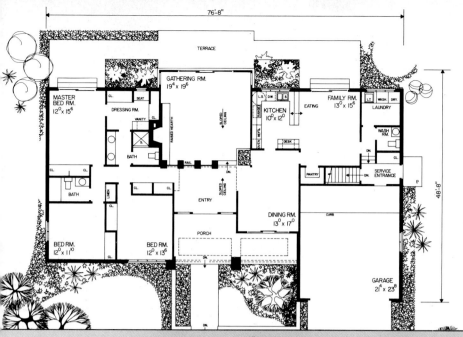

Design 42717
2,310 Sq. Ft.; 51,680 Cu. Ft.

● The "work efficient" kitchen in this plan features a built-in desk and appliances, a large pantry plus a pass-through to the family room for added convenience. A first floor laundry, too, with adjacent washroom and stairs to the basement. Entering this home, there's a sloped ceiling in the entry hall plus a delightful "over the railing" view of the sunken gathering room. The gathering room itself is more than 19' by 19' with a sloped ceiling, raised hearth fireplace and sliding glass doors to the rear terrace. A 13' by 17' formal dining room, too. A lot of extras are featured in the master bedroom. Two more bedrooms and a bath are for the younger generation.

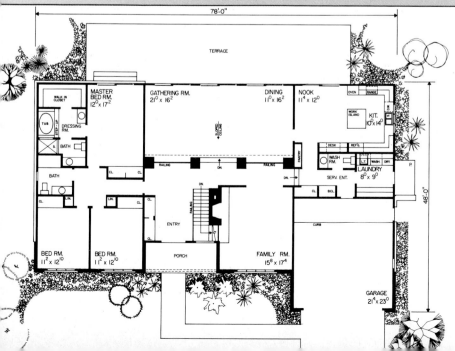

Design 42756
2,652 Sq. Ft.; 51,540 Cu. Ft.

● This one-story will serve your family with great ease. It will assure the best in contemporary living with its many fine features. Notice the bath with tub and stall shower, dressing room and walk-in closet featured with the master bedroom. Two more family bedrooms. The sunken gathering/dining room is highlighted by the sloped ceiling and sliding glass doors to the large, rear terrace. The formal area is a full 32' by 16'. Imagine the great furniture placement that can be done in this area. In addition to the gathering room, there is an informal family room with fireplace. You will enjoy the efficient kitchen and get much use out of the work island, pantry and built-in desk.

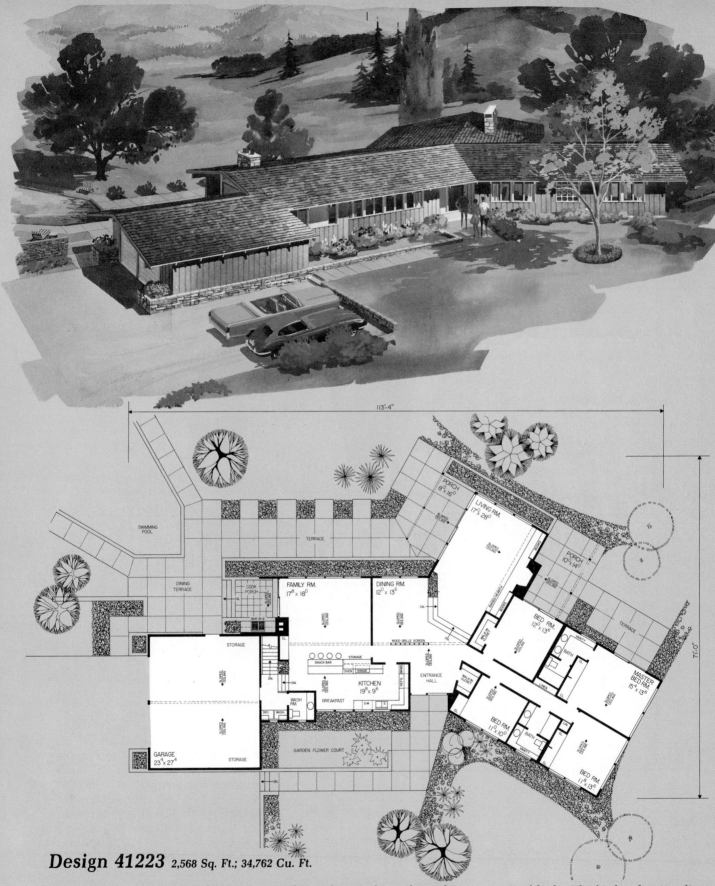

Design 41223 2,568 Sq. Ft.; 34,762 Cu. Ft.

● Indeed, it is very easy to believe that this is one of the most popular designs. It has a pleasing and refreshing exterior, highlighted by its most interesting shape and low pitched, wide-overhanging roof. Its interior is spacious, well-zoned and features outstanding indoor-outdoor relationships. Observe the three covered porches and the terraces. Sloped ceilings and delightful, large glass areas contribute to the cheerful atmosphere of the interior. The four bedroom sleeping wing offers excellent storage and two compartmented baths. The kitchen has its adjacent breakfast area and enjoys a view of the front yard. The family room with its snack bar and sliding glass doors to the cook porch is nearby. Note the indoor, built-in planting units. There is a partial basement.

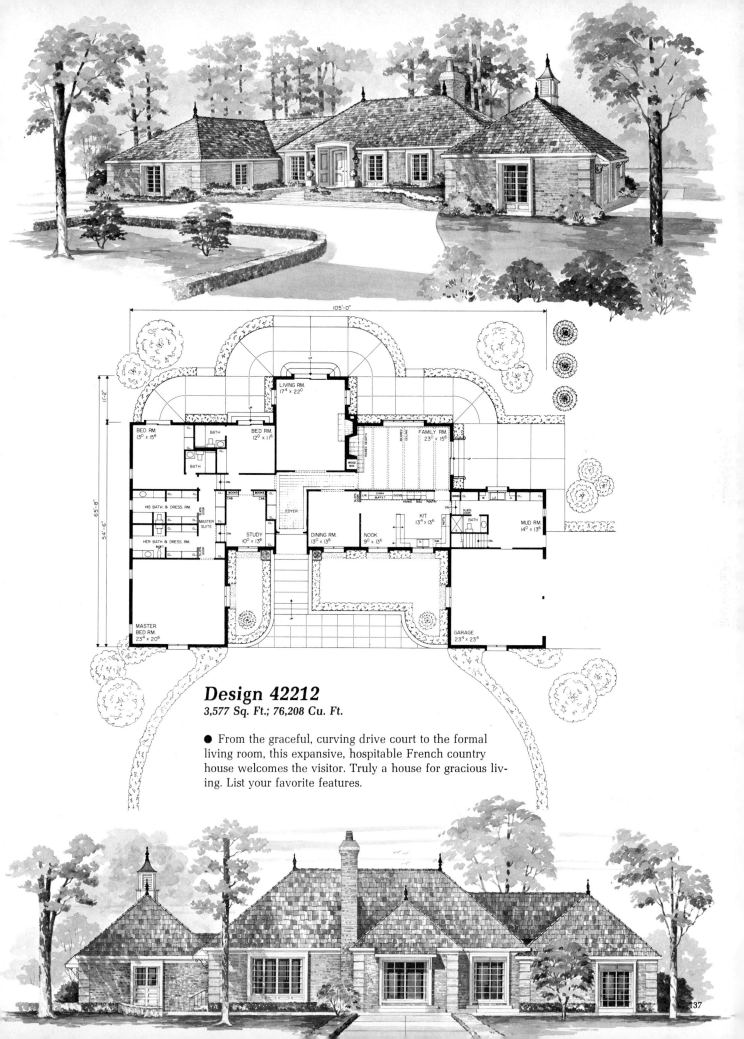

Design 42212

3,577 Sq. Ft.; 76,208 Cu. Ft.

● From the graceful, curving drive court to the formal living room, this expansive, hospitable French country house welcomes the visitor. Truly a house for gracious living. List your favorite features.

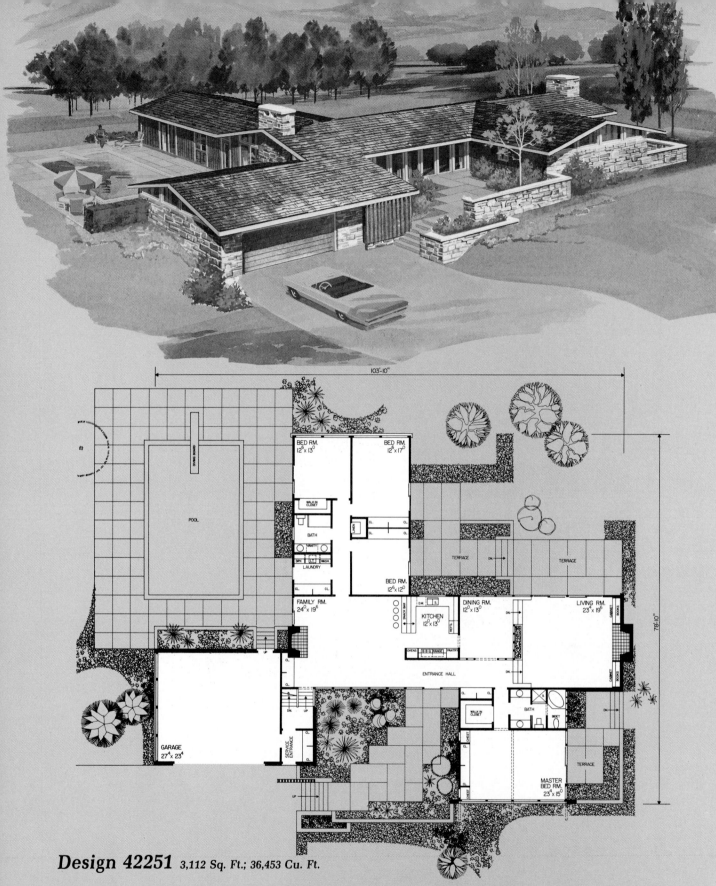

Design 42251 3,112 Sq. Ft.; 36,453 Cu. Ft.

● It will not matter at all where this distinctive ranch home is built. Whether located in the south, east, north or west, the exterior design appeal will be breathtakingly distinctive and the interior livability will be delightfully different. The irregular shape is enhanced by the low-pitched, wide overhanging roof. Two wings project to help form an appealing entrance court from the main living area of the house. Variations in grade result in the garage being on a lower level. The plan reflects an interesting study in zoning and a fine indoor-outdoor relationship of the various areas. Notice the bedroom wing and the family room and how these young people's areas function with the pool development. Observe the isolation of the master bedroom with its bath.

Design 42832
2,805 Sq. Ft. - Excluding Atrium; 52,235 Cu. Ft.

● The advantage of passive solar heating is a significant highlight of this contemporary design. The huge skylight over the atrium provides shelter during inclement weather, while permitting the enjoyment of plenty of natural light to the atrium below and surrounding areas. Whether open to the sky, or sheltered by a glass or translucent covering, the atrium becomes a cheerful spot and provides an abundance of natural light to its adjacent rooms. The stone floor will absorb an abundance of heat from the sun during the day and permit circulation of warm air to other areas at night. During the summer, shades afford protection from the sun without sacrificing the abundance of natural light and the feeling of spaciousness. Sloping ceilings highlight each of the major rooms, three bedrooms, formal living and dining and study. The conversation area between the two formal areas really will be something to talk about. The broad expanses of roof can accommodate solar panels should an active system be desired to supplement the passive features of this design.

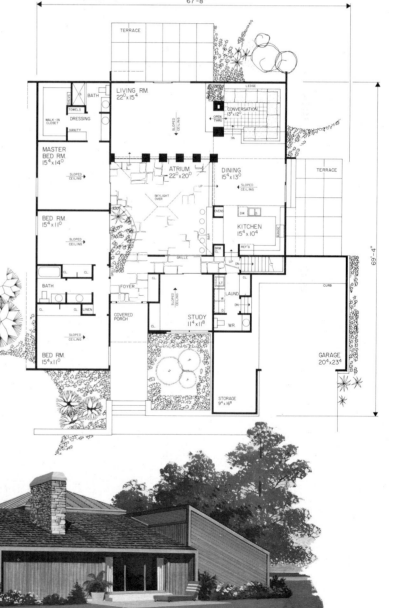

Design 42823

1,370 Sq. Ft. - First Floor
927 Sq. Ft. - Second Floor
34,860 Cu. Ft.

● The street view of this contemporary design features a small courtyard entrance as well as a private terrace off the study. Inside the livability will be outstanding. This design features spacious first floor activity areas that flow smoothly into each other. In the gathering room a raised hearth fireplace creates a dramatic focal point. An adjacent covered terrace, featuring a skylight, is ideal for outdoor dining and could be screened in later for an additional room.

Design 42858
2,231 Sq. Ft.; 28,150 Cu. Ft.

● This sun oriented design was created to face the south. By doing so, it has minimal northern exposure. It has been designed primarily for the more temperate U.S. latitudes using 2 x 6 wall construction. The morning sun will brighten the living and dining rooms, along with the adjacent terrace. Sun enters the garden room by way of the glass roof and walls. In the winter, the solar heat gain from the garden room should provide relief from high energy bills. Solar shades allow you to adjust the amount of light that you want to enter in the warmer months. Interior planning deserves mention, too. The work center is efficient. The kitchen has a snack bar on the garden room side and a serving counter to the dining room. The breakfast room with laundry area is also convenient to the kitchen. Three bedrooms are on the northern wall. The master bedroom has a large tub and a separate shower with a four foot square skylight above. When this design is oriented toward the sun, it should prove to be energy efficient and a joy to live in.

Design 42379 1,525 Sq. Ft. - First Floor; 748 Sq. Ft. - Second Floor; 26,000 Cu. Ft.

● A house that has "everything" may very well look just like this design. Its exterior is well-proportioned and impressive. Inside the inviting double front doors there are features galore. The living room and family room level are sunken. Separating these two rooms is a dramatic thru fireplace. A built-in bar, planter and beamed ceiling highlight the family room. Nearby is a full bath and a study which could be utilized as a fourth bedroom. The fine functioning kitchen has a pass-thru to the snack bar in the breakfast nook. The adjacent dining room overlooks the living room and has sliding doors to the covered porch. Upstairs three bedrooms, two baths and an outdoor balcony. Blueprints for this design include optional basement details.

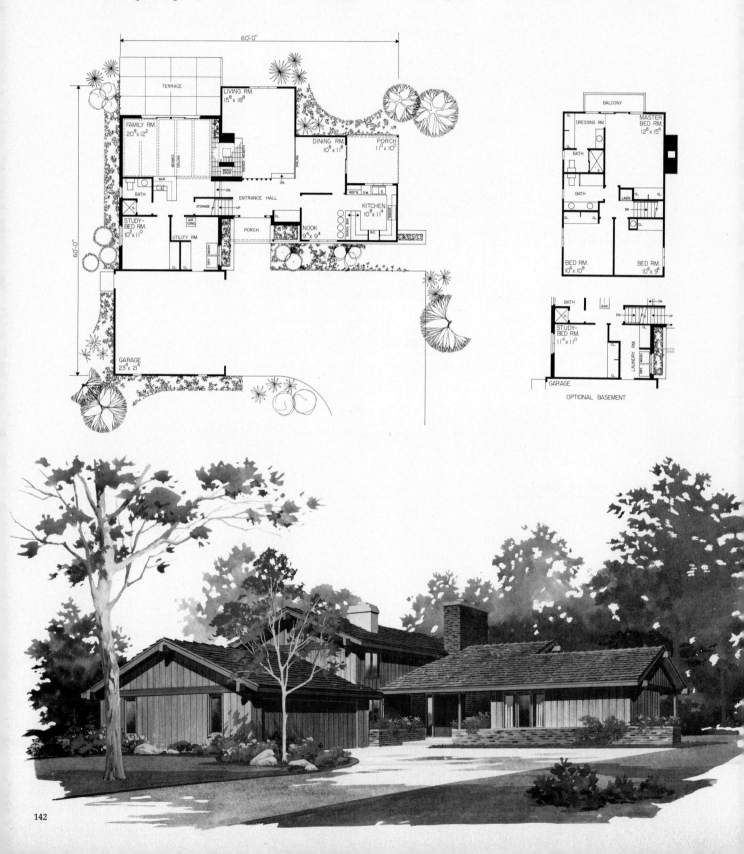

THIRD-STORY LIVABILITY ...

is worthy of consideration here by virtue of the so called attic space potential for developing bonus livability. Many two-story homes because of their high-pitched roof design end up with unused area. The development of this third attic level can make just as much economic sense as developing and exposing a basement lower level. As the designs on the following pages show, this area can become a playroom, studio, study, guest room, hobby area or an additional bedroom. When developed, along with the basement, the two-story can become a house with four stacked levels of livability - all between the same roof and foundation.

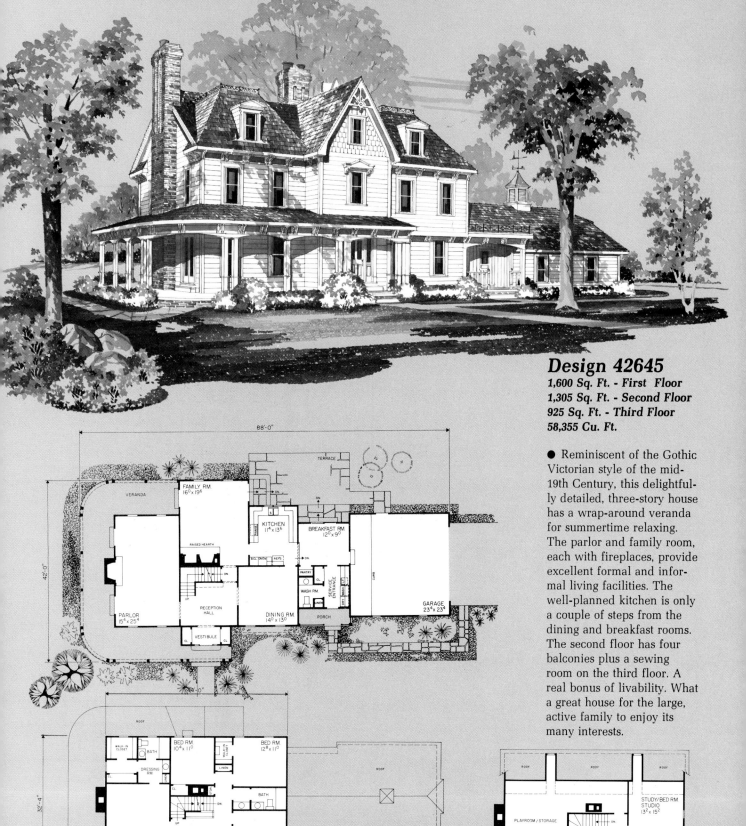

Design 42645

1,600 Sq. Ft. - First Floor
1,305 Sq. Ft. - Second Floor
925 Sq. Ft. - Third Floor
58,355 Cu. Ft.

● Reminiscent of the Gothic Victorian style of the mid-19th Century, this delightfully detailed, three-story house has a wrap-around veranda for summertime relaxing. The parlor and family room, each with fireplaces, provide excellent formal and informal living facilities. The well-planned kitchen is only a couple of steps from the dining and breakfast rooms. The second floor has four balconies plus a sewing room on the third floor. A real bonus of livability. What a great house for the large, active family to enjoy its many interests.

Design 42192

1,884 Sq. Ft. - First Floor
1,521 Sq. Ft. - Second Floor
58,380 Cu. Ft.

● This is surely a fine adaptation from the 18th Century when formality and elegance were by-words. The authentic detailing of this design centers around the fine proportions, the dentils, the window symmetry, the front door and entranceway, the massive chimneys and the masonry work. The rear elevation retains all the grandeur exemplary of exquisite architecture. The appeal of this outstanding home does not end with its exterior elevations. Consider the formal living room with its corner fireplace. Also, the library with its wall of bookshelves and cabinets. Further, the dining room highlights corner china cabinets. Continue to study this elegant plan.

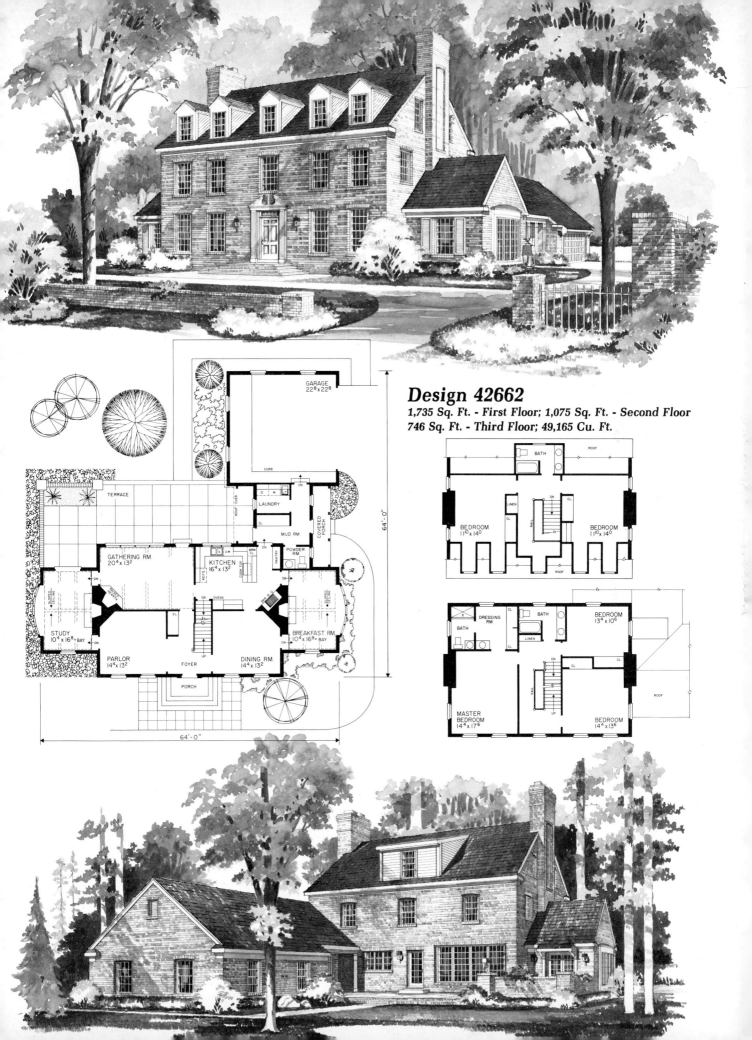

Design 42662
1,735 Sq. Ft. - First Floor; 1,075 Sq. Ft. - Second Floor
746 Sq. Ft. - Third Floor; 49,165 Cu. Ft.

GARAGE
22⁸ x 22⁸

TERRACE

LAUNDRY

MUD RM

COVERED PORCH

GATHERING RM.
20⁴ x 13²

KITCHEN
16⁴ x 13²

PANTRY

POWDER RM.

STUDY
10⁴ x 16⁸ BAY

PARLOR
14⁴ x 13²

FOYER

OVENS

DINING RM.
14⁴ x 13²

BREAKFAST RM.
10⁴ x 16⁸ BAY

PORCH

64'-0"

64'-0"

BATH
ROOF

BEDROOM
11¹⁰ x 14⁰

LINEN
CL

RAIL

CL

BEDROOM
11¹⁰ x 14⁰

ROOF

DRESSING RM.

BATH

BATH

LINEN

BEDROOM
13⁴ x 10⁶

MASTER BEDROOM
14⁴ x 17⁶

RAIL

CL

ROOF

BEDROOM
14⁴ x 13⁶

WALK - IN
CLOSET

GUEST
BEDROOM
11⁰ x 20⁶

BATH

LINEN

DN

STUDY
11⁰ x 13⁰

BASEMENT

WASH
RM.

GAME
STOR.

WINE
CELLAR

UP

ACTIVITIES RM.
17⁸ x 21⁰

RAISED HEARTH

● Here is an adaptation
of the 18th-Century
"Single House" so popu-
lar in Charleston, SC. In
its original form, the
house was but a single
room wide. This up-dated
version features the
kitchen/garage wing.

PIAZZA

MASTER
BEDROOM
19⁴ x 13⁰

ROOF

ATTIC

BATH

CL

CL

BATH

CL

BEDROOM
14⁰ x 13⁰

BEDROOM
13⁴ x 11⁸

CL

LINEN

BATH

ATTIC

DN

UP

ROOF

BEDROOM
19⁴ x 13⁰

90'-0"

40'-0"

50'-0"

TERRACE

PIAZZA

GATHERING RM.
19⁴ x 15⁰

COVERED
PORCH

DINING RM.
13⁴ x 12⁰

NICHE

KITCHEN
12⁰ x 12⁰

BRKFST. RM.
9⁸ x 12⁰

68'-0"

FOUNTAIN

PDR.
RM.

CL

BOOKS

LAUNDRY

OVEN

PANTRY DESK PANTRY

CURB

COURTYARD

CL

FOYER

OPEN

DN

UP

GARAGE
21⁸ x 22⁰

PARLOR
19⁴ x 13⁰

PORCH

Design 42660 1,479 Sq. Ft. - First Floor
1,501 Sq. Ft. - Second Floor; 912 Sq. Ft. - Third Floor
556 Sq. Ft. - Activities Room Area; 57,440 Cu. Ft.

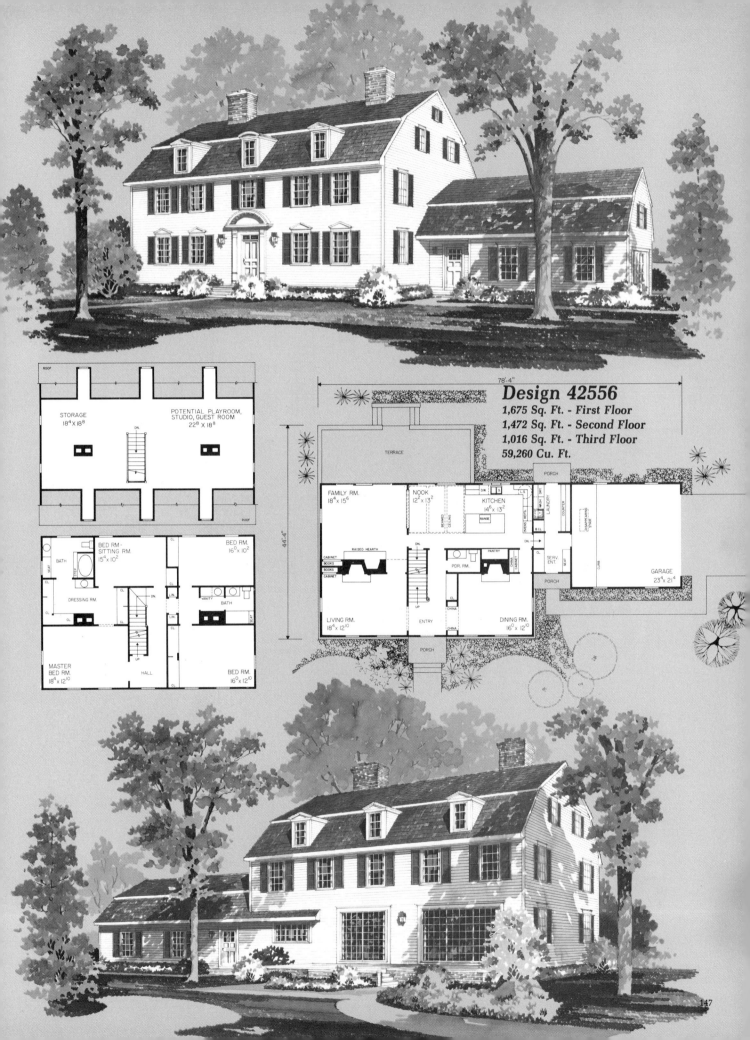

STORAGE
18⁴ X 18⁸

POTENTIAL PLAYROOM, STUDIO, GUEST ROOM
22⁸ X 18⁸

BED RM.-SITTING RM.
15⁴ x 10²

BED RM.
16⁰ x 10²

DRESSING RM.

MASTER BED RM.
18⁴ x 12¹⁰

HALL

BED RM.
16⁰ x 12¹⁰

78'-4"

44'-4"

Design 42556

1,675 Sq. Ft. - First Floor
1,472 Sq. Ft. - Second Floor
1,016 Sq. Ft. - Third Floor
59,260 Cu. Ft.

TERRACE

PORCH

FAMILY RM.
18⁴ x 15⁶

NOOK
12² x 13²

KITCHEN
14⁶ x 13²

RANGE

LAUNDRY

COUNTER

GARAGE
23⁴ x 21⁴

RAISED HEARTH

BOOKS

CABINET

PDR. RM.

PANTRY

SERV. ENT.

LIVING RM.
18⁴ x 12¹⁰

ENTRY

DINING RM.
16⁰ x 12¹⁰

CHINA

PORCH

Design 42659
1,023 Sq. Ft. - First Floor; 1,008 Sq. Ft. - Second Floor
467 Sq. Ft. - Third Floor; 31,510 Cu. Ft.

● The facade of this three-storied, pitch-roofed house has a symmetrical placement of windows and a restrained but elegant central entrance. The central hall, or foyer, expands midway through the house to a family kitchen. Off the foyer are two rooms, a living room with fireplace and a study. The windowed third floor attic can be used as a study and studio. Three bedrooms are housed on the second floor.

Design 42633
1,338 Sq. Ft. - First Floor
1,200 Sq. Ft. - Second Floor
506 Sq. Ft. - Third Floor; 44,525 Cu. Ft.

● This is a pleasing Georgian. Its facade features a porch with simple wooden posts. The garage wing has a sheltered service entry and brick facing. Sliding glass doors link the terrace and family room, providing an indoor/outdoor area for entertaining. The floor plan has been designed to serve the family efficiently. The stairway in the foyer leads to four second-floor bedrooms. The third floor is windowed and can be used as a studio and study.

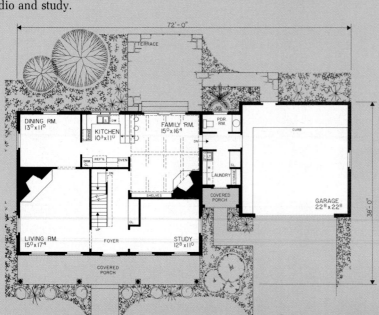

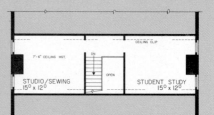

148

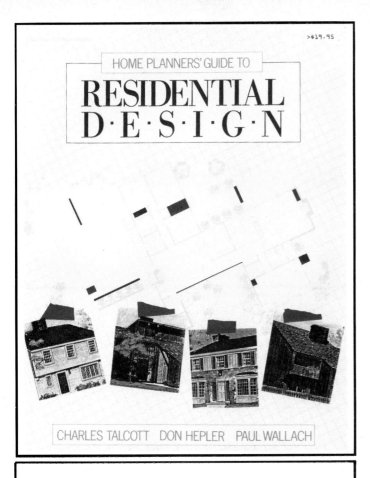

HOME PLANNERS' GUIDE TO

RESIDENTIAL D·E·S·I·G·N

>$19.95

CHARLES TALCOTT   DON HEPLER   PAUL WALLACH

Contents

Preface
Illustrated Designs Index

PART ONE

Principles of Residential Design

CHAPTER ONE **Introduction**

Reading Architectural Drawings   3
  Pictorial drawings   3
  Multiview drawings   3
  Elevation drawings   4
  Floor plans   5
  Architectural symbols   7
Design Factors   10
  Principles of floor plan design   10
  Area planning   11
  Traffic patterns   11
  Room locations   14
  Effect of levels on room locations   24
  Room sizes   26
  Floor plan sizes   29
  Fundamentals of elevation design   32
  Elements of design   33
  Principles of design   37

CHAPTER TWO **Defining Personal Requirements**

Assessing Lifestyles   41
Determining Needs and Wants   41
General Financial Considerations   46
  Site   46
  Building materials   46
  Specifications   46
  Labor costs   47
  Estimating costs   47
  Mortgage planning   47
  Expandable plans   48

CHAPTER THREE **Site Considerations**

Orientation   53
Solar Planning   55
Earth Sheltered Housing   60
Building Code Considerations   63

CHAPTER FOUR **Area Planning**

Living Area   65
Service Area   65
Sleeping Area   68
Types of Plans   69
Levels   70
  Bi-level   74
  Split-level   80
  Story-and-a-half   83
  Lofts   85
Basement Plans   85

CHAPTER FIVE **Guidelines for Room Planning**

Room Sizes   89
Room Functions   89
Room Locations   96

Room Shapes   100
  Living room shapes   100
  Kitchen shapes   104
  Utility room shapes   107
  Garage shapes   107
  Bedroom and bath shapes   107
Storage   111
  Closets   111
  Built-in storage facilities   111
  Furniture storage   114
Windows and Doors   114
  Windows   114
  Doors   115
Fireplaces   116
Fixtures and Appliances   125
  Kitchen appliances   125
  Laundry appliances   128
  Bath appliances and fixtures   132
Traffic Patterns   136
  External Traffic   136
  Internal Traffic   142
Lighting   148
  Lighting fixtures   148
  Illumination planning   149

CHAPTER SIX **Design Skills**

The Architect's Scale   151
Dimensioning   155
Sketching   156

PART TWO

Residential Design Practices

CHAPTER SEVEN **Plan Selection**

Satisfying Basic Needs and Wants   161
Short-Cutting Process   161
Financial Considerations   165
  Methods of controlling costs   167
Checklist for Plan Selection   167

CHAPTER EIGHT **Altering Plans**

Methods of Making Changes   175
Types of Design Alterations   175
  Altering room sizes   176
  Room location changes   182
  Altering room shapes   182
  Moving doors and windows   182
  Altering traffic space   188
  Expanding living space   191
  Solar adaptations   197

CHAPTER NINE **Adapting Elevation Styles**

Elevation Design   203
  Form and space   203
  Roof styles   205
  Design adjustment guidelines   205
A Final Word on Styles   214
  European styles   214
  Early American styles   215
  Later American styles   215
  Contemporary styles   215
Index

Announcing-

A "MUST" Book for Anyone Involved in the Planning of a New Home

This book features a wealth of information vital to the successful planning of a new home. Discussed in a highly illustrated manner, is a great variety of subjects concerning residential design and planning. Written and edited specifically for use during the early planning and pre-construction stages of the building program, this book may save you many times its cost. In addition to giving a layman's overview of the architectural side of residential design, it helps the reader give due consideration to the innumerable budgetary and livability aspects of the planning process. A CHECKLIST FOR PLAN SELECTION lists over 650 items that will guide and help assure proper decision-making which involve the myriad of subjects influencing proper residential design and planning.
224 pages, soft cover.

A Most Rewarding and Money-Saving Book.

$19.95
Postpaid

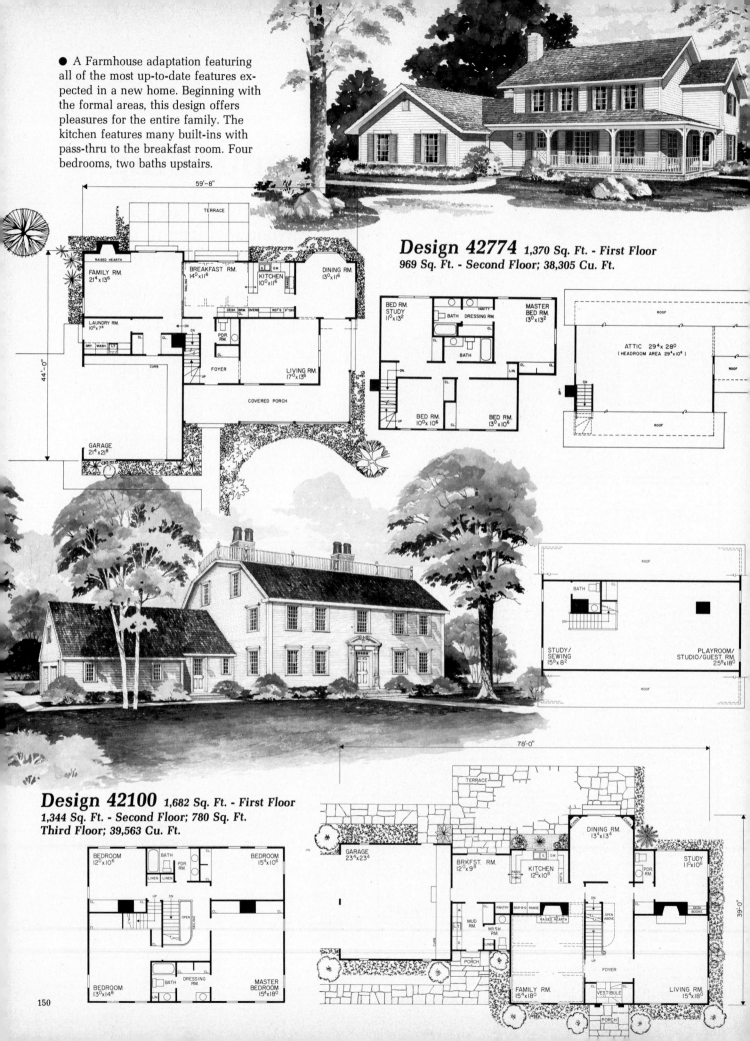

● A Farmhouse adaptation featuring all of the most up-to-date features expected in a new home. Beginning with the formal areas, this design offers pleasures for the entire family. The kitchen features many built-ins with pass-thru to the breakfast room. Four bedrooms, two baths upstairs.

Design 42774 1,370 Sq. Ft. - First Floor
969 Sq. Ft. - Second Floor; 38,305 Cu. Ft.

TERRACE

RAISED HEARTH

FAMILY RM. 21⁴x13⁶

BREAKFAST RM. 14⁰x11⁶

KITCHEN 10⁰x11⁶

DINING RM. 13⁰x11⁶

LAUNDRY RM. 10⁰x7⁶

DESK BRM. OVENS REF'G P'TRY

DRY. WASH.

PDR. RM.

FOYER

LIVING RM. 17⁰x13⁶

GARAGE 21⁴x21⁸

COVERED PORCH

59'-8"

44'-0"

BED RM. STUDY 11⁰x13²

BATH

VANITY

DRESSING RM.

MASTER BED RM. 13⁰x13²

BATH

LIN.

BED RM. 10⁰x10⁶

BED RM. 13⁰x10⁶

ROOF

ATTIC 29⁴x 28⁰ (HEADROOM AREA 29⁴x10⁶)

ROOF

DN.

ROOF

BATH

STUDY/ SEWING 15⁸x8²

PLAYROOM/ STUDIO/GUEST. RM. 25⁸x18⁰

ROOF

78'-0"

Design 42100 1,682 Sq. Ft. - First Floor
1,344 Sq. Ft. - Second Floor; 780 Sq. Ft.
Third Floor; 39,563 Cu. Ft.

BEDROOM 12⁰x10⁶

BATH

PDR. RM.

LINEN LINEN

BEDROOM 15⁴x10⁶

UP DN OPEN

BEDROOM 13⁰x14⁸

BATH

DRESSING RM.

MASTER BEDROOM 15⁴x18⁰

TERRACE

GARAGE 23⁴x23⁴

BRKFST. RM. 12⁰x9⁸

KITCHEN 12⁰x10⁸

DINING RM. 13⁴x13⁴

STUDY 11⁰x10⁶

PDR. RM.

PASS THRU

MUD RM.

WASH RM.

PANTRY

BAR-B-Q RANGE

RAISED HEARTH

OPEN ABOVE

DESK BOOKS

DN

FAMILY RM. 15⁴x18⁰

VESTIBULE

FOYER

LIVING RM. 15⁴x18⁰

PORCH

PORCH

39'-0"

150

All The "TOOLS" You And Your Builder Need

. . . to, first select an exterior and a floor plan for your new house that satisfy your tastes and your family's living patterns . . .

. . . then, to review the blueprints in great detail and obtain a construction cost figure . . . also, to price out the structural materials required to build . . . and, finally, to review and decide upon the specifications to which your home is to be built. Truly, an invaluable set of "tools" to launch your home planning and building programs.

1. THE PLAN BOOKS

Home Planners' unique Design Category Series makes it easy to look at and study only the types of designs for which you and your family have an interest. Each of six plan books features a specific type of home, namely: Two-Story, 1½ Story, One-Story Over 2000 Sq. Ft., One-Story Under 2000 Sq. Ft., Multi-Levels and Vacation Homes. In addition to the convenient Design Category Series, there is an impressive selection of other current titles. While the home plans featured in these books are also to be found in the Design Category Series, they, too, are edited for those with special tastes and requirements. Your family will spend many enjoyable hours reviewing the delightfully designed exteriors and the practical floor plans. Surely your home or office library should include a selection of these popular plan books. Your complete satisfaction is guaranteed.

2. THE CONSTRUCTION BLUEPRINTS

There are blueprints available for each of the designs published in Home Planners' current plan books. Depending upon the size, the style and the type of home, each set of blueprints consists of from five to ten large sheets. Only by studying the blueprints is it possible to give complete and final consideration to the proper selection of a design for your next home. The blueprints provide the opportunity for all family members to familiarize themselves with the features of all exterior elevations, interior elevations and details, all dimensions, special built-in features and effects. They also provide a full understanding of the materials to be used and/or selected. The low-cost of our blueprints makes it possible and indeed, practical, to study in detail a number of different sets of blueprints before deciding upon which design to build.

3. THE MATERIALS LIST

A list of materials is an integral part of the plan package. It comprises the last sheet of each set of blueprints and serves as a handy reference during the period of construction. Of course, at the pricing and the material ordering stages, it is indispensable.

4. THE SPECIFICATION OUTLINE

Each order for blueprints is accompanied by one Specification Outline. You and your builder will find this a time-saving tool when deciding upon your own individual specifications. An important reference document should you wish to write your own specifications.

The Category Series

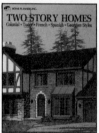

360 TWO STORY HOMES

English Tudors, Early American Salt Boxes, Gambrels, Farmhouses, Southern Colonials, Georgians, French Mansards, Contemporaries. Interesting floor plans for both small and large families. Efficient kitchens, 2 to 6 bedrooms, family rooms, libraries, extra baths, mud rooms. Homes for all budgets.

1.

288 Pages, $6.95

150 1½ STORY HOMES

Cape Cod, Williamsburg, Georgian, Tudor and Contemporary versions. Low budget and country-estate feature sections. Expandable family plans. Formal and informal living and dining areas along with gathering rooms. Spacious, country kitchens. Indoor-outdoor livability with covered porches and functional terraces.

2.

128 Pages, $3.95

210 ONE STORY HOMES OVER 2,000 Sq. Ft.

All popular styles. Including Spanish, Western, Tudor, French, and other traditional versions. Contemporaries. Gracious, family living patterns. Sunken living rooms, master bedroom suites, atriums, courtyards, pools. Fine indoor-outdoor living relationships. For modest to country-estate budgets.

3.

192 Pages, $4.95

315 ONE STORY HOMES UNDER 2,000 Sq. Ft.

A great selection of traditional and contemporary exteriors for medium and restricted budgets. Efficient, practical floor plans. Gathering rooms, formal and informal living and dining rooms, mud rooms, indoor-outdoor livability. Economically built homes. Designs with bonus space livability for growing families.

4.

192 Pages, $4.95

215 MULTI-LEVEL HOMES

For new dimensions in family living. A captivating variety of exterior styles, exciting floor plans for flat and sloping sites. Exposed lower levels. Balconies, decks. Plans for the active family. Upper level lounges, excellent bath facilities. Sloping ceilings. Functional outdoor terraces. For all building budgets.

5.

192 Pages, $4.95

223 VACATION HOMES

Features A-Frames, Chalets, Hexagons, economical rectangles. One and two stories plus multi-levels. Lodges for year 'round livability. From 480 to 3238 sq. ft. Cottages sleeping 4 to 22. For flat or sloping sites. Spacious, open planning. Over 600 illustrations. 120 Pages in full color. Cluster home selection. For lakeshore or woodland leisure living.

6.

176 Pages, $4.95

The Exterior Style Series

120 EARLY AMERICAN PLANS

and Other Colonial Adaptations is an outstanding and unique plan book for the home and professional library. Devoted exclusively to Early American architectural interpretations adapted for today's living patterns. Exquisitely detailed exteriors retain all the charm of a proud heritage. One-story, 1½ and two-story and multi-level designs for varying budgets.

7.

112 Pages, $2.95

125 CONTEMPORARY HOME PLANS

Here is an exciting book featuring a wide variety of home designs for the 1980's and far beyond. The exteriors of these delightfully illustrated houses are refreshing with their practical and progressive "new look". The floor plans offer new dimensions in living highlighting such features as gathering rooms, cathedral ceilings and interior balconies. House designs of all sizes.

8.

112 Pages, $2.95

135 ENGLISH TUDOR HOMES

and other Popular Family Plans is a favorite of many. The current popularity of the English Tudor home design is phenomenal. Here is a book which is loaded with Tudors for all budgets. There are one-story, 1½ and two-story designs, plus multi-levels and hillsides from 1,176 to 3,849 sq. ft. There is a special 20 page section of Early American Adaptations.

9.

104 Pages, $2.95

The Budget Series

175 LOW BUDGET HOMES

A special selection of home designs for the modest or restricted building budget. An excellent variety of Traditional and Contemporary designs. One-story, 1½ and two-story and split-level homes. Three, four and five bedrooms. Family rooms, extra baths, formal and informal dining rooms. Basement and non-basement designs. Attached garages and covered porches.

11.

96 Pages, $2.95

165 AFFORDABLE HOME PLANS

This outstanding book was specially edited with a wide selection of houses and plans for those with a medium building budget. While none of these designs are considered low-cost; neither do they require an unlimited budget to build. Square footages range from 1,428. Exteriors of Tudor, French, Early American, Spanish and Contemporary are included.

12.

112 Pages, $2.95

142 HOME DESIGNS FOR EXPANDED BUILDING BUDGETS

A family's ability to finance and need for a larger home grows as its size and income increases. This selection highlights designs which house an average square footage of 2,551. One-story plans average 2,069; two-stories, 2,735; multi-levels, 2,825. Spacious homes featuring raised hearth fireplaces, open planning and efficient kitchens.

13.

112 Pages, $2.75

Full Color Series

116 TRADITIONAL and CONTEMPORARY PLANS

A beautifully illustrated home plan book in complete, full color. One, 1½, two-story and split-level designs featured in all of the most popular exterior styles. Varied building budgets will be satisfied by the numerous plans for all budget sizes. Designs for flat and hillside sites, including exposed lower levels. It will make an ideal gift item.

14.

96 Pages in Full Color, $5.95

122 HOME DESIGNS

This book has full color throughout. More than 120 eye-pleasing, colored illustrations. Tudor, French, Spanish, Early American and Contemporary exteriors featuring all design types. The interiors house efficient, step-saving floor plans. Formal and informal living areas along with convenient work centers. Two to six bedroom sleeping areas. A delightful book for one's permanent library.

15.

96 Pages in Full Color, $5.95

114 TREND HOMES

Heritage Houses, Energy Designs, Family Plans - these, along with Vacation Homes, are in this new plan book in full color. The Trend Homes feature unique living patterns. The revered Heritage Houses highlight the charm and nostalgia of Early America. Solariums, greenhouses, earth-sheltered and super-insulated houses are the Energy Designs. Vacation homes feature A-frames and chalets.

16.

104 Pages in Full Color, $5.95

450 HOUSE PLANS

For those who wish to review and study perhaps the largest selection of designs available in a single volume. This edition will provide countless hours of enjoyable family home planning. Varying exterior styles, plus interesting and practical floor plans for all building budgets. Formal, informal living patterns; indoor-outdoor livability; small, growing and large family facilities.

17.

320 Pages, $8.95

136 SPANISH & WESTERN HOME DESIGNS

Stucco exteriors, arches, tile roofs, wide-overhangs, courtyards and rambling ranches are characteristics which make this design selection distinctive. These sun-country designs highlight indoor-outdoor relationships. Solar oriented livability is featured. Their appeal is not limited to the Southwest region of our country.

10.

120 Pages, $2.95

The Plan Books

. . . are a most valuable tool for anyone planning to build a new home. A study of the hundreds of delightfully designed exteriors and the practical, efficient floor plans will be a great learning and fun-oriented family experience. You will be able to select your preferred styling from among Early American, Tudor, French, Spanish and Contemporary adaptations. Your ideas about floor planning and interior livability will expand. And, of course, after you have selected an appealing home design that satisfies your long list of living requirements, you can order the blueprints for further study of your favorite design in greater detail. Surely the hours spent studying the portfolio of Home Planners' designs will be both enjoyable and rewarding ones.

1 Frontal Sheet

2 Foundation Plan

3 Detailed Floor Plan

FIRST FLOOR PLAN

SECOND FLOOR PLAN

4 House Cross-Sections

CROSS SECTION C-C

CROSS SECTION D-D

5 Interior Elevations

6 Exterior Elevations

LEFT SIDE

7 Material List

home planners, inc.

The Blueprints

1. FRONTAL SHEET.
Artist's landscaped sketch of the exterior and ink-line floor plans are on the frontal sheet of each set of blueprints.

2. FOUNDATION PLAN.
¼" Scale basement and foundation plan. All necessary notations and dimensions. Plot plan diagram for locating house on building site.

3. DETAILED FLOOR PLAN.
¼" Scale first and second floor plans with complete dimensions. Cross-section detail keys. Diagrammatic layout of electrical outlets and switches.

4. HOUSE CROSS-SECTIONS.
Large scale sections of foundation, interior and exterior walls, floors and roof details for design and construction control.

5. INTERIOR ELEVATIONS.
Large scale interior details of the complete kitchen cabinet design, bathrooms, powder room, laundry, fireplaces, paneling, beam ceilings, built-in cabinets, etc.

6. EXTERIOR ELEVATIONS.
¼" Scale exterior elevation drawings of front, rear, and both sides of the house. All exterior materials and details are shown to indicate the complete design and proportions of the house.

7. MATERIAL LIST.
Complete lists of all materials required for the construction of the house as designed are included in each set of blueprints.

THIS BLUEPRINT PACKAGE
will help you and your family take a major step forward in the final appraisal and planning of your new home. Only by spending many enjoyable and informative hours studying the numerous details included in the complete package, will you feel sure of, and comfortable with, your commitment to build your new home. To assure successful and productive consultation with your builder and/or architect, reference to the various elements of the blueprint package is a must. The blueprints, material list and specification outline will save much consultation time and expense. Don't be without them.

The Material List

With each set of blueprints you order you will receive a material list. Each list shows you the quantity, type and size of the non-mechanical materials required to build your home. It also tells you where these materials are used. This makes the blueprints easy to understand.

Influencing the mechanical requirements are geographical differences in availability of materials, local codes, methods of installation and individual preferences. Because of these factors, your local heating, plumbing and electrical contractors can supply you with necessary material take-offs for their particular trades.

Material lists simplify your material ordering and enable you to get quicker price quotations from your builder and material dealer. Because the material list is an integral part of each set of blueprints, it is not available separately.

Among the materials listed:

• Masonry, Veneer & Fireplace • Framing Lumber • Roofing & Sheet Metal • Windows & Door Frames • Exterior Trim & Insulation • Tile Work, Finish Floors • Interior Trim, Kitchen Cabinets • Rough & Finish Hardware

The Specification Outline

This fill-in type specification lists over 150 phases of home construction from excavating to painting and includes wiring, plumbing, heating and air-conditioning. It consists of 16 pages and will prove invaluable for specifying to your builder the exact materials, equipment and methods of construction you want in your new home. One Specification Outline is included free with each order for blueprints. Additional Specification Outlines are available at $3.00 each.

CONTENTS
• General Instructions, Suggestions and Information • Excavating and Grading • Masonry and Concrete Work • Sheet Metal Work • Carpentry, Millwork, Roofing, and Miscellaneous Items • Lath and Plaster or Drywall Wallboard • Schedule for Room Finishes • Painting and Finishing • Tile Work • Electrical Work • Plumbing • Heating and Air-Conditioning

Before You Order

1. STUDY THE DESIGNS . . . found in Home Planners current publications. As you review these delightful custom homes, you should keep in mind the total living requirements of your family — both indoors and outdoors. Although we do not make changes in plans, many minor changes can be made prior to the period of construction. If major changes are involved to satisfy your personal requirements, you should consider ordering one set of blueprints and having them redrawn locally. Consultation with your architect is strongly advised when contemplating major changes.

2. HOW TO ORDER BLUEPRINTS . . . After you have chosen the design that satisfies your requirements, or if you have selected one that you wish to study in more detail, simply clip the accompanying order blank and mail with your remittance. However, if it is not convenient for you to send a check or money order, you can use your credit card, or merely indicate C.O.D. shipment. Postman will collect all charges, including postage and C.O.D. fee. C.O.D. shipments are not permitted to Canada or foreign countries. Should time be of essence, as it sometimes is with many of our customers, your telephone order usually can be processed and shipped in the next day's mail. Simply call toll free 1-800-521-6797, (Michigan residents call collect 0-313-477-1854).

3. OUR SERVICE . . . Home Planners makes every effort to process and ship each order for blueprints and books within 48 hours. Because of this, we have deemed it unnecessary to acknowledge receipt of our customers orders. See order coupon for the postage and handling charges for surface mail, air mail or foreign mail.

4. A NOTE REGARDING REVERSE BLUEPRINTS . . . As a special service to those wishing to build in reverse of the plan as shown, we do include an extra set of reversed blueprints for only $25.00 additional with each order. Even though the lettering and dimensions appear backward on reversed blueprints, they make a handy reference because they show the house just as it's being built in reverse from the standard blueprints — thereby helping you visualize the home better.

5. OUR EXCHANGE POLICY . . . Since blueprints are printed up in specific response to your individual order, we cannot honor requests for refunds. However, the first set of blueprints in any order (or the one set in a single set order) for a given design may be exchanged for a set of another design at a fee of $10.00 plus $3.00 for postage and handling via surface mail; $4.00 via air mail.

TO: HOME PLANNERS, INC., 23761 RESEARCH DRIVE FARMINGTON HILLS, MICHIGAN 48024

Please rush me the following:

____ SET(S) BLUEPRINTS FOR DESIGN NO(S). _____ $_____
Single Set, $95.00; Additional Identical Sets in Same Order $25.00 ea.
4 Set Package of Same Design, $145.00 (Save $25.00)
7 Set Package of Same Design, $180.00 (Save $65.00)
(Material Lists and 1 Specification Outline included)

____ SPECIFICATION OUTLINES @ $3.00 EACH . . . . $_____

Michigan Residents add 4% sales tax $_____

FOR POSTAGE AND HANDLING PLEASE CHECK ✓ & REMIT	☐ $3.00 Added to Order for Surface Mail (UPS) – Any Mdse.
	☐ $4.00 Added for Priority Mail of One-Three Sets of Blueprints.
	☐ $6.00 Added for Priority Mail of Four or more Sets of Blueprints.
	☐ For Canadian orders add $2.00 to above applicable rates

$_____

☐ C.O.D. PAY POSTMAN
(C.O.D. Within U.S.A. Only)

TOTAL in U.S.A. funds $_____

PLEASE PRINT
Name _____
Street _____
City _____ State _____ Zip _____

CREDIT CARD ORDERS ONLY: Fill in the boxes below   Prices subject to change without notice

Credit Card No. [ ][ ][ ][ ][ ][ ][ ][ ][ ][ ][ ][ ][ ][ ]   Expiration Date Month/Year [ ][ ][ ][ ]

CHECK ONE: ☐ **VISA** ☐ **MasterCard**

Order Form Key NCV4   Your Signature _____

BLUEPRINT ORDERS SHIPPED WITHIN 48 HOURS OF RECEIPT!

TO: HOME PLANNERS, INC., 23761 RESEARCH DRIVE FARMINGTON HILLS, MICHIGAN 48024

Please rush me the following:

____ SET(S) BLUEPRINTS FOR DESIGN NO(S). _____ $_____
Single Set, $95.00; Additional Identical Sets in Same Order $25.00 ea.
4 Set Package of Same Design, $145.00 (Save $25.00)
7 Set Package of Same Design, $180.00 (Save $65.00)
(Material Lists and 1 Specification Outline included)

____ SPECIFICATION OUTLINES @ $3.00 EACH . . . . $_____

Michigan Residents add 4% sales tax $_____

FOR POSTAGE AND HANDLING PLEASE CHECK ✓ & REMIT	☐ $3.00 Added to Order for Surface Mail (UPS) – Any Mdse.
	☐ $4.00 Added for Priority Mail of One-Three Sets of Blueprints.
	☐ $6.00 Added for Priority Mail of Four or more Sets of Blueprints.
	☐ For Canadian orders add $2.00 to above applicable rates

$_____

☐ C.O.D. PAY POSTMAN
(C.O.D. Within U.S.A. Only)

TOTAL in U.S.A. funds $_____

PLEASE PRINT
Name _____
Street _____
City _____ State _____ Zip _____

CREDIT CARD ORDERS ONLY: Fill in the boxes below   Prices subject to change without notice

Credit Card No. [ ][ ][ ][ ][ ][ ][ ][ ][ ][ ][ ][ ][ ][ ]   Expiration Date Month/Year [ ][ ][ ][ ]

CHECK ONE: ☐ **VISA** ☐ **MasterCard**

Order Form Key NCV4   Your Signature _____

How many sets of blueprints should be ordered?

This question is often asked. The answer can range anywhere from 1 to 7 sets, depending upon circumstances. For instance, a single set of blueprints of your favorite design is sufficient to study the house in greater detail. On the other hand, if you are planning to get cost estimates, or if you are planning to build, you may need as many as seven sets of blueprints. Because the first set of blueprints in each order is $95.00, and because additional sets of the same design in each order are only $25.00 each (and with package sets even more economical), you save considerably by ordering your total requirements now. To help you determine the exact number of sets, please refer to the handy check list.

How Many Blueprints Do You Need?

___ **OWNER'S SET**

___ **BUILDER** (Usually requires at least 3 sets: 1 as legal document; 1 for inspection; and at least 1 for tradesmen — usually more.)

___ **BUILDING PERMIT** (Sometimes 2 sets are required.)

___ **MORTGAGE SOURCE** (Usually 1 set for a conventional mortgage; 3 sets for F.H.A. or V.A. type mortgages.)

___ **SUBDIVISION COMMITTEE** (If any.)

___ **TOTAL NO. SETS REQUIRED**

Blueprint Ordering Hotline –

Phone toll free: 1-800-521-6797. Orders received by 11 a.m. (Detroit time) will be processed the same day and shipped to you the following day. Use of this line restricted to blueprint ordering only. Michigan residents simply call collect 0-313-477-1854.

Kindly Note: When ordering by phone, please state Order Form Key No. located in box at lower left corner of blueprint order form.

In Canada Mail To:
Home Planners, Inc., 20 Cedar St. North Kitchener, Ontario N2H 2W8
Phone: (519) 743-4169

HILLSIDE HOMES . . .

when effectively planned, take advantage of the contours of the site on which they stand. A hillside house can be a one or a two-story; a split or a bi-level. It can have its lower level exposed to the front, the rear, or the sides of the house. For the development of the most private indoor-outdoor living relationships, exposing the lower level to the rear is best. Unless the building site is very large permitting the house to be located far from the street, rear outdoor living delivers the most privacy. Many houses with basements designed for a flat site can be adapted to hillside living by merely exposing the basement and installing windows. This is a fine way to pick-up additional living space.

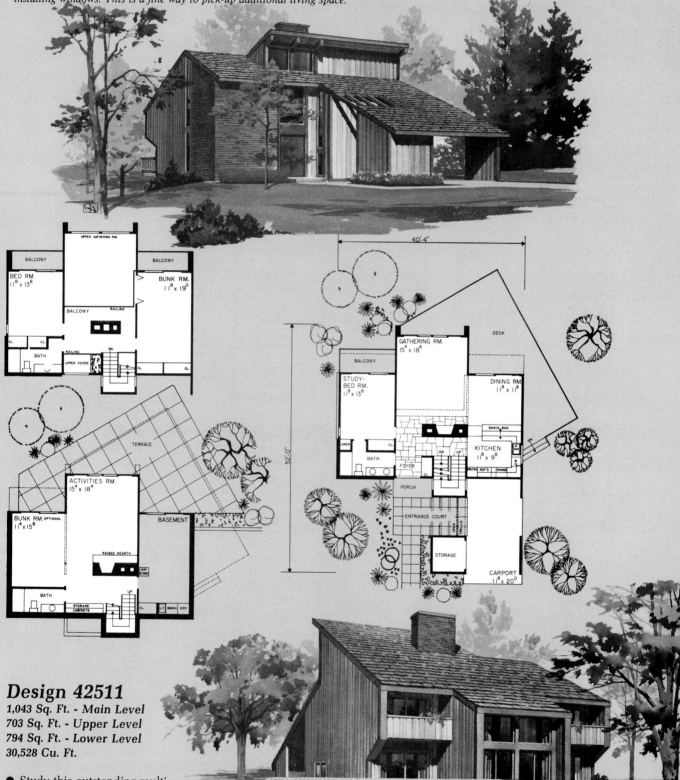

Design 42511

1,043 Sq. Ft. - Main Level
703 Sq. Ft. - Upper Level
794 Sq. Ft. - Lower Level
30,528 Cu. Ft.

● Study this outstanding multi-level with its dramatic outdoor deck and balconies. This home is ideal if you are looking for a home that is new and exciting. The livability that it offers will efficiently serve your family.

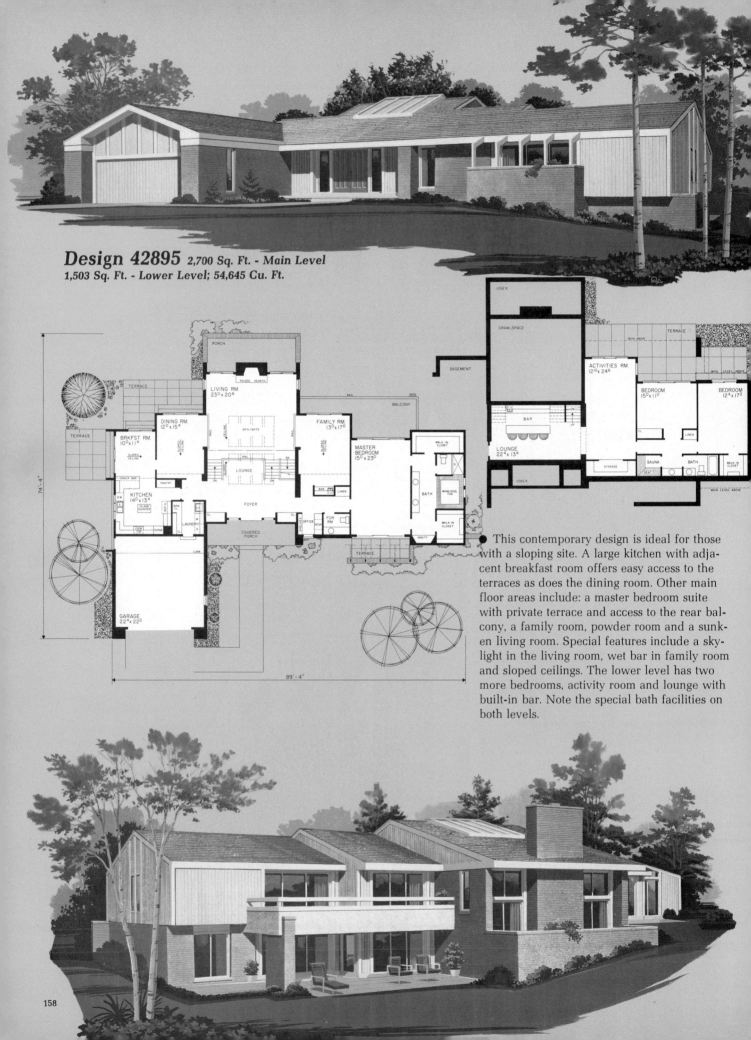

Design 42895 2,700 Sq. Ft. - Main Level
1,503 Sq. Ft. - Lower Level; 54,645 Cu. Ft.

● This contemporary design is ideal for those with a sloping site. A large kitchen with adjacent breakfast room offers easy access to the terraces as does the dining room. Other main floor areas include: a master bedroom suite with private terrace and access to the rear balcony, a family room, powder room and a sunken living room. Special features include a skylight in the living room, wet bar in family room and sloped ceilings. The lower level has two more bedrooms, activity room and lounge with built-in bar. Note the special bath facilities on both levels.

Design 42896
1,856 Sq. Ft. - Main Level; 1,454 Sq. Ft. - Lower Level; 43,390 Cu. Ft.

● This design is very inviting with its contemporary appeal. A large kitchen with an adjacent snack bar makes light meals a breeze. The adjoining breakfast room offers a scenic view through sliding glass doors. Notice the sloped ceiling in the dining and gathering rooms. A fireplace in the gathering room adds a cozy air. An interesting feature is the master bedroom's easy access to the study. Also, take note of the sliding doors in the master bedroom which lead to a private balcony. On the lower level, a large activities room will be a frequently used spot by family members. The fireplace and wet bar add a nice touch for entertaining friends. Also, notice the sliding glass doors which lead to the terrace. Take note of the two or optional three bedrooms - the choice is yours.

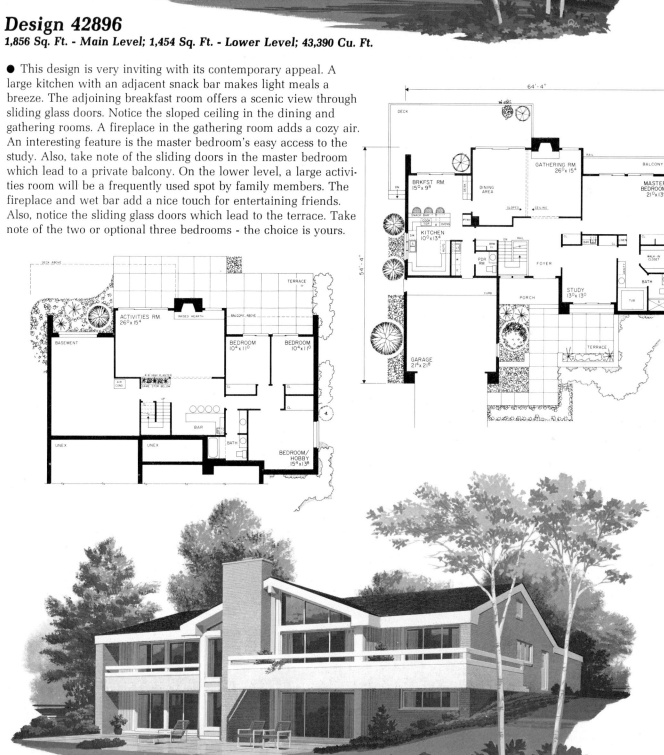

Design 42719

2,363 Sq. Ft. - Main Level
1,523 Sq. Ft. - Lower Level; 47,915 Cu. Ft.

● If you have a flair for something different and useful at the same time, then expose the basement for hillside living. This design offers three large living areas: gathering room, family room and all-purpose activity room. Note the features in each of the three: balcony, sloping ceiling and thru-fireplace in the gathering room; deck and eating area in the family room; terrace and raised hearth fireplace in the activities room. The staircase to the lower level is delightfully open which adds to the spacious appeal of the entry hall. Cabinets and shelves are also a delightful feature of this area. Three bedrooms, the master bedroom suite on the main level with the other two on the lower level. An efficient U-shaped kitchen to easily serve the eating area of the family room and the formal dining room. The laundry is just a step away. The front projection of the two-car garage reduces the size of the lot required to build this exciting contemporary home.

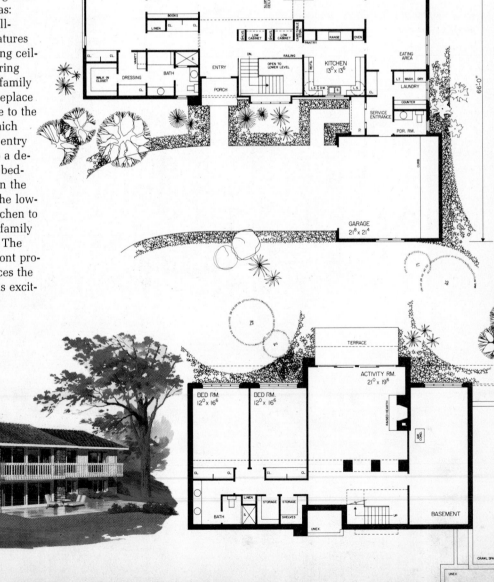

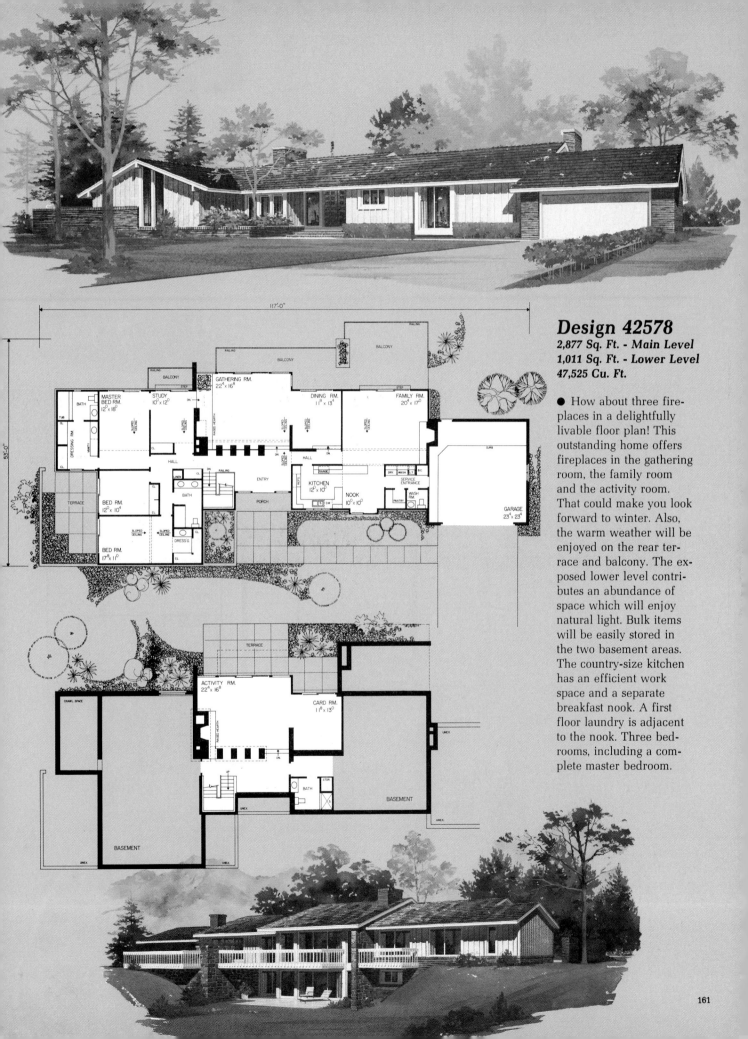

Design 42578
2,877 Sq. Ft. - Main Level
1,011 Sq. Ft. - Lower Level
47,525 Cu. Ft.

● How about three fireplaces in a delightfully livable floor plan! This outstanding home offers fireplaces in the gathering room, the family room and the activity room. That could make you look forward to winter. Also, the warm weather will be enjoyed on the rear terrace and balcony. The exposed lower level contributes an abundance of space which will enjoy natural light. Bulk items will be easily stored in the two basement areas. The country-size kitchen has an efficient work space and a separate breakfast nook. A first floor laundry is adjacent to the nook. Three bedrooms, including a complete master bedroom.

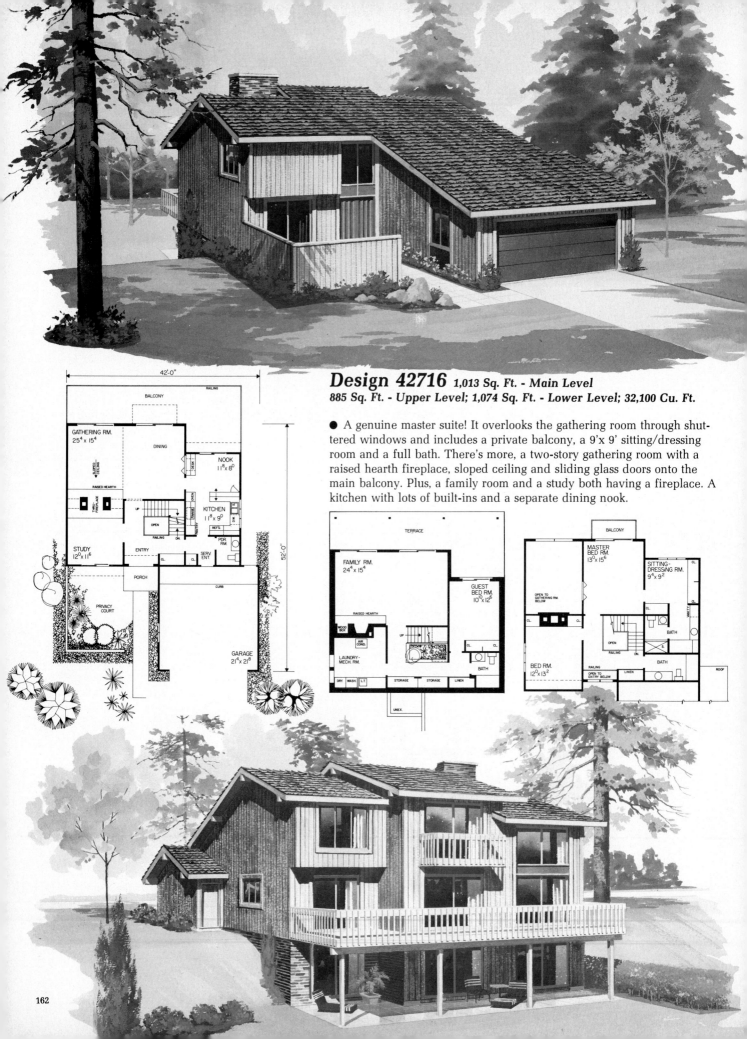

Design 42716 1,013 Sq. Ft. - Main Level
885 Sq. Ft. - Upper Level; 1,074 Sq. Ft. - Lower Level; 32,100 Cu. Ft.

● A genuine master suite! It overlooks the gathering room through shuttered windows and includes a private balcony, a 9'x 9' sitting/dressing room and a full bath. There's more, a two-story gathering room with a raised hearth fireplace, sloped ceiling and sliding glass doors onto the main balcony. Plus, a family room and a study both having a fireplace. A kitchen with lots of built-ins and a separate dining nook.

Design 42552 1,437 Sq. Ft. - Main Level; 1,158 Sq. Ft. - Upper Level; 1,056 Sq. Ft. - Lower Level; 43,000 Cu. Ft.

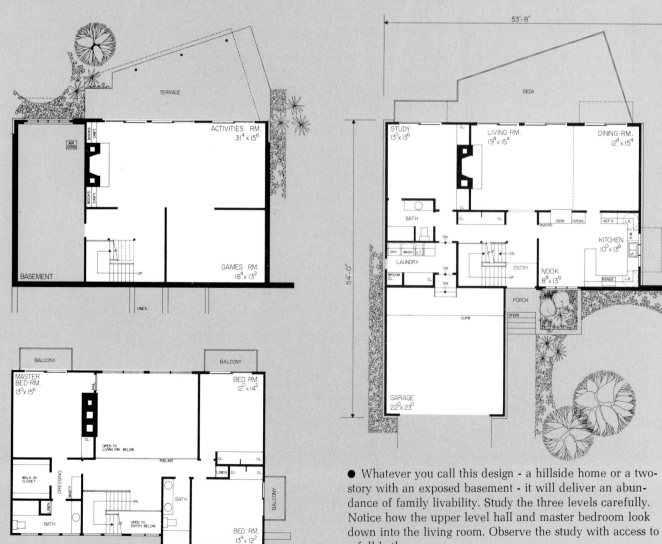

TERRACE

ACTIVITIES RM.
31⁴ x 15⁶

BOOKS CABT.

AIR COND.

BOOKS CABT.

BASEMENT

GAMES RM.
18⁴ x 13²

UP

UNEX.

53'-8"

DECK

STUDY
13⁰ x 13⁶

LIVING RM.
19⁴ x 15⁴

DINING RM.
12⁴ x 15⁴

CL

CL

CL

BATH

PANTRY

DESK

OVENS

REF'G.

L.S.

DRY.

WASH

DN.

DN.

KITCHEN
10⁰ x 13⁶

LAUNDRY

ENTRY

NOOK
8⁸ x 13⁶

RANGE

L.S.

BROOM CL.

CL

DN.

UP

54'-0"

PORCH

CURB

STEPS

GARAGE
22⁰ x 23⁰

BALCONY

BALCONY

MASTER BED RM.
13⁰ x 15⁶

RAIL

CL

OPEN TO LIVING RM. BELOW

BED RM.
12⁰ x 14²

RAILING

LINEN

CL

CL

CL

WALK IN CLOSET

DRESSING

VANITY

BATH

DN.

BATH

OPEN TO ENTRY BELOW

BALCONY

BED RM.
13⁴ x 12²

● Whatever you call this design - a hillside home or a two-story with an exposed basement - it will deliver an abundance of family livability. Study the three levels carefully. Notice how the upper level hall and master bedroom look down into the living room. Observe the study with access to a full bath.

Design 42848 *2,028 Sq. Ft. - Main Level; 1,122 Sq. Ft. - Lower Level; 45,695 Cu. Ft.*

● This contemporary design is characterized by the contrast in diagonal and vertical wood siding. The private front court adjacent to the covered porch is a nice area for evening relaxation and creates an impressive entry. Once inside the house, the livability begins to unfold. Three bedrooms are arranged to one side of the entry with two baths sharing back-to-back plumbing. The master bedroom has a balcony. A view of the front court will be enjoyed from the kitchen and breakfast room. Along with the breakfast room, both the formal dining room and the screened porch will have easy access to the kitchen. A formal living room will be enjoyed on many occasions. It is detailed by a sloped ceiling and the warmth of a fireplace. A fourth bedroom is on the lower level. This level is opened to the outdoors by three sets of sliding glass doors. A second fireplace, this one with a raised hearth, is in the family room. A full bath and two work rooms also are located on the lower level.

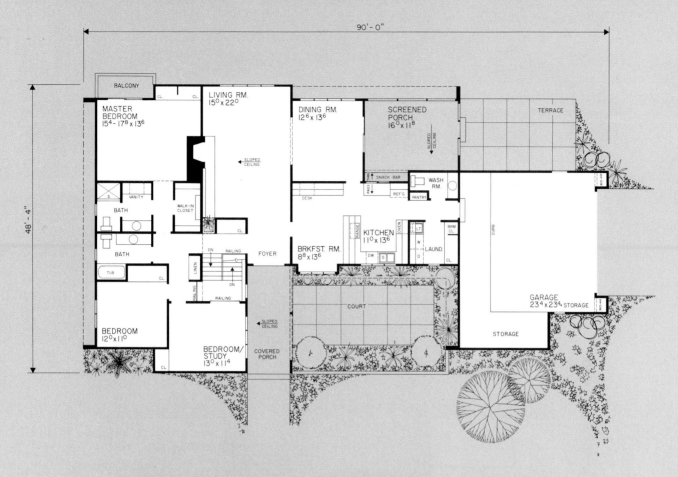

Contemporary Hillside Living

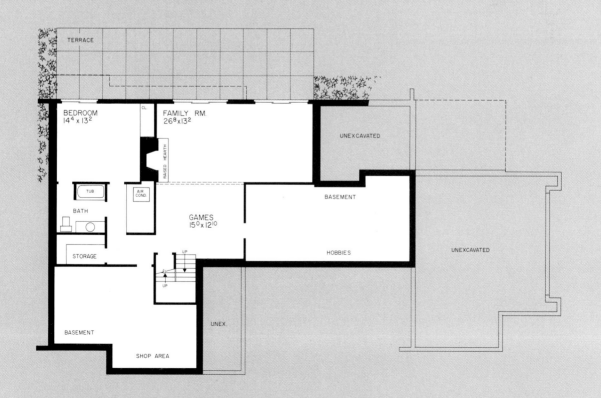

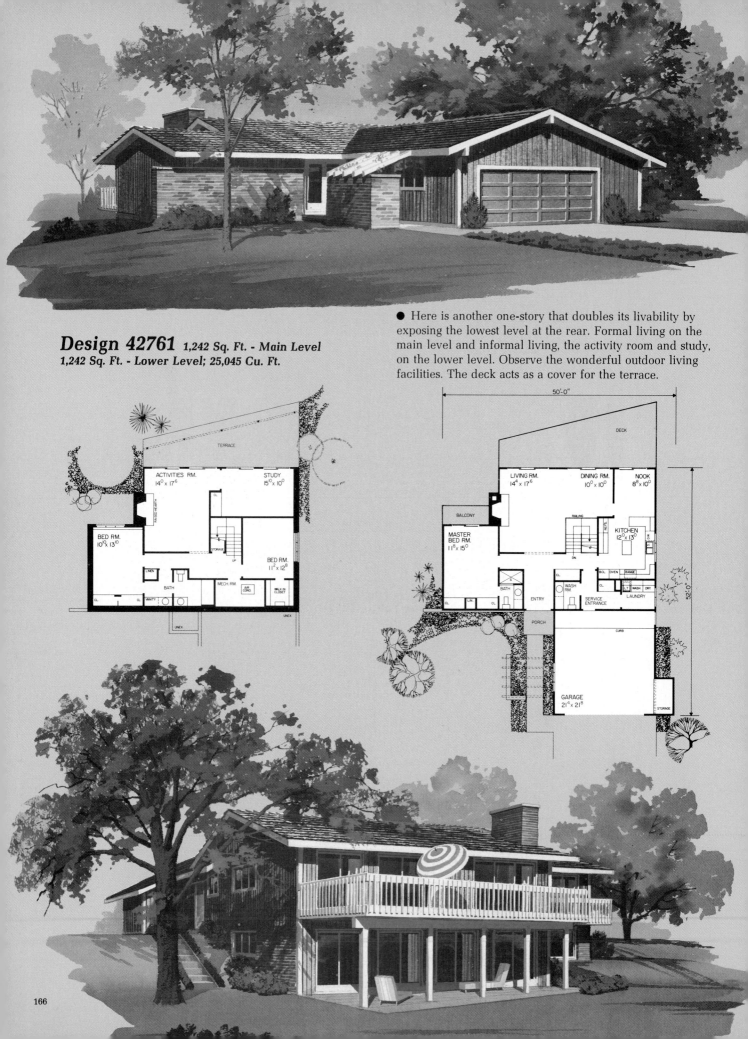

Design 42761 1,242 Sq. Ft. - Main Level
1,242 Sq. Ft. - Lower Level; 25,045 Cu. Ft.

● Here is another one-story that doubles its livability by exposing the lowest level at the rear. Formal living on the main level and informal living, the activity room and study, on the lower level. Observe the wonderful outdoor living facilities. The deck acts as a cover for the terrace.

TERRACE

ACTIVITIES RM.
14⁰ x 17⁶

STUDY
15¹⁰ x 10⁰

BED RM.
10⁰ x 13¹⁰

BED RM.
11² x 12⁸

STORAGE   UP

LINEN

BATH

VANITY

MECH. RM.

AIR COND.

WALK IN CLOSET

UNEX.

50'-0"

DECK

LIVING RM.
14⁴ x 17⁶

DINING RM.
10⁰ x 10⁰

NOOK
8⁸ x 10⁰

BALCONY

RAILING

MASTER BED RM.
11⁸ x 15⁰

KITCHEN
12⁰ x 13⁰

DN

BATH

WASH RM.

ENTRY

SERVICE ENTRANCE

OVEN RANGE

WASH DRY

LAUNDRY

52'-0"

PORCH

CURB

GARAGE
21⁴ x 21⁸

STORAGE

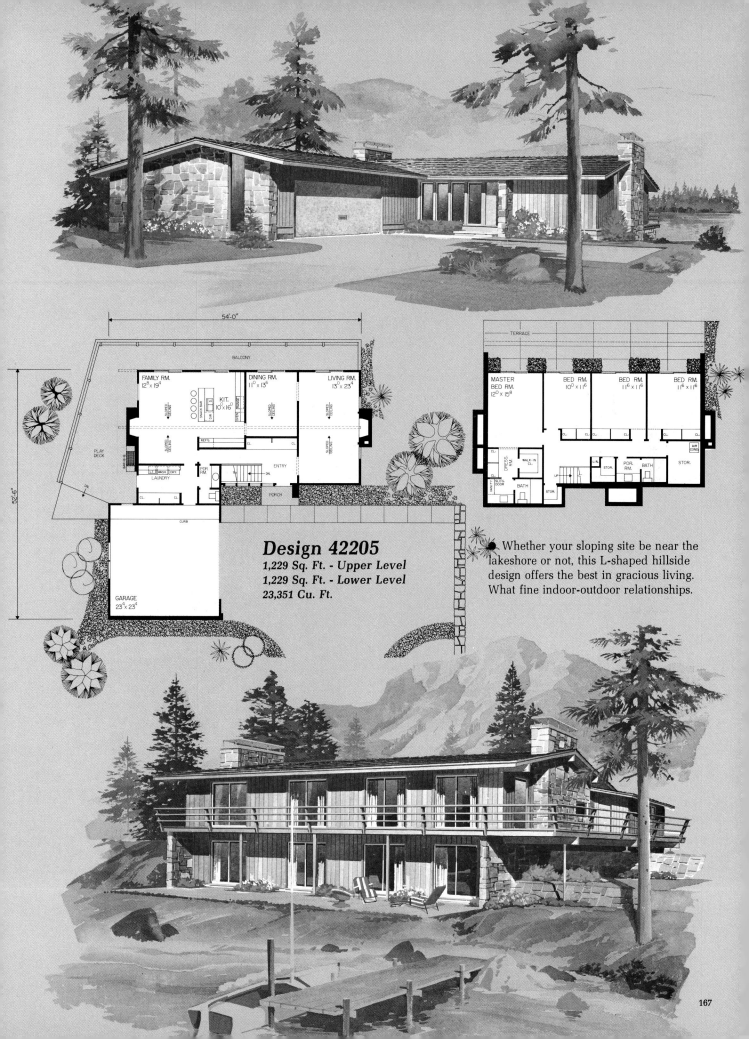

Design 42205

1,229 Sq. Ft. - Upper Level
1,229 Sq. Ft. - Lower Level
23,351 Cu. Ft.

Whether your sloping site be near the lakeshore or not, this L-shaped hillside design offers the best in gracious living. What fine indoor-outdoor relationships.

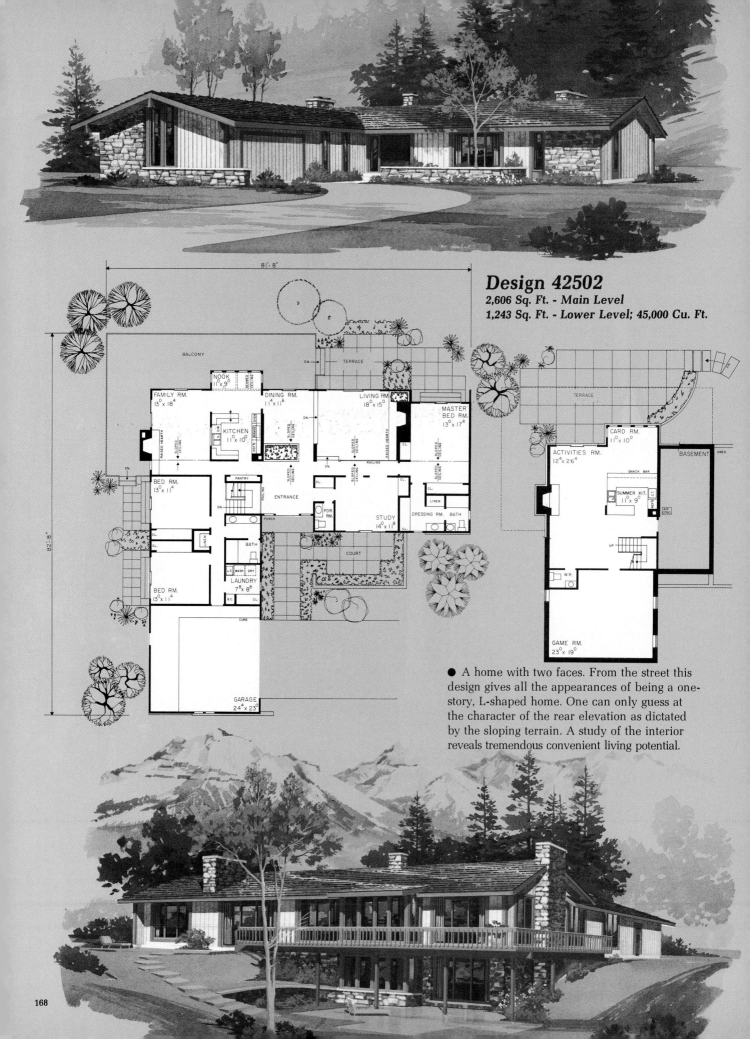

Design 42502

2,606 Sq. Ft. - Main Level
1,243 Sq. Ft. - Lower Level; 45,000 Cu. Ft.

● A home with two faces. From the street this design gives all the appearances of being a one-story, L-shaped home. One can only guess at the character of the rear elevation as dictated by the sloping terrain. A study of the interior reveals tremendous convenient living potential.

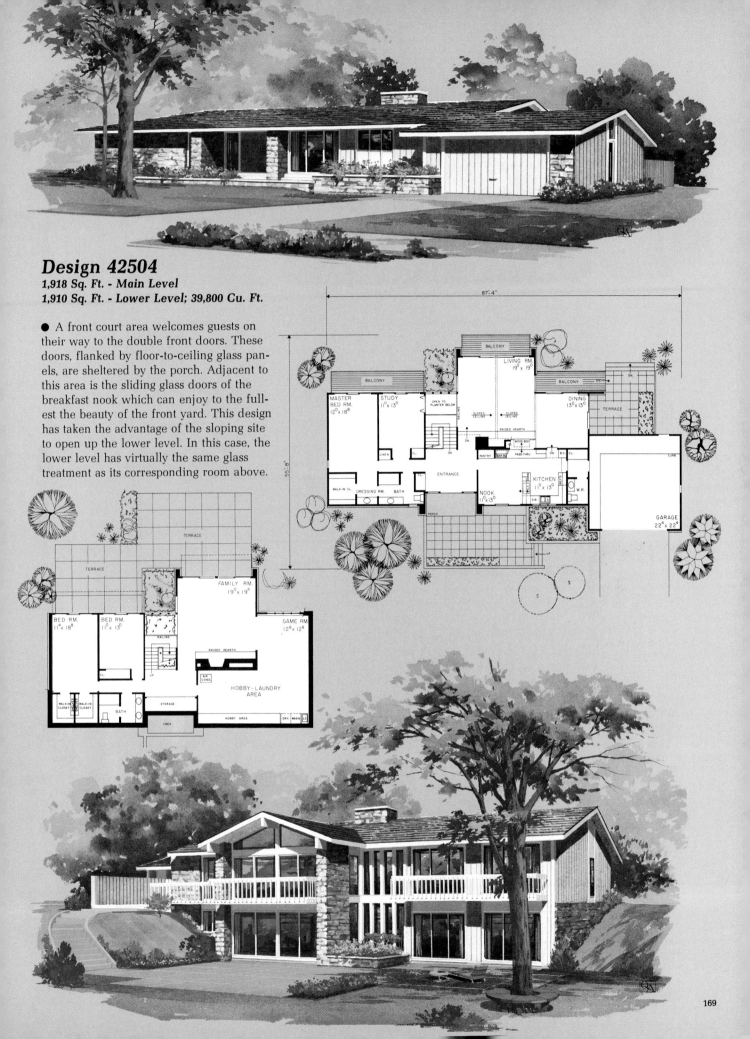

Design 42504

1,918 Sq. Ft. - Main Level
1,910 Sq. Ft. - Lower Level; 39,800 Cu. Ft.

● A front court area welcomes guests on their way to the double front doors. These doors, flanked by floor-to-ceiling glass panels, are sheltered by the porch. Adjacent to this area is the sliding glass doors of the breakfast nook which can enjoy to the fullest the beauty of the front yard. This design has taken the advantage of the sloping site to open up the lower level. In this case, the lower level has virtually the same glass treatment as its corresponding room above.

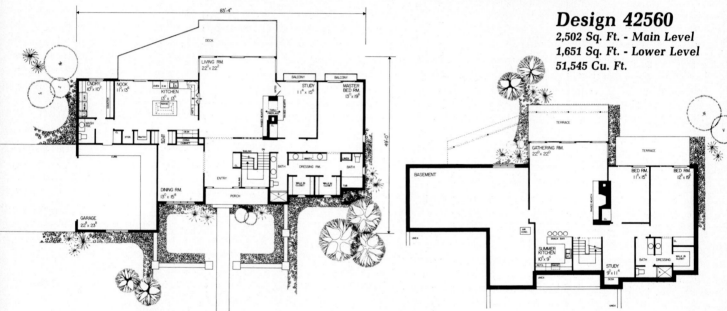

Design 42560
2,502 Sq. Ft. - Main Level
1,651 Sq. Ft. - Lower Level
51,545 Cu. Ft.

● This traditionally styled hillside home has two distinctively different facades. Each belies the existence of the other. The formal, double front doors open to a spacious center entry which effectively routes traffic to assure exceptional two-level living. There are features galore. Note the two fireplaces, the two studies, the two large living areas and the two kitchens. List other highlights which appeal to you.

Design 42576 *2,805 Sq. Ft. - Main Level; 785 Sq. Ft. - Lower Level; 41,562 Cu. Ft.*

● This delightfully styled hip-roofed house features all the living facilities on one level with an additional lower level housing an activity room, powder room, laundry and garage. The result is a very captivating design. Formal living patterns will prevail in this house.

The living room and dining room will have a delightful view of the rear yard, possess a dramatic thru-fireplace and has natural light through the openness that the sliding glass doors provide, along with access to the terrace. Two full baths serve the three bedrooms

and the cozy study/bedroom. Food preparation could hardly have better facilities than those offered by this well-planned front, U-shaped kitchen. The pass-thru from the kitchen to the nook make the quick, informal meal an enjoyable one.

Design 42760

1,483 Sq. Ft. - Main Level
1,483 Sq. Ft. - Lower Level; 33,080 Cu. Ft.

● Here is contemporary design at its simple, yet dramatic, best. The modern adaptation of the mansard roof produces results that are interesting, indeed. The top of the roof itself is virtually flat and built-up with a gravel surface. The overhanging portion is made up of metal. While this is predominantly a frame house with vertical siding, there are brick masses which offer an attractive contrast. The rear view is unique with glass areas effectively shaded by overhanging roofs and balconies. Two of the terraces are covered, thus permitting inclement weather use. No rained-out cookouts here! A thru-fireplace separates the dining room from the sunken living room.

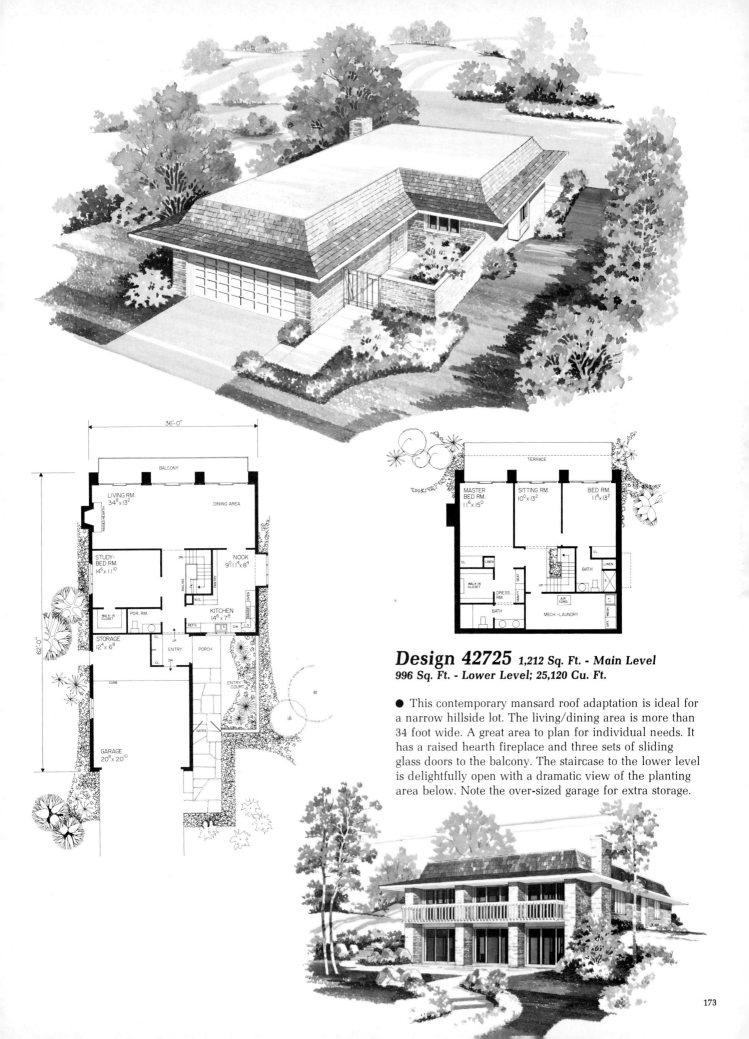

Design 42725 1,212 Sq. Ft. - Main Level
996 Sq. Ft. - Lower Level; 25,120 Cu. Ft.

● This contemporary mansard roof adaptation is ideal for a narrow hillside lot. The living/dining area is more than 34 foot wide. A great area to plan for individual needs. It has a raised hearth fireplace and three sets of sliding glass doors to the balcony. The staircase to the lower level is delightfully open with a dramatic view of the planting area below. Note the over-sized garage for extra storage.

Rear Living Enjoys Maximum View

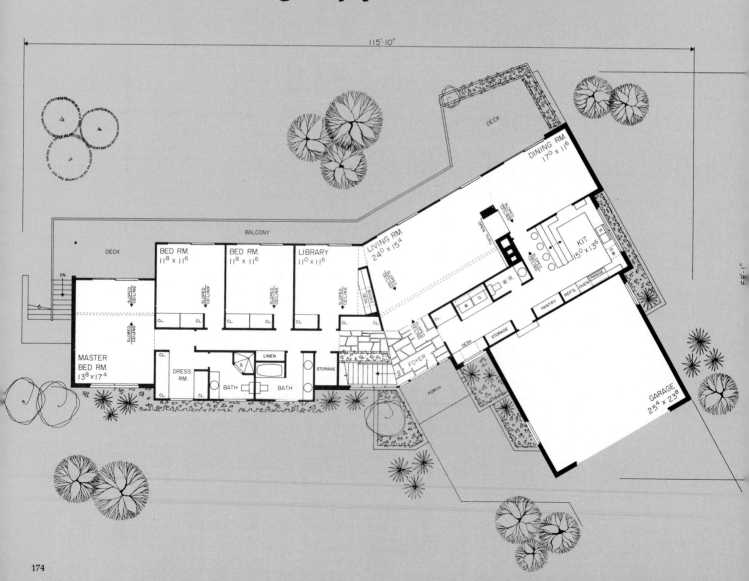

115'-10"

69'-11"

DECK

BALCONY

DECK

DN.

BED RM.
11⁸ x 11⁶

BED RM.
11⁸ x 11⁶

LIBRARY
11⁰ x 11⁶

LIVING RM.
24⁰ x 15⁴

DINING RM.
17⁰ x 11⁶

KIT.
15⁰ x 13⁶

SLOPED CEILING

SLOPED CEILING

SLOPED CEILING

SLOPED CEILING

SLOPED CEILING

SLOPED CEILING

SLOPED CEILING

OPEN THRU

W.R.

CL.

CL.

CL.

CL.

CL.

CL.

CL.

RANGE

REF'G

OVEN

PANTRY

DESK

STORAGE

MASTER
BED RM.
13⁸ x 17⁴

CL.

CL.

DRESS.
RM.

CL.

BATH

LINEN

BATH

STORAGE

FOYER

PORCH

GARAGE
25⁴ x 23⁸

174

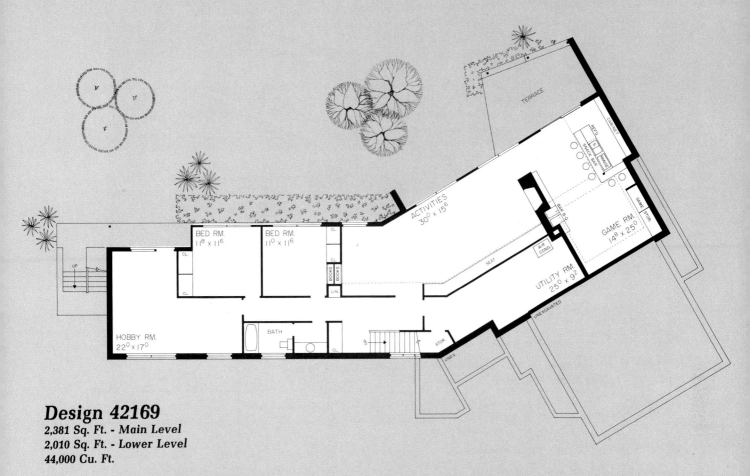

Design 42169
2,381 Sq. Ft. - Main Level
2,010 Sq. Ft. - Lower Level
44,000 Cu. Ft.

● Behold, the view! If, when looking toward the rear of your site, nature's scene is breathtaking or in any way inspiring, you may wish to maximize your enjoyment by orienting your living areas to the rear of your plan. In addition to greater enjoyment of the landscape, such floor planning will provide extra privacy from the street. The angular configuration can enhance the enjoyment of a particular scene, plus it adds appeal to the exterior of the design. A study of both levels reveals that the major living areas look out upon the rear yard. Further, the upper level rooms have direct access to the decks and balcony. The kitchen with its large window over the sink is not without its view. With five bedrooms, plus a library, a game, activities and hobby room, the active family will have an abundance of space to enjoy individualized pursuits. Can't you envision your family living in this house?

Design 42546 1,143 Sq. Ft. - Main Level; 746 Sq. Ft. - Upper Level
1,143 Sq. Ft. - Lower Level; 31,128 Cu. Ft.

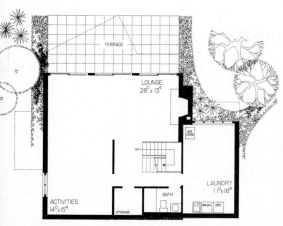

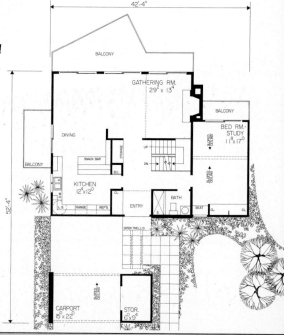

Design 42770
1,182 Sq. Ft. - Main Level
998 Sq. Ft. - Upper Level
25,830 Cu. Ft.

● If you are looking for a home with loads of livability, then consider these two-story contemporary homes which have an exposed lower level.

Design 42548 1,109 Sq. Ft. - Main Level; 739 Sq. Ft. - Upper Level
869 Sq. Ft. - Lower Level; 31,370 Cu. Ft.

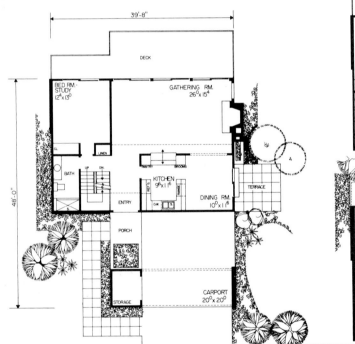

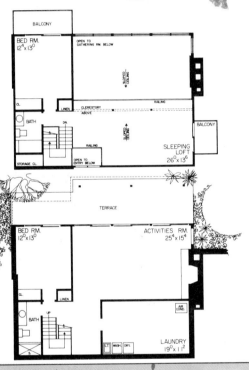

● This hillside home gives all the appearances of being a one-story ranch home; and what a delightful one at that! Should the contours of your property slope to the rear, this plan permits the exposing of the lower level. This results in the activities room and bedroom/study gaining direct access to outdoor living. Certainly a most desirable aspect for active, outdoor family living. The large and growing family will be admirably served with five bedrooms and three baths. An extra washroom and separate laundry add to the convenient living potential.

Design 42549
2,260 Sq. Ft. - Main Level
1,406 Sq. Ft. - Lower Level; 51,857 Cu. Ft.

Design 42213
1,671 Sq. Ft. - Upper Level
1,033 Sq. Ft. - Lower Level; 27,249 Cu. Ft.

● Whether you locate this contemporary bi-level home on a sloping or flat site, it will certainly command its share of attention and provide the family with wonderful living patterns. The front entry is a separate level with stairs leading directly to the lower and the upper levels.

The most captivating feature of this home may very well be the spacious living and dining areas. An exposed beam is the apex of sloped ceilings. The projecting, glass-gabled end allows for a full measure of natural light. Two pairs of sliding glass doors open onto the balcony. The living balcony wraps around both front and rear to provide appealing planting areas. The kitchen is an efficient one in which to work, while the breakfast nook is but a step away. The sleeping zone has three bedrooms plus two full baths. Don't overlook the fireplace with its wood box.

Design 42847 1,874 Sq. Ft. - Main Level
1,131 Sq. Ft. - Lower Level; 44,305 Cu. Ft.

● This is an exquisitely styled Tudor, hillside design. It is designed to serve its happy occupants for many years. Complete livability is on the main level. Bonus space will be found on the lower level.

78'-8"

DECK

DINING RM.
11⁰ x 11⁶

LIVING RM.
14⁰ x 19⁴

MASTER BEDROOM
15⁰ x 12⁰

BREAKFAST
11⁰ x 12⁰

THRU FIREPLACE

RAILING

CURB

CHINA

PANTRY BRM CL

OVEN

DN

BATH

KITCHEN
16⁸ x 9⁴

CONSOLE

DW

REF'G

LINEN

BATH

42'-0"

GARAGE
23⁶ x 23⁴

LAUNDRY

COVERED PORCH

FOYER

CL

CL

CL

CL

BEDROOM
11⁴ x 11⁰

BEDROOM
11⁸ x 13⁰

TERRACE

BEDROOM/STUDY
10⁸ x 11⁶

FAMILY RM.
14⁰ x 22¹⁰

BASEMENT

SAUNA/HOT TUB/DRESSING ROOM
10⁶ x 15⁴

RAISED HEARTH

AIR COND

CL

UP

UNEX.

BATH

LINEN

STORAGE

SEAT

SNACK BAR

UNEX.

SUMMER KITCHEN
13⁴ x 7⁰

RANGE

S

REF'G

STORAGE

SHOP AREA

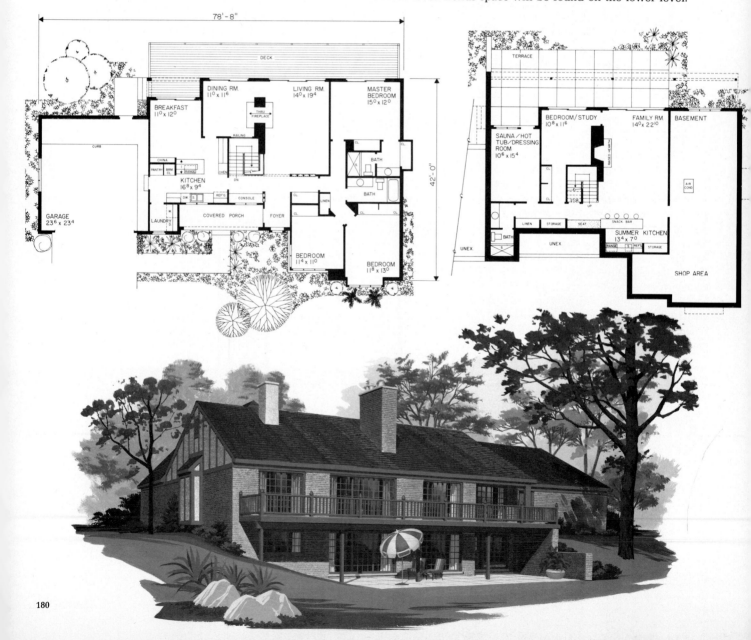

Design 42846
2,341 Sq. Ft. - Main Level; 1,380 Sq. Ft. - Lower Level; 51,290 Cu. Ft.

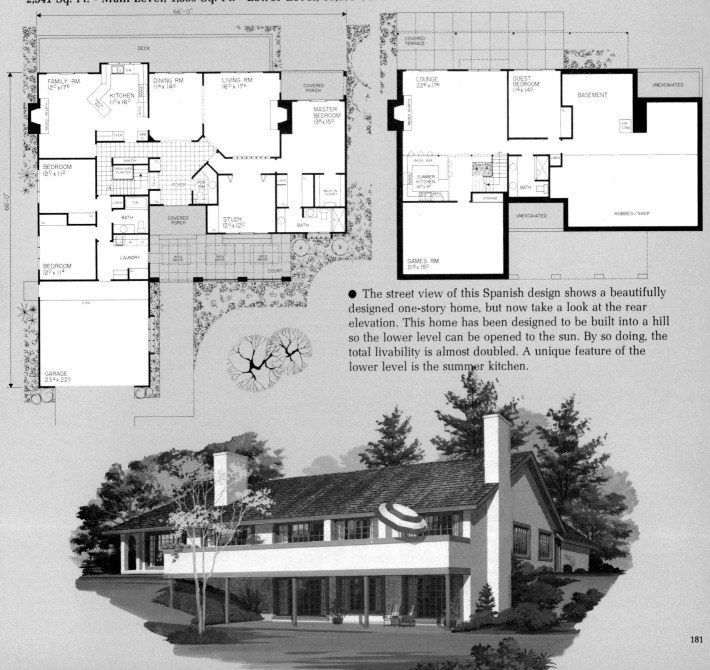

● The street view of this Spanish design shows a beautifully designed one-story home, but now take a look at the rear elevation. This home has been designed to be built into a hill so the lower level can be opened to the sun. By so doing, the total livability is almost doubled. A unique feature of the lower level is the summer kitchen.

Elegance And Grandeur On Two Levels

● The above illustrations of the front and rear views of this hillside contemporary design are impressive. And indeed rightly so! For the varied design features are so numerous and they are so delightfully incorporated under the wide overhanging roofs that the result is almost breathtaking at first glance. Consider the basic L-shape of the house and garage. Note how it lends itself to a large drive court. Observe the simplicity of the masses of brick and vertical character of the glass areas. Notice the inviting recessed double front doors. Around to the rear, the architectural interest is indeed extremely exciting. The glass areas are as dramatic as is the wood deck. The covered porch and the two covered terraces complete the facilities for gracious outdoor living fun.

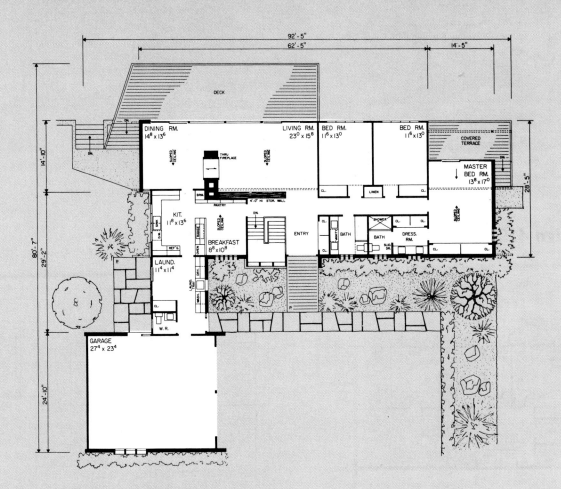

Design 41963 2,248 Sq. Ft. - Main Level; 1,948 Sq. Ft. - Lower Level; 42,422 Cu. Ft.

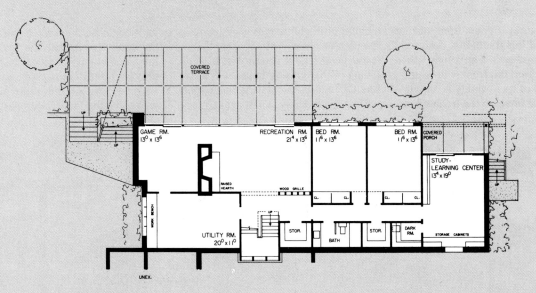

● Over four thousand square feet are available for use by the young, active family. And use them, they certainly will! There are five bedrooms to sleep a large active crew. The living areas are varied and numerous. In addition to the conventional formal living and dining rooms, there is a study/learning center. This is where all the mechanical paraphenalia like the tape recorder, film and slide projectors, phonograph, radio and television will be kept. A great way to keep all the equipment together. Note adjacent dark room. Then there is the recreation room with raised hearth fireplace. The game room will house the pool table, while the utility room will cater to the hobbyists. There are three full baths, plus an extra wash room and laundry adjacent to the kitchen.

Design 41974 1,680 Sq. Ft. - Main Level; 1,344 Sq. Ft. - Lower Level; 34,186 Cu. Ft.

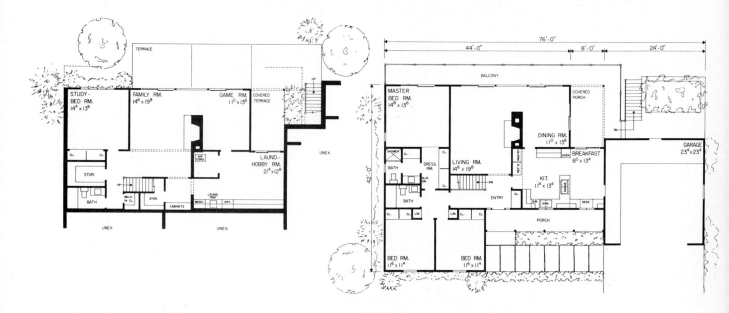

● You would never guess from looking at the front of this traditional design that it possessed such a strikingly different rear. From the front, you would guess that all of its livability is on one floor. Yet, just imagine the tremendous amount of livability that is added to the plan as a result of exposing the lower level - 1,344 square feet of it. Living in this hillside house will mean fun. Obviously, the most popular spot will be the balcony. Then again, may- be it could be the terrace adjacent to the family room. Both the terrace and the balcony have a covered area to provide protection against unfavorable weather. The interior of the plan also will serve the family with ease.

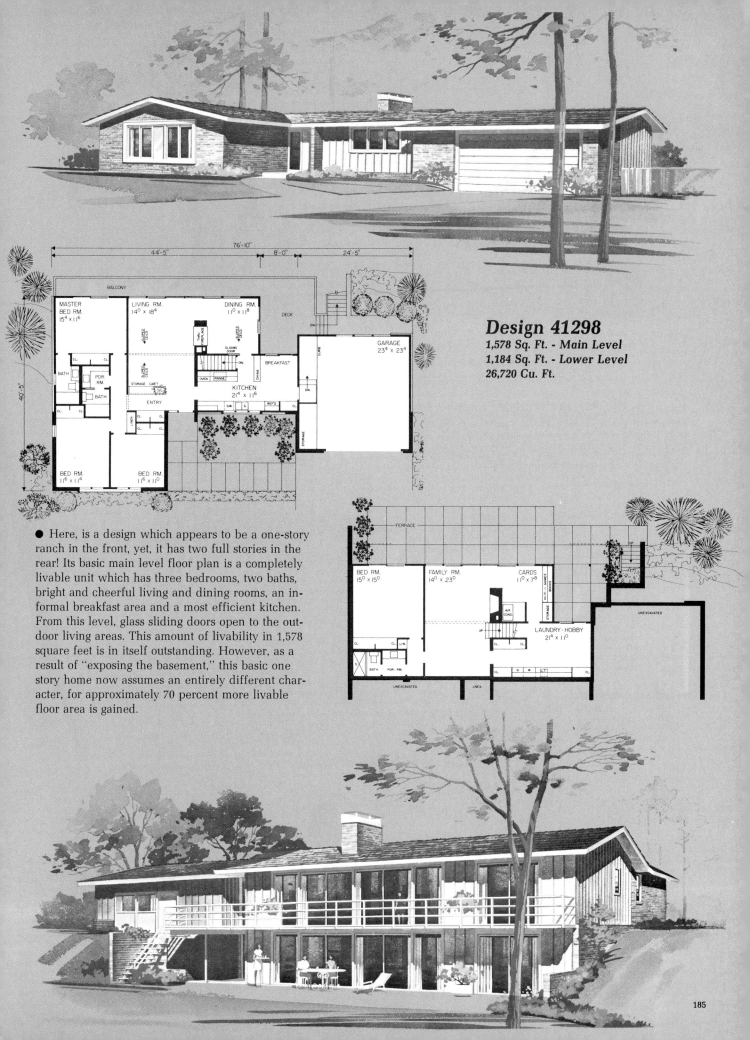

Design 41298
1,578 Sq. Ft. - Main Level
1,184 Sq. Ft. - Lower Level
26,720 Cu. Ft.

● Here, is a design which appears to be a one-story ranch in the front, yet, it has two full stories in the rear! Its basic main level floor plan is a completely livable unit which has three bedrooms, two baths, bright and cheerful living and dining rooms, an informal breakfast area and a most efficient kitchen. From this level, glass sliding doors open to the outdoor living areas. This amount of livability in 1,578 square feet is in itself outstanding. However, as a result of "exposing the basement," this basic one story home now assumes an entirely different character, for approximately 70 percent more livable floor area is gained.

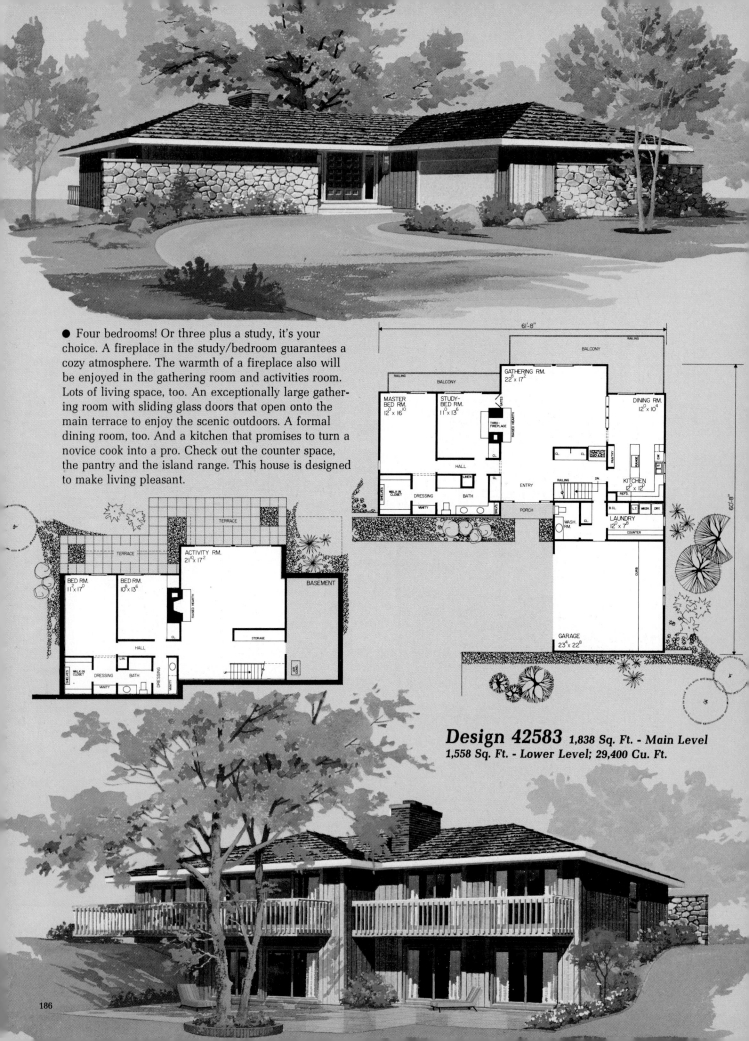

● Four bedrooms! Or three plus a study, it's your choice. A fireplace in the study/bedroom guarantees a cozy atmosphere. The warmth of a fireplace also will be enjoyed in the gathering room and activities room. Lots of living space, too. An exceptionally large gathering room with sliding glass doors that open onto the main terrace to enjoy the scenic outdoors. A formal dining room, too. And a kitchen that promises to turn a novice cook into a pro. Check out the counter space, the pantry and the island range. This house is designed to make living pleasant.

Design 42583 1,838 Sq. Ft. - Main Level
1,558 Sq. Ft. - Lower Level; 29,400 Cu. Ft.

Design 42769 *1,898 Sq. Ft. - Main Level*
1,134 Sq. Ft. - Lower Level; 41,910 Cu. Ft.

● This traditional hillside design has fine architectural styling. It possesses all of the qualities that a great design should have to serve its occupants fully.

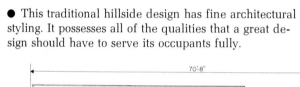

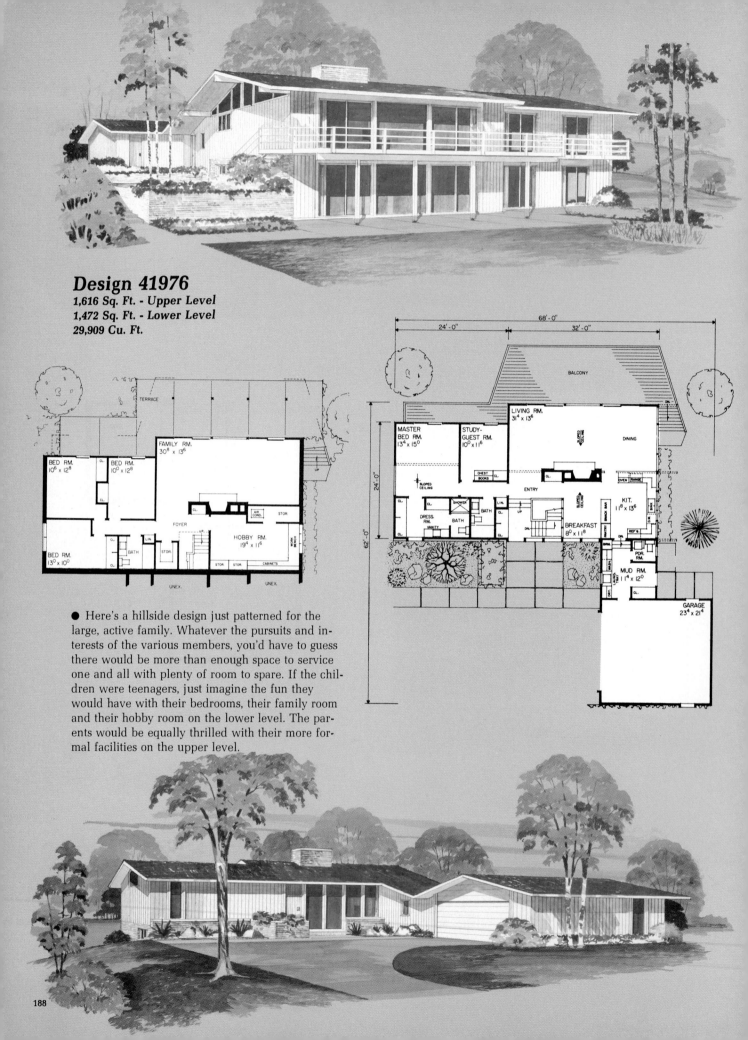

Design 41976

1,616 Sq. Ft. - Upper Level
1,472 Sq. Ft. - Lower Level
29,909 Cu. Ft.

● Here's a hillside design just patterned for the large, active family. Whatever the pursuits and interests of the various members, you'd have to guess there would be more than enough space to service one and all with plenty of room to spare. If the children were teenagers, just imagine the fun they would have with their bedrooms, their family room and their hobby room on the lower level. The parents would be equally thrilled with their more formal facilities on the upper level.

Design 41739 1,281 Sq. Ft. - Main Level; 857 Sq. Ft. - Sleeping Level; 687 Sq. Ft. - Lower Level; 37,624 Cu. Ft.

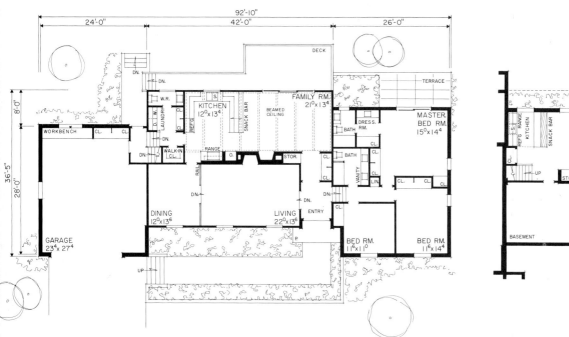

A Lifetime of Exciting, Contemporary Living Patterns

● Here is a home for those with a bold, contemporary living bent. The exciting exteriors give notice of an admirable flair for something delightfully different. The varying roof planes and textured blank wall masses are distinctive. Two sets of panelled front doors permit access to either level. The inclined ramp to the upper main level is dramatic, indeed. The rear exterior highlights a veritable battery of projecting balconies. This affords direct access to outdoor living for each of the major rooms in the house. Certainly an invaluable feature should your view be particularly noteworthy. Notice two covered outdoor balconies plus a covered terrace. Indoor-outdoor living at its greatest.

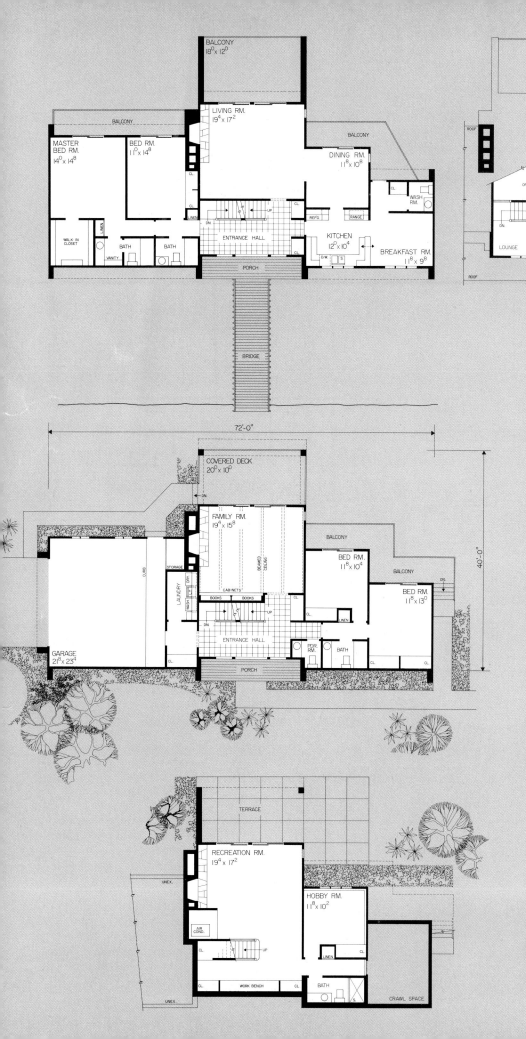

BALCONY
18⁰ x 12⁰

LIVING RM.
19⁴ x 17²

MASTER BED RM.
14⁰ x 14⁸

BED RM.
11⁰ x 14⁸

BALCONY

DINING RM.
11⁸ x 10⁸

BALCONY

CL

CL

CL

CL

WASH RM.

LINEN

DN.

UP

REF'G

RANGE

WALK-IN CLOSET

LINEN

BATH

BATH

VANITY

ENTRANCE HALL

KITCHEN
12⁰ x 10⁴

D.W.

S.

CL

BREAKFAST RM.
11⁸ x 9⁸

PORCH

BRIDGE

ROOF

ROOF

ROOF

STUDIO
11⁸ x 12⁸

ROOF

OPEN TO LIVING RM. BELOW

RAILING

DN.

CL

LOUNGE

ROOF

ROOF

72'-0"

40'-0"

COVERED DECK
20⁰ x 10⁰

DN.

FAMILY RM.
19⁴ x 15⁸

BEAMED CEILING

CABINETS

BOOKS

BOOKS

STORAGE

LAUNDRY

DRY

WASH

BALCONY

BED RM.
11⁸ x 10⁴

BALCONY

BED RM.
11⁸ x 13⁰

CL

UP

DN.

DN.

ENTRANCE HALL

PDR. RM.

BATH

LINEN

CL

CL

CL

GARAGE
21⁸ x 23⁴

CURB

CL

PORCH

TERRACE

RECREATION RM.
19⁴ x 17²

UNEX.

AIR COND.

CL

UP

HOBBY RM.
11⁸ x 10²

LINEN

CL

UNEX.

WORK BENCH

CL

BATH

S.

CRAWL SPACE

Design 42392
1,691 Sq. Ft. - Main Level
1,127 Sq. Ft. - Lower Entry Level
396 Sq. Ft. - Upper Level
844 Sq. Ft. - Lower Level
40,026 Cu. Ft.

● Try to imagine the manner in which you and your family will function in this four-level hillside design. Surely it will be an adventure in family living that will be hard to surpass. For instance, can you picture a family member painting or sewing in the upper level studio, while another is building models or developing pictures in the lower level hobby room? Or, can you visualize a group in quiet conversation in the living room, another lounging in the family room, while a third plays table tennis or pool in the recreation room? Be sure not to overlook the fireplace in each of these living areas. As for sleeping and bath facilities, your family will have plenty, four bedrooms and four baths, plus a powder room and a wash room. They also will enjoy the eating facilities with a breakfast room, a dining room and an outdoor balcony nearby. Then, too, there is the lounge of the upper level.

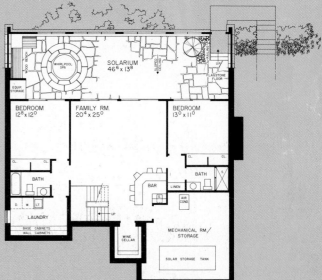

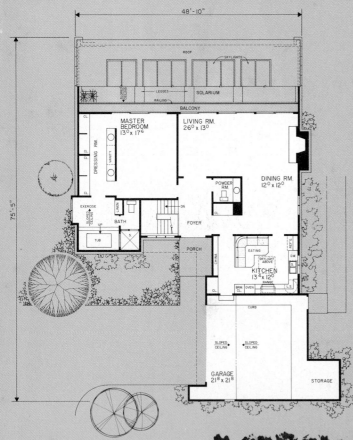

Design 42835
1,626 Sq. Ft. - Main Level
2,038 Sq. Ft. - Lower Level; 50,926 Cu. Ft.

● Passive solar techniques with the help of an active solar component - they can work together or the active solar component can act as a back-up system - heat and cool this striking contemporary design. The lower level solarium is the primary passive element. It admits sunlight during the day for direct-gain heating. The warmth, which was absorbed into the thermal floor, is then radiated into the structure at night. The earth berms on the three sides of the lower level help keep out the winter cold and summer heat. The active system uses collector panels to gather the sun's heat. The heat is transferred via a water pipe system to the lower level storage tank where it is circulated throughout the house by a heat exchanger. Note that where active solar collectors are a design OPTION, which they are in all of our active/passive designs, they must be contracted locally. The collector area must be tailored to the climate and sun angles that characterize your building location.